First World War
and Army of Occupation
War Diary
France, Belgium and Germany

3 CAVALRY DIVISION
6 Cavalry Brigade
1st Dragoons (Royals)
19 September 1914 - 31 March 1919

WO95/1153/1

The Naval & Military Press Ltd
www.nmarchive.com
Published in association with The National Archives

Published by

The Naval & Military Press Ltd

Unit 10 Ridgewood Industrial Park,

Uckfield, East Sussex,

TN22 5QE England

Tel: +44 (0) 1825 749494

www.naval-military-press.com

www.nmarchive.com

This diary has been reprinted in facsimile from the original. Any imperfections are inevitably reproduced and the quality may fall short of modern type and cartographic standards.

© Crown Copyright

Images reproduced by permission of The National Archives, London, England, 2015.

Contents

Document type	Place/Title	Date From	Date To
Heading	WO95/1153/1 3 Cavalry Division 6 Cavalry Brigade 1 Royal Dragoons Sep 1914-Mar. 1919		
Heading	1914-1919 3rd Cavalry Division 6th Cavalry Brigade. 1st Royal Dragoons. Sep 1914-mar 1919 to Dragoons Bde Box. 1166		
Heading	B.E.F. France & Flanders. 3 Cavalry Division 6 Cavalry Brigade. 1 Royal Dragoons. 1914 Sept To 1919 Mar. 3 Dragoon Guards. 1914 Oct To 1919 Jan. 10 Hussars. 1918 Mar To 1919 Mar. 1/1 North Somerset Yeomanry. 1914 Nov To 1918 Mar.		
Heading	1st Royal Dragoons 3rd Cavalry Division 6 Cavalry Brigade Vol I. 1909-31.10.14 Mar 1919		
War Diary		19/09/1914	31/10/1914
Heading	Lt Leckie's Story of 1st Dragoon Is In 1st Division of 1914		
Heading	Lt Leckie 1 Dragoons 1914-15		
Miscellaneous	Copy of the diary of the late Lieutenant J.h. Leckie 1st Dragoons. 6th Cavalry Brigade 3rd Cav. D Wison		
Miscellaneous	DU.		
Heading	1/Dragoons Lt Leckie Story in 1914 War Diary		
Miscellaneous			
Miscellaneous	Copy of the diary of the late Lieutenant J.H. Leckie. 1st Dragoons 6th Cavalry Brigade 3rd Cavalry W W.		
Heading	1st Royal Dragoons 6th Cav. Brigade 3 Cav Div Vol II 1-30.11.14		
War Diary		01/11/1914	30/11/1914
Heading	6th Cavalry Brigade 1st Royal Dragoon Vol III 1-31.12.14.		
War Diary	Cappel Boom North France	01/12/1914	31/12/1914
Heading	6th Cavalry Brigade 1st Royal Dragoon Vol IV & V 1.1-28.2.15		
War Diary		01/01/1915	28/02/1915
Heading	6th Cavalry Brigade 1st (Royal) Dragoons Vol VI 2-27.3.15 Ni		
War Diary	Blaringhem-North France	02/03/1915	11/03/1915
War Diary	Merville-Estaires	12/03/1915	12/03/1915
War Diary	Blaringhem-N.France	14/03/1915	22/03/1915
War Diary	Merville-Estaires	12/03/1915	13/03/1915
War Diary	Blaringhem-N.France	22/03/1915	27/03/1915
Heading	6th Cavalry Brigade 1st Royal Dragoon Vol VII 1-30.4.15		
War Diary	Blaringhem	01/04/1915	12/04/1915
War Diary	Thiennes	12/04/1915	26/04/1915
War Diary	Vlammertinge	27/04/1915	30/04/1915
Heading	3rd 6/Cavalry Division 1st Royal Dragoons Vol VIII 1-31.5.15		
War Diary		01/05/1915	31/05/1915
Miscellaneous	1st Royal Dragoons. War Diary Vol. VIII Appendix I Casualties of Actions of 12th 14th May		

Type	Description	Start	End
Miscellaneous	1st (Royal) Dragoons. War Diary-Vol. VIII-Appendix 1 (Sheet 2). Casualties of Action of 12th 14th May	29/06/1915	29/06/1915
Miscellaneous	1st (Royal) Dragoons War Diary Volume VIII Appendix II Honour Awards Mentions for Good Work in the field S.c. 12th-14th May	29/06/1915	29/06/1915
Miscellaneous	1st (Royal) Dragoons War Diary Volume VIII Appendix III Casualties & Action & period	29/06/1915	29/06/1915
Miscellaneous	1st (Royal) Dragoons War Diary Volume VIII Appendix IV Reinforcements joined during may, 1915	29/06/1915	29/06/1915
Heading	3rd Cavalry Division 1st Royal Dragoons Vol IX June 15 June 1915		
War Diary	N of Zillebeke J. B.C.	01/06/1915	06/06/1915
War Diary	General	06/06/1915	06/06/1915
War Diary	Thiennes	07/06/1915	30/06/1915
Miscellaneous	1st. (Royal) Dragoons. War Diary Vol. IX Appendix No. 1 Casualties of Period 1st to 30th. June, 1915	04/08/1915	04/08/1915
Miscellaneous	1st. (Royal) Dragoons. War Diary Vol. IX Appendix No. II Reinforcements received during period 1st. to 30th. June/15.	04/08/1915	04/08/1915
Miscellaneous	1st. (Royal) Dragoons.1st. (Royal) Dragons. War Diary Vol' IX Appendix NO. III. Honours and Rewards, Mentions for Good Work in the Field,&c. 1st. -30th /6/15		
Heading	3rd Cavalry Division 1st Royals Vol X From 1st To 31st July 1915		
War Diary	Thiennes	01/07/1915	31/07/1915
Miscellaneous	The Royal Dragoons. War Diary-Vol. X-1st.-31st. July Appendix I. Reinforcements received During the Month of July, 1915.		
Heading	3rd Cavalry Division 1st Royal Dragoon Vol XI August 15		
War Diary	Thiennes	01/08/1915	03/08/1915
War Diary	Amettes Area Armentieres	13/08/1915	31/08/1915
War Diary	Armentieres	13/08/1915	31/08/1915
Miscellaneous	The Royal Dragoons. War Diary, Volume XI, 1st. 31st. August, 1915 Appendix I. 'Honour And Rewards"	15/09/1915	15/09/1915
Miscellaneous	The Royal Dragoons. War Diary, Volume XI, 1st. 31st. August, 1915. Appendix II. Reinforcements Received.	15/09/1915	15/09/1915
Heading	6th Cav. Bde. 3rd Cav. Div War Diary 1st (Royal) Dragoons. September 1915 Attached: Appendices I, II & III		
War Diary		01/09/1915	30/09/1915
Miscellaneous	Appendices I, II & III		
Miscellaneous	The Royal Dragoons. War Diary-Volume XII-1-30th. September, 1915. Appendix I: Casualties.	03/11/1915	03/11/1915
Miscellaneous	The Royal Dragoons.War Diary-Volume XII-1st./30th. September, 1915. Appendix II Reinforcements.	03/11/1915	03/11/1915
Miscellaneous	The Royal Dragoons. War Diary-Volume XII-September 1st./30th., 1915. Appendix III-Honours & Rewards.	03/11/1915	03/11/1915
Heading	3rd Cavalry Division 1st (Royal) Dragoons Oct 1915 Vol XIII		
War Diary	Bruay	01/10/1915	03/10/1915
War Diary	Cauchy A La Tour	03/10/1915	16/10/1915
Miscellaneous	1st. (Royal) Dragoons Appendix A. War Diary, Vol. XIII, October, 1915. Reinforcements Joined.	29/11/1915	29/11/1915

Miscellaneous	1st. (Royal) Dragoons. Appendix B War Diary, Vol. XIII, October 1915. Honours And Decoration.	29/11/1915	29/11/1915
Heading	3rd Cavalry Division 1st (Royal) Dragoons Nov. 1915 Vol XIV		
War Diary	Ligny Les Aire	01/11/1915	10/11/1915
War Diary	Crequy	16/11/1915	30/11/1915
War Diary	Ligny-Lez-Aire	03/11/1915	11/11/1915
Miscellaneous	The Royal Dragoons.War Diary Vol. XIV. Appendix I. Reinforcements. November, 1915	24/12/1915	24/12/1915
Miscellaneous	The Royal Dragoons. War Diary. Vol. XIV. Appendix II. Honours And Rewards. November, 1915	24/12/1915	24/12/1915
Miscellaneous	The Royal Dragoons. War Diary. Vol. XIV. Appendix III. Casualties. November, 1915.	24/12/1915	24/12/1915
Heading	3 Cav Royal Dragoons Dec 1915 Vol. XV		
War Diary	Crequy North France	01/12/1915	31/12/1915
Heading	War Diary The Royal Dragoons. Volume XV. December, 1915 Reinforcements Received. Appendix 1.	10/01/1916	10/01/1916
War Diary		01/01/1916	29/01/1916
Miscellaneous	The Royal Dragoons Appendix 1-War Diary. Volume XVI. Casualties. January, 1916	00/02/1916	00/02/1916
Miscellaneous	The Royal Dragoons Appendix II-War Diary. Volume XVI. Honours And Rewards. January, 1916.	00/02/1916	00/02/1916
Miscellaneous	The Royal Dragoons Appendix III-War Diary. Volume XVI. Reinforcements Received. January, 1916.	00/02/1916	00/02/1916
War Diary		01/02/1916	28/02/1916
Miscellaneous	The Royal Dragoons. War Diary Volume XVII. Reinforcements Received. Appendix 1 February, 1916.	26/03/1916	26/03/1916
Miscellaneous	The Royal Dragoons. War Diary. Volume XVII. Casualties. Appendix III. February, 1916	26/03/1916	26/03/1916
War Diary	Crequy N France	03/03/1916	30/03/1916
Heading	War Diary The Royal Dragoons. Appendix I. Vol.XVIII. Reinforcements. March, 1916	08/05/1916	08/05/1916
Miscellaneous	War Diary The Royal Dragoons Appendix II Volume XVIII Casualties. March, 1916.	08/05/1916	08/05/1916
Miscellaneous	War Diary The Royal Dragoons Appendix III. Vol.XVIII. Honours and Rewards. March, 1916.	08/05/1916	08/05/1916
War Diary	Crequy N France	10/04/1916	29/04/1916
War Diary	General	01/04/1916	30/04/1916
Miscellaneous	War Diary The Royal Dragoons Appendix 1. Vol. XIX. Reinforcements. April, 1916.	08/05/1916	08/15/1916
War Diary	In the Field	06/05/1916	29/06/1916
War Diary	Bonnay	01/07/1916	03/07/1916
War Diary	Allery	04/07/1916	09/07/1916
War Diary	Vaux-Sur-Somme	10/07/1916	10/07/1916
War Diary	Vaux	11/07/1916	19/07/1916
War Diary	La Neuville	20/07/1916	31/07/1916
War Diary	Vaux	15/07/1916	30/07/1916
War Diary	Bonnay	01/07/1916	30/07/1916
War Diary	Lamesge	01/08/1916	01/08/1916
War Diary	Neuf Moulin	02/08/1916	03/08/1916
War Diary	Maintenay	04/08/1916	04/08/1916
War Diary	Fressin	05/08/1916	08/09/1916
War Diary	Dominois	10/09/1916	10/09/1916
War Diary	Drucat	11/09/1916	11/09/1916
War Diary	La Chaussee	12/09/1916	13/09/1916

War Diary	Bussy-Les-Daours	14/09/1916	14/09/1916
War Diary	W. of Bonnay	15/09/1916	15/09/1916
War Diary	Pont-Noyelles	17/09/1916	20/09/1916
War Diary	Le-Mesge	21/09/1916	21/09/1916
War Diary	Beauvoir Riviere	22/09/1916	22/09/1916
War Diary	Raye	23/09/1916	25/09/1916
War Diary	St Josse	29/09/1916	29/09/1916
War Diary	Ovillers	31/08/1916	31/10/1916
War Diary		06/11/1916	29/11/1916
War Diary	St. Josse	02/12/1916	15/12/1916
War Diary	Verton	16/12/1916	17/12/1916
War Diary	St Josse	18/12/1916	22/12/1916
War Diary	Plumoison	27/12/1916	30/12/1916
War Diary	Plumoison	01/01/1917	05/04/1917
War Diary	Fortel	07/04/1917	07/04/1917
War Diary	Fortel Fosseux	08/04/1917	08/04/1917
War Diary	Fosseux Duisans Arras Duisans	09/04/1917	09/04/1917
War Diary	Duisans Arras Hill 100	10/04/1917	10/04/1917
War Diary	Hill 100	11/04/1917	11/04/1917
War Diary	W. of Arras	11/04/1917	11/04/1917
War Diary	Arras (Racecourse) Fosseux	12/04/1917	12/04/1917
War Diary	Fosseux	13/04/1917	13/04/1917
War Diary	Fosseux Le Ponchel	16/04/1917	16/04/1917
War Diary	Le Ponchel Vron	19/04/1917	19/04/1917
War Diary	Vron	21/04/1917	30/04/1917
War Diary	Duplicate	10/04/1917	11/04/1917
War Diary	Plumoison	05/04/1917	05/04/1917
War Diary	Vron	21/04/1917	11/05/1917
War Diary	Dominois	12/05/1917	12/05/1917
War Diary	Frohen-Le-Petit	13/05/1917	13/05/1917
War Diary	Berteaucourt	14/05/1917	14/05/1917
War Diary	La Neuville	15/04/1917	15/04/1917
War Diary	Bayonvillers	17/05/1917	17/05/1917
War Diary	N of Buire	19/05/1917	31/05/1917
War Diary	Buire	02/06/1917	09/06/1917
War Diary	Neighbourhood of Epehy	10/06/1917	26/06/1917
War Diary	Buire	27/06/1917	30/06/1917
War Diary	Ontports D 2 Sub Sector	14/06/1917	25/06/1917
War Diary	D 2 Sub Sector	25/06/1917	30/06/1917
Miscellaneous	Report on Raid Carried out by Man of Royal Dragoons With Scouts of 6th. Cav& Bde. And Details of 3rd. D.Gds.And 3rd. Field Squadron R.E. on The Morning of 25/6/19. Ref.Le Catelet Map. 1/20.000.	25/06/1917	25/06/1917
Miscellaneous	Report on Raid Carried out Night 24th/25th. by A. Party.		
Miscellaneous	Raid Carried out on The Night of June 24/25th. 1917 by The Royal Dragoons		
Miscellaneous	Report on B. Raiding Party "Jack" (map attached)	26/06/1917	26/06/1917
Diagram etc	Sketch		
Diagram etc	Scale (Rough) 20 Yds		
War Diary	Buire	01/07/1917	02/07/1917
War Diary	Buire-Suzanne	03/07/1917	03/07/1917
War Diary	Suzanne-Mericourt	04/07/1917	04/07/1917
War Diary	Mericourt-Amplier	05/07/1917	05/07/1917
War Diary	Amplier-Rebruviette	06/07/1917	06/07/1917
War Diary	Rebreuviette-Lapugnoy	07/07/1917	07/07/1917

War Diary	Lapugnoy	07/07/1917	16/07/1917
War Diary	Haverskerque	16/07/1917	31/07/1917
War Diary	D Sector	05/07/1917	17/07/1917
War Diary	Haverskerque	01/08/1917	19/10/1917
War Diary	E.P.S	22/11/1917	22/11/1917
War Diary	Boubers	23/11/1917	23/11/1917
War Diary	Berneuil	24/11/1917	24/11/1917
War Diary	Long	25/11/1917	30/11/1917
Miscellaneous	The Royal Dragoons Appendix 1.	04/11/1917	04/11/1917
War Diary	Long	03/11/1917	17/11/1917
War Diary	Contay	18/11/1917	18/11/1917
War Diary	Suzanne	19/11/1917	28/11/1917
War Diary	Wargnies	24/11/1917	30/11/1917
War Diary	In the Field	01/12/1917	31/12/1917
War Diary	In the Field	01/01/1918	31/01/1918
Miscellaneous	Appendix "I"-Casualties.		
War Diary	In The Field	01/02/1918	28/02/1918
Miscellaneous	Appendix I-Casualties. Nil. Appendix II-Honours And Rewards.		
War Diary	In the Field	01/03/1918	31/03/1918
Miscellaneous	Strength of Regiment.		
Heading	War Diary The Royal Dragoons. April 1918		
War Diary	In The Field	01/04/1918	30/04/1918
Miscellaneous	Appendices I, II and III.		
Miscellaneous	Appendix I.-Casualties.		
Miscellaneous	Appendix III.-Reinforcement.		
War Diary	In the Field	01/05/1918	31/05/1918
War Diary	In The Field	01/06/1918	30/06/1918
War Diary	In The Field	01/07/1918	30/07/1918
Miscellaneous	Appendix I-Casualties.		
War Diary	In The Field	01/08/1918	30/09/1918
Miscellaneous	Appendix-I.-Casualties.		
War Diary	In The Field	02/10/1918	31/10/1918
Miscellaneous	Appendix I.-Casualties.		
War Diary	In The Field	01/11/1918	30/11/1918
Miscellaneous	Appendix-I.-Casualties.		
War Diary	In The Field	07/12/1918	30/12/1918
Miscellaneous	Casualties-Appendix I.		
War Diary		01/01/1919	30/01/1919
Miscellaneous	Appendix I. Nil. Appendix 2.		
War Diary	Jehay-Bodegnee	01/02/1919	18/03/1919
War Diary	Sprimont	19/03/1919	19/03/1919
War Diary	Theux	20/03/1919	20/03/1919
War Diary	Raeren	21/03/1919	21/03/1919
War Diary	Warden	22/03/1919	22/03/1919
War Diary	Oberembt	23/03/1919	23/03/1919
War Diary	Cologne	24/03/1919	31/03/1919
War Diary	Paffendorf	31/03/1919	31/03/1919

(1)

WO 95/1153

3 Cavalry Division

6 Cavalry Brigade.

1 Royal Dragoons

Sep. 1914 – Mar. 1919.

1914-1919
3RD CAVALRY DIVISION
6TH CAVALRY BRIGADE.

1ST ROYAL DRAGOONS.

SEP 1914-MAR 1919

TO DRAGOON WE
Box 1166

B.E.F. FRANCE & FLANDERS.
3 CAVALRY DIVISION.

6 CAVALRY BRIGADE.
1 ROYAL DRAGOONS.
1914 SEPT TO 1919 MAR.
3 DRAGOON GUARDS.
1914 OCT TO 1919 JAN.
10 HUSSARS.
1918 MAR TO 1919 MAR.
1/1 NORTH SOMERSET
YEOMANRY.
1914 NOV TO 1918 MAR.

15th Oct - As moved motorbikes with cavalry
26th Oct - Difficulties in identifying friendly aeroplanes

6/3

Seen by M.T. 2

1st Royal Dragoons

121/2489

3rd Cavalry Division. 6 Cavalry Brigade

Vol I. 1914 — 31.10.14

Mar 1919

Army Form C. 2118.

WAR DIARY
or
INTELLIGENCE SUMMARY.
(Erase heading not required.)

Instructions regarding War Diaries and Intelligence Summaries are contained in F.S. Regs., Part II. and the Staff Manual respectively. Title pages will be prepared in manuscript.

Hour, Date, Place	Summary of Events and Information	Remarks and references to Appendices
19 September 1914	Regiment landed at Southampton from South Africa per S.S. Dunluce Castle and a few details and families on the Guildford Castle, & proceeded to Windmill Hill Camp Ludgershall.	
20 September 1914	Officers from Cavalry School Netheravon on leave reported.	
	13 Reservists rejoined Regt.	
26"	W.O.'s N.C.O.'s & men not present with Regt. i.e. left behind in South Africa on command and or on leave not likely to rejoin for service struck off strength.	
	21 Horses considered unfit for service struck off charge.	
	177 Horses arrived from South Ireland & one Hotchkiss Derby Yeomanry.	
27"	8 N.C.O.s & men & 4 horses transferred to VI Signal Troop.	
30"	32 Horses Cavt. 60 Draught horses arrived & taken on strength.	
1st October "	100 horses arrived and taken on strength.	
2nd " "	18 N.C.O. & men arrived from York. Grandsons made to War Establ. from 20/9/14 viz date of mobilization.	
3rd " "	11 horses from Woolwich received for machine guns, trench colours. 1st reinforcements 16th. Surplus horses (six hundred) over to detachment 8 Dragoon Guards.	
6 October 1914	The Regiment received orders to move for Active Service in 4 trains. Squadrons left with the following order: "A", "B", "C" H.Q. machine gun and were entrained from AMESBURY at intervals of 1 hour from 3:30 A.M. to 6:30 A.M.
	The first train arrived Southampton about 10 A.M. "A" Squadron had horses entrained on the S.S. Lord Charlemont, the remaining two squadrons

Forms/C. 2118/10

Army Form C. 2118.

WAR DIARY
or
INTELLIGENCE SUMMARY.
(Erase heading not required.)

Instructions regarding War Diaries and Intelligence Summaries are contained in F.S. Regs, Part II. and the Staff Manual respectively. Title pages will be prepared in manuscript.

Hour, Date, Place	Summary of Events and Information	Remarks and references to Appendices
6th October 1914 (Cont)	Squadrons and HQ Quarters embarked after the S.S. Irdore by 2.30 p.m. On this ship were also 1 Squadron 2/Life Guards, 1 Squadron 1/Life Guards with their Head Quarters. Lt. Col. FERGUSON, 2/Life Guards in Command. The ship was well fitted for horses though some of the Boxes and Gangways were a little difficult. Owing to the confusion of different units, Embarkation took longer than would otherwise have been the case.	
7th October 1914	Our ship sailed at 5 a.m. reaching DEAL in the afternoon. The fleet consisted of about 8 Ships. Escorted by many men-of-war. Left DEAL at 9.30 p.m.	
8th October 1914	Stood by at 10.30 a.m. ready to disembark at ZEEBRUGE but were delayed some time. Eventually disembarked by 12.30 p.m. After long delay received orders to move at 3.30 p.m. via BLANKENBURG where we watered and fed. Orders received to move on OSTEND where we reached at dusk. Lt Golding & Stannors conducted us to Race Course where we bivouacced as Brigade. March 16 miles. Dismount got in at 10 p.m.	
9th October 1914	A. Squadron came in aft. Changing their horses on to OSTEND. Moved at 1.30 p.m. via LEFINGHE into billets at SNELLEGHEM. VARSENNAERE and ST MICHEL – 16 miles	
10th October 1914	Patrol under Lieut Browne sent out at 6.30 a.m. to THOUROUT and ROULERS. – No news. Moved out of billets at 12.30 p.m. to rendezvous at LOPHEM 2 pm. Hence to THOUROUT where we billeted at 5 pm – march 12 miles. 12 noon 'A' Squadron under Lieut Waterhouse sent to LICHTERVEDE on outpost	

Forms/C. 2118/10

WAR DIARY
or
INTELLIGENCE SUMMARY.
(Erase heading not required.)

Army Form C. 2118.

Hour, Date, Place	Summary of Events and Information	Remarks and references to Appendices
11th October 1914	Outpost troops relieved by troops "B" Squadron, who were ordered to cover found from LICHTERVELDE to COPTEMARCK. Car Armington sent out at 8.30 A.M. in armoured motor with machine gun to reconnoitre South of ROULERS. Now received fall of ANTWERP but successful removal of garrison. So far we have not got in touch with enemy. Our Force came under command of Sir John French yesterday. Still in billets at THOUROUT. Lieut. Col. Channing 1st returned with 5 German Uhlans captured near YPRES.	
12th October 1914	Left THOUROUT at 6.30 A.M. Marched via ROULERS to OOSTNIEUWKERKE MOORSLEDE ZONNEBEKE with Uhlans post at WEST ROOSEBEKE - about 11 miles.	
13th October 1914	Marched via ST. JULIEN to YPRES where we billeted for 1 hour. Thence via GHERUVELT to billets at DADIZEELE and LEDEGHEM - about 20 miles. A few scattered Uhlans reported at different points. Major McHuie rejoined the Regiment.	
14th October 1914	Left at 6.30 A.M. for YPRES. Regiment as advanced guard took up position line VOORMEZEELE to VLAMERTINGHE. Then to WYSCHATE - LACLYTTE. Brigade brought down a Taube aeroplane near YPRES, with 3 bombs in it. Billets up at KEMMEL by a Jas Carman. C Squadron surrounded house and armoured with allure fired from front, flank 2 troops of C Squadron killed by machine allure at NEUVE EGLISE about 200 German reported. 5 killed by machine allure - since we met 18th Hussars. We had crossed. Half part of the 3rd & 5th Cavalry Brigades. Billets at WYSCLAETE. Lt. BAKER & Sgt. reconnoitred the line. Lance badly wounded.	
15th October 1914	Remained in billets. Reconnaissance by 5th Cavalry Bde. Shewed missing some LYS destroyed. Being by Germans in distance.	

WAR DIARY or INTELLIGENCE SUMMARY.

Army Form C. 2118.

(Erase heading not required.)

Instructions regarding War Diaries and Intelligence Summaries are contained in F.S. Regs., Part II. and the Staff Manual respectively. Title pages will be prepared in manuscript.

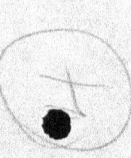

Hour, Date, Place	Summary of Events and Information	Remarks and references to Appendices
16 October 1914	Received orders to move at 8 A.m. via YPRES to POELCAPPELLE where we halted for 5 hours. At 8.15 p.m. we moved off into billets E of ZONNEBEKE on the PASSCHENDAELE ROAD. We arrived in the dark. Distance 14 miles.	
17 October 1914	Remained in billets.	
18 October 1914	Infantry outposts at ZONNEBEKE were drawn close to village. "B" Squadron took up point of observation at MOORSLEDE. Regiment remained at ZONNEBEKE until 8 p.m. "C" Sqn sent in some Uhlans captured, including an officer also belonging to a German escort. There was continual sniping almost all day between "C" Squadron & the enemy just before dark. Lieut de Gunzbourg's troop bagged a few, but three were not picked up at the time. Next morning 2 were found dead. At dusk remainder of the Regiment moved into billets. All 3 Squadrons providing outposts near MOORSLEDE. During the night heavy firing was heard on our left where troops (should have been) got hurt, the 7th Cav Brigade. They, however, were not there. They were attacked "A" Sqn. on our right. Here we joined with the Divisional Cavalry of the 7 Division.
19 October 1914	Regiment concentrated at dawn and moved on ROULERS-MENIN ROAD to ST PIETERS with the object of observing towards LEDEGHEM and ROLLEGHEM-CAPPELLE. On arrival at St PIETERS a patrol of the 7 Cavalry Brigade told us that their brigade was 2 miles on our left. This information subsequently proved incorrect. By owe right we were in touch with the 7nd Infantry Bde. "B" Squadron proceeded to LEDEGHEM and were sniped at continuously, reported Northern end of village clear. Sergt GRAY two severely wounded. Lt LESLIE slightly wounded.

WAR DIARY or INTELLIGENCE SUMMARY

Army Form C. 2118.

Hour, Date, Place	Summary of Events and Information	Remarks and references to Appendices
19 October 1914 (Cont'd)	Wounded. Corp FITCH & Corp WEST were also wounded. Rfn. GRIGGLESTONE missing. A Sqdn. went towards ROLLEGHEM-CAPPELLE and remained on the level crossing. They received an order to retire about 11-30pm but again reoccupied that position until the troop near windmill near ST PIETERS. This post was useful for observation. Commander SAMPSONS 3 bombs & that alliance also came into action on same night with 'C' Battery R.H.A. a little further to the right. YE M. Gun was established on the ROULERS – MENIN Road facing NORTH. The Germans in considerable force crossed the road North of his getting point over left which was in the "out" & the M.g fired at intervals without much result. Remarkable message told that the 20th Inf. Brigade had retired from LEDEGHEM together with 10th Hussars. B. I.C Squadron retired first 'A' holding the enemy to the EAST whilst they assumed in considerable force. (C. or B. Battalion). The Infantry was along the road towards MOORSLEDE and was on similar manoeuvre afterwards by A Squadron who were fired at heavily from the left flank without, however, losing more than 7 horses. 2 Troops (2Lt de Graffenried) were cut off for a time, and did not return until next day. 2Lt de Graffenried's horse was killed, but he had no casualties. A Squadron on this front as was reported the following casualties:— Pte HARRISON killed. Sgt. LOCK wounded. Sjnt. MEASURES L.Cpl. MURKIN. Cpl. PROTTS. L.Cpl. PETHERICK. WIDE and McCULLUM. – missing. Rolleghem-Capelle Banner from Germans who held houses near ROLLEGHEM-CAPPELLE	

WAR DIARY or INTELLIGENCE SUMMARY.

(Erase heading not required.)

Army Form C. 2118.

Hour, Date, Place	Summary of Events and Information	Remarks and references to Appendices

19th October 1914 (cont.) He subsequently returned to PASSCHENDAELE covering retirement of 4 Cavalry Brigade from MOORSLEDE. Billets after and at POELCAPPELLE (at troops on outposts)

This was our first day in action and in trying one or both our flanks were already exposed and the German infantry were in great force on our front and left.

Our retirement from the Cross Roads at ST PIETERS was most gallantly covered by an officer (Roos) of the Welsh Guards with merely 1 miteraillese and it is from him we are indebted for our small number of casualties.

20 October 1914 Left before dawn to take up a trenched line from WEST ROOSEBEKE inclusive to a point about 600 × N. of PASSCHENDAELE. The line was held by 2 Squadrons of guns and M. Guns and one Squadron of 10 Hussars. We had to dig ourselves in before dawn and with a limited number of tools this took time. Remainder of 10 Hussars and ourselves in intrench Support.

We heard that the Infantry would be up to be in position. They did not arrive. Our left was supposed to be held by the French but most of them had moved to the rear. Capt CHARRINGTON was early killed by Shrapnel in The trenches. YEOMANS who came in for Sergt Henry Shrapnel. Qr GOODALL and CAMDION were wounded and 6 horses were killed. The Machine Gun was soon put-down as it was doing no good. There were no hostile infantry to fire at and the enemy used only Shrapnel.

About 3 pm the Brigade retired slowly by alternate squadrons and took up a line from LANGEMARK to ST JULIEN. At about 4 pm we moved into billets at LANGEMARK + ST JULIEN. "C Squadron on outpost

WAR DIARY or INTELLIGENCE SUMMARY.

(Erase heading not required.)

Army Form C. 2118.

(7)

Hour, Date, Place	Summary of Events and Information	Remarks and references to Appendices
20th October 1914 (cont)	Outposts at Cross Roads ST JULIEN spent a troubled night with hostile infantry close to them and a fierce fight raging within rifle shot of the 7th Division. During the night they were reinforced by half Company of Zouaves. 2nd Lt RYDER was killed, Pte HANNE wounded. A Squadron reported Sgt LEVINE wounded.	
21st October 1914	Regiment received orders to move at daybreak to YPRES and CONCENTRATE at YPRES at 6.30 A.M. to draw supplies. It subsequently moved to HOOGE and off saddled for 2 hours. There to VERBRANDEN MOLEN in a position of readiness with C Squadron holding bridge over Canal N of HOLLEBEKE. At dark we were ordered to ZANDVOORDE to take over the trenches from 2nd Scots Guards. This we did, pulling almost every man into the firing line, keeping a few only to look after the horses in the village.	
22nd October 1914	Remained in trenches. Led horses had to be constantly shifted owing to attention of hostile air-craft and big howitzers. Subsequently found a fairly safe concealed position for horses near wood just N of Nieuwe ZANDVOORDE. Troops spent the night here.	
23rd October 1914	We were ordered to hand over trenches to 1 Cav. Brigade. Relief N of village were easily carried out, but 2 of our troops have on the extreme SW side & subject to heavy shrapnel fire. One of these troops Ssgt 2/Lt HENDERSON slightly wounded. Pte CLARKE killed and Ptes SOLLETT, WALLACE & S1155 and SS DAVIS wounded in trying to get out of the trenches. Eventually this troop did not get away till dark. Ssgt STUART of A Sqdn reported killed during previous night. The Regiment went into bivouac near KLEINE ZILLEBEKE and were constantly annoyed by fire from enemy's heavy howitzer.

Army Form C. 2118.

WAR DIARY
or
INTELLIGENCE SUMMARY.
(Erase heading not required.)

Instructions regarding War Diaries and Intelligence Summaries are contained in F.S. Regs., Part II. and the Staff Manual respectively. Title pages will be prepared in manuscript.

Hour, Date, Place	Summary of Events and Information	Remarks and references to Appendices
October 23rd 1914 (cont)	Kortewilde, but hostile suffered no casualties. During the night especially, the fire was frequent and we employed stars & Verey lamps etc. for signalling.	
October 24th 1914	Remained as before. Only annoyed occasionally by shell fire.	
October 25th 1914	Left at ZILLEBEKE about 3 p.m. and returned to Trenches at ZANDVOORDE with "A" Squadron and machine gun at HOLLEBEKE CHATEAU, which they reported had been looted. "B" & "C" Squadron W. of ZANDVOORDE. a good deal of firing during the night on our left but very little on our immediate front.	
October 26th 1914	Remained as before. Heavy firing at intervals by guns but no rifle fire on our immediate front. Machine gun Lieut R.C. COUPER killed H.A.L. COBB slightly wounded by shrapnel. About mid-day some stragglers from Border Reg. & Scots Guards reported their Brigade to have been cut up as CRUISEIK, undoubtedly this Brigade had been heavily engaged but hope no worse than that. About 4 p.m. aeroplane was observed on our left dropping coloured lights over our guns. The WARWICKS opened a fire and brought it down — one of our own craft, but error was quite pardonable. At 4.30 p.m. 2 Squadrons of the "Blues" were sent out through our line, mounted to demonstrate towards KORTEWILDE and clear the fire. This they did most gallantly with "B" Squadron "Blues". Came back half an hour later having had a fearful time and lost heavily from rifle & shrapnel fire. During the night all was quiet.	

WAR DIARY or INTELLIGENCE SUMMARY.

Army Form C. 2118.

Hour, Date, Place	Summary of Events and Information	Remarks and references to Appendices
27 October 1914	All quiet during the morning except for the usual Gun fire. A second line of trenches were prepared during the day by Field Troops in rear of original line. We hear that during the night the "Gordons" had their third drawn from the left of our Brigade leaving no "in the air" for 2 hours. When the became known troops were hurried up from the 1st Army to take their place. About 5 PM our outpost line was withdrawn & relieved by the 7th Cavalry Brigade. Spent the night at KLEINE ZILLEBEKE. A Sqdn & M. Gun were left out at the CHATEAU HOLLEBEKE. 2Lt BRYAN was wounded.	
28 October 1914.	Remained at K ZILLEBEKE only worried by a few shells. In afternoon 2 troops and Co the adjt went to CHATEAU HOLLEBEKE to bring back A Sqdn & horses. Scarcely smoke when did not give a good field of fire. Especially Cap't HOUSTOUNS who was badly handicapped by a house only 50 x to his front. We had asked to Endeavor the position then house for demolition but nothing had been done. The smoke generally were somewhat too wide and not deep enough. Astride Mons the Railway there machine guns were able to enfilade but Commander SAMPSON had he hunt guns were still on the bridge. Germans probably thought retired 2 miles. Their ranging was excellent. On the way back left horses got 4 shells close to them, luckily, only one horse was hit. The Enemy must have seen the road obviously while aeroplane reported to have been brought down. Their casualties 20 men and 25 horses joined. A quiet night.	

WAR DIARY or INTELLIGENCE SUMMARY

Army Form C. 2118.

Hour, Date, Place	Summary of Events and Information	Remarks and references to Appendices
29th October 1914	About 4.30 am heavy guns started firing. At 5 am we were told to stand "to arms". At 10 am. he were ordered to saddle up & understood that Counter attack is being allowed in direction of GHELUVELDT. At 12.30 pm. moved up in support of the 7th Division who were supposed to be counter-attacking in direction of KRUSSIK. This attack did not lead to much. Regiment returned to bivouac at KLEINE ZILLEBEKE 8 pm. All quiet at the CHATEAU.	Moved to the village of ZANDVOORDE
30th October 1914	Moved off at 11.30 am dismounted to take up a line of supporting trenches in rear of the CHATEAU. The ZANDVOORDE line was reported to have been given up and 2 Squadrons of the 7th Brigade were ordered to have been cut off. The CHATEAU had been heavily attacked during the morning, at first by Shell fire and afterwards by Infantry who were in considerable force and worked round our right into HOLLEBEKE. A Squadron was ordered to leave the CHATEAU about 3 pm and retired gradually after doing very good work, especially at Watehouse on the right at the Railway Crossing where his troops fired about 350 rounds apiece doing great execution. Capt. JUMP was severely wounded in the thigh and shoulder and could not be got away, 2 Lieut BURN was killed when "C" Squadron went up in Support, and also could not be got away. The Machine Gun limber had seriously been shot back and the gun was brought out of action by hand. It he had one good target of about 500 but otherwise fired very little. About 4 pm "D" & "C" Sqdn with HQ" were occupying the second line in front of KLEINE ZILLEBEKE to the Railway just NORTH of HOLLEBEKE. The Germans did not come on though we saw several of their snipers, luckily for us he have a very thin line.	

WAR DIARY or INTELLIGENCE SUMMARY.

(Erase heading not required.)

Army Form C. 2118.

Hour, Date, Place	Summary of Events and Information	Remarks and references to Appendices
30th October 1914 (Cont.)	Just after midnight we were relieved by the Canadian Scouts who had dug themselves in behind us and refused to leave anything to do with our line. Major LEIGHTON and 2/Lieut SWIRE had both been hit in our trenches owing to the Germans having got into the front of HOLLEBEKE. Genl. GOUGH apparently further to our right had been very heavily engaged and who obliged to draw back. This hindered the withdrawal from HOLLEBEKE and consequently caused our flank, what was, for a time, in a very critical condition there. Lieut HEWETT was also hit in the CHATEAU. In addition we suffered the following casualties among the ranks are file during the 29th & 30th. 29.10.14. Wounded: Pte. DREW, GROVE, DIXON. 30.10.14. Killed: Sgt. VANSON, S.S. SOWDEN, Pte. DUDGEON, L/Sgt. HEWITT, Pte. CLIFFE (Chesh: Regt. attached) MacCAW, NAIRN. Was also killed. and also Cpl. VANSON. 67 Bge: HQ Quarters. 30.10.14. Wounded: Pte. DUNLOP, BOWERS, MEASURES (and missing) JONES. L/Sgt. MARLOW (and missing.) Pte. HEBNER, NEWTON, RIDDING, DOWNIE. Sgts. NEWTON + MILLER. Pte. WATSON, CHASE, FAIRBURN, THOMPSON, NORTH. Cpl. MONKHOUSE. L/Cpl. MORGAN, Lcpl. BROWN. Cpl. SMITH. Sgt M. GRADY. L. Cpl. TREACHER + Pte ALLEN. 30-10-14 - Missing Sgt. HENDERSON. Pte EDEN. 31st October 1914. At 2 a.m. we got back to bivouac at ZILLEBEKE. We turned out at dawn after a short night and moved forward in time to avoid a salvo of "Jack Johnson's" which heavily shelled the village of ZILLEBEKE. We were moved on to HOOGE in reserve to the Army. At first it was thought we might be required in support of General GOUGH near WYTSCHAETE but later we were that to support Gen'l. BULFIN near KLEINE ZILLEBEKE and clear the wood. The German Infantry had nearly got through the wood but with our support Gen'l. BULFIN drove them back and only had time been a little more light he might be have squashed the lot. As it was the Germans suffered heavily and we also a good number of prisoners. Gen'l. BULFIN's Bge: had also suffered heavily	

WAR DIARY
or
INTELLIGENCE SUMMARY.

Army Form C. 2118.

(12)

Hour, Date, Place	Summary of Events and Information	Remarks and references to Appendices
31st October 1914 (Cont)	heavily and his Regiments were very weak. They had, practically, no officers left. About dawn Br. BULFIN led apparently re-organised and not reformed troops to bivouac in wood just SOUTH of HOOGE. F.B.C. 10 am Fitzgerald Capt. + Adjt. 4th Royal Dragoons	

Lt. Leekie's Story of 1st Dragoons is in 1 Dly Disem of 1914

Lt J H Leeke
1 Dragoons

1914 - 15

NOT FOR
VISITORS

Copy of the diary of the late Lieutenant J.H.Leckie,
1st Dragoons.
6th Cavalry Brigade 3rd Cav. Division

October 6th 1914. Received orders to entrain at Amesbury. Left Windmill Hill at 1 a.m. Left Amesbury at 5 a.m. and reached Southampton somewhere about 7.30. Spent all day in embarking on 'Indore'. On board there were two squadrons 2nd Life Guards, two squadrons Royal Dragoons and one squadron 1st Life Guards.

October 7th. Sailed from Southampton at 5 a.m. and stopped first off Dover and then on to Deal for sailing orders. 'Indore' not much of a boat, but being only a cattle boat one cannot expect too much.

October 8th. Arrived at Zeebrugge, just beyond Ostend, at 6 a.m. It was a real cold night and a goodish bit of wind. Took a long time disembarking the horses. Moved off from Zeebrugge about 4.30 p.m. Had a huge reception from the 'Belgies' all along the road. They rushed out with cigarettes, biscuits and drinks. Watered in Brandenberge and then on to Ostend where we arrived at 9.30 and bivouacked on the race course. Horses were tied up to the rails.

October 9th. There are a lot of aeroplanes on the race course, mostly Belgian I fancy. They are pretty clever in getting up and landing in a comparatively confined space. Left Ostend about 1 p.m. and marched to Vassanaere and billetted in a convent, horses in the open. Arrived after dark about 7 or 8.

October 10th. Left Vassanaere about noon for Thurout via Lophem. The hospitality of the 'Belgies' is really rather a nuisance. They positively hurl fruit and biscuits at you. Got very good billets in Thurout, the horses in stables, the men in Pubs. and ourselves in three houses and very comfortable.

October 11th. Went out on outpost to Lichtersde. Several armoured motors came in in the evening with a few captured Uhlans in them. Received orders to remain out during the night, so pushed the horses and ourselves into a farm close by the railway. Had one post on the cross roads. As I was going round at night a shot was loosed off, must have been Belgian, as I dont fancy the Huns are anywhere near.

October 12th. Regiment moved at 8.30 and we all set off on flank guard via Costemarck and Hooglede to Oostnienkerke. Got in about noon.

October 13th. Brigade moved off in the morning to Ypres, where we waited for a long time in the market square. A very fine square with good buildings. Went on eventually to Dadizeche. I with my troop was boosted off at once on outpost to the cross roads just outside the town. Had some difficulty in getting there as it was a pitch dark night and there was a tremendous block of transport on the road. No alarms during the night except for Corporal Evans who brought in two harmless civilians, imagining, I suppose, that they were spies.

October 14th. Brigade moved off early via Ypres to a line of protection just south. Moved on to Neuve Eglise and waited just behind the firing line. Brigade was not wanted so after dark moved into billets in Wytschaete. Horses in the open.

October 15th. Brigade remained in billets in Wytschaete. The day's rest has done the horses a lot of good. They always seem to move us into billets after dark which makes it a good deal harder, but I suppose there must be something in it.

October 16th. Our Division moved early to Poelcapelle, waited for about four hours outside the village in the most fearful cold. We were waiting apparently to support the Household Cavalry Brigade, who were playing about in the Forêt d'Houthoulst

October 17th. Remained in our billets outside Zonnebeke all day.

October 18th. Received orders to move into Zonnebeke which we did at 5.30 a.m. and spent the day at the cross roads just outside the village. Moved into Moorslede late that evening. Had three troops on outpost as the woods all round were reported to be full of Huns. No alarms during the night.

October 19th. Brigade moved to St.Pieters. Two troops went on as advanced guard by different roads. On getting to the beginning of the village an inhabitant told me there were about 12 Uhlans feeding in a farm house. I went on a few hundred yards when volleys of shots began. Went up with my troop and had shots at them as they bolted from the farm to the cow-house, where their horses were evidently. Kept on potting them whenever they showed themselves and dropped about 6 altogether I should say. They waved a white flag from the cow-house so we advanced to round them up and were promptly fired on by their people behind, so we had to retire after catching a couple of them. Again lined the road. Grenfell and his troop advanced parallel to the road through the roots, but were held up by heavy fire. Rest of squadron lined out on the other side of the road. Grenfell eventually got into the farm at the end of the road, and the remainder got in behind a cottage on the road. After some time retired and withdrew to St.Pieters. The Huns were coming on across the railway in thousands. Retired back through Moorslede and billetted in Poelcapelle.

October 20th. Brigade moved early to dig trenches and occupy a line near Westroosebeke. Remained in the trenches until about 1 p.m. when the French, who were in Westroosebeke on our left, retired, so we had to follow suit. Retired behind Poelcapelle and were just going to billet by squadrons in the farm handy when a French officer arrived to say the Huns were still advancing and were about 1½ miles the other side of the village. They then started shelling so the whole brigade moved back and we billetted in St.Julien in a perfectly filthy farm. The kitchen had just been vacated by Belgians and was inches deep in mud & filth.

October 21st. A lot of firing during the night. "C" squadron had a pretty sharp night attack. Went early into Ypres to replenish supplies and forage in the square by the station. The whole brigade moved out to Hooge in support. In the afternoon received orders to go to Zanvoorde and occupy the trenches there and took them over from the infantry about 10 p.m. Horses were left up in the village.

October 22nd. In the supporting trenches at Zanvoorde all day. No excitement of any kind except that the horses were shelled in Zandvoorde and had to be moved down to the big wood.

October 23rd. Were relieved in the trenches by the Household Cavalry about 10 a.m. and went back to Klein Zillebeke. Spies in the houses were signalling with lamps to the Huns, so we turned them all out and marched them up.

October 24th. Remained at Klein Zillebeke all day. They had been putting 'Jack Johnsons' over us all night, pitching them just over the crest the other side of the road. To-night they got them nearer, so we had to shift after dark, only a few hundred yards away to the next farm.

October 25th. A lot of firing during the night.

October 26th. I was sent up with my troop to "A" Squadron in the Chateau of Hollebeke. Very peaceful night, practically no firing.

October 27th. Returned to Klein Zillebeke.

October 28th. Slept inside a farm cottage, first night indoors for a week.

October 29th. Saddled up and went out in support up to Zandvoorde. Back again to Klein Zillebeke after dark.

October 30th. Went into the trenches in support of Chateau early and got a fairly bad shelling, but nothing like what "A" Squadron had in the Chateau. We retired to the trenches on the edge of a wood where we remained from about 5 p.m. until 12 at night, when we were relieved by the Grenadiers. Retired to Zillebeke.

October 31st. Shelled out of our place early by 'Jack Johnsons'. Brigade moved up beyond Hooge in support. In the afternoon took up a line of trenches to cover the retirement of the 7th Division. This was unnecessary and we were soon moved out to the Division's assistance in the big woods. Bivouacked in the wood.

November 1st. Huns started shelling our wood so we had to clear out. Went back to the woods to support the Irish Guards, found they had had absolute hell in the trenches from shell fire. Took over their trenches about 3 p.m. while they reorganized themselves and were relieved by the French about 11 p.m.

November 2nd. Brigade moved off about 5 a.m. into the big wood in support. Remained there all day and got back to our bivouac about 7 p.m.

November 3rd. Back to another part of the wood at 6 a.m. Moved after a bit behind the Hooge - Ypres road. Germans were shelling the Ypres road to some tune. Bivouacked in a new farm just across the line.

November 4th. Turned out in the middle of the night on a message being sent in that the Germans had broken through; it turned out to be a false alarm.

November 5th. Was sent off with an orderly to General Cavan, 4th Guards Brigade, near Zillebeke, recalled at 3.30 p.m. as the brigade was going into trenches near Gheluvelt.

November 6th. In supporting trenches all day. Relieved at 2.30 a.m. and got back to bivouac at 4 a.m.

November 7th. Moved off at 12 noon to take place of Household Brigade. At night turned out to support Cavan, a false alarm.

November 8th. In trenches. had a few shells over during the night.

November 9th. Regiment in trenches at Klein Zillebeke. French made an attack into the wood in front of our trenches in the evening. Regiment got back about 10 p.m.

November 10th. Turned out at 1 a.m. and went up to Zillebeke and waited until dark because the Germans were supposed to be massing for an attack. Went on into the trenches after drawing rations. Most awful block on the road caused by French cavalry.

November 11th. In firing line trenches all day. Pretty heavy shelling. Relieved and got back to our farm at 11 p.m.

November 12th. Paraded for trenches again at 5 p.m. We were
in support a short way in front of Zillebeke just behind the
trenches we were in before.

November 13th. In trenches all day. Heavy shelling with short
bursts and lulls in between. Relieved early by the 1st Life
Guards. Back to camp where we found that they had been shelling
our horses pretty considerably all day. A lot of horses
were hit.

November 14th. Brigade moved about 1.30 through Ypres, where
the Huns had done a goodish bit of damage with 'Jack Johnsons'
to new billets in some farms just the other side of Vlamertinghe.
The Cathedral and Cloth Hall are still standing at
Ypres.

November 15th. Stood to at 6.30 and gave the horses some
exercise. Moved off at 2.30; road blocked with transport and
French motor transport. Rode as far as Ypres where we left
the horses. Marched from Ypres to Zillebeke along the line
and then on into the firing line trenches beyond Cavan's
headquarters. The Huns are within about 100 yards of us.

November 16th. Remained in the trenches all day. There was a
certain amount of shooting during the morning, but on the
whole it was a very quiet day

November 17th Germans made an attack all along the line lasting
from 12 to 3 p.m. They failed to break through and suffered
pretty severe losses. After dark a perfect fusilade started
and the Huns threw up lights. We discovered afterwards that
they do this when they expect a counter-attack. Later on went
up to conduct the relieving party from H.Q. We started at
9 p.m. with 1st Herts. Territorials and eventually got them
into the trenches and got away ourselves at 11 p.m.

November 18th. Remained in camp all day.

November 19th. According to present arrangements we go back
to Hazebrouck to-morrow to rest and refit. The French seem
to have taken over the whole of our line in this part of the

world.

November 20th. Wagons started off at 6.30 a.m. for billeting area. Left at 3.30 p.m. Came through Poperinghe, Mont Rouge, Westoutre, Vieux Berquin. Our new billets are from Vieux Berquin through Verte Rue and on just past Candescure.

November 21st. The horses are out in the open, but the men are quite comfortable in barns and ourselves very comfortable in two farms.

November 22nd. Arms inspected in the morning.

November 23rd. Walked over to H.Q. with the letters in the morning and to Vieux Berquin in the afternoon.

November 24th. Spent all day looking for billets for horses.

November 25th. Spent the afternoon in looking for lodgings for the men.

November 26th. Started for Headquarters and found we were to go out on a reconnaissance. First went to Brigade Headquarters and then started off through Merville, Beaupré, Gorgue, Lestrem, Pont Riqual, Fosse, Vieille Chapelle, La Vert Lannot, Locon. Returned at 5 p.m.

November 27th. Have received orders to go to-morrow as Corps Escort to Cavalry Corps Headquarters at La Motte.

November 28th. I started at 10.30 for La Motte and Bois and took over Cavalry Corps Escort from a troop of the 5th Lancers. The Staff are living in a magnificent chateau surrounded by Daimlers and Rolls-Royces. Every spare shed in the village is a garage.

November 29th. Sent out a patrol in the morning and afternoon through the woods to stop people shooting the pheasants with rifles and revolvers.

November 30th. A very quiet day.

December 1st. The King was driving through on his way from Merville to Hazebrouck, so I had some of my troop in the village keeping the roads clear. He came through about 4.30 a.m. Apparently to-morrow is going to be a hell of an affair.

December 2nd. Had ten men mounted along the Vieux Berquin road to keep the road clear, also a guard on each gate of the Chateau. The King arrived about 10.30 and had apparently walked most of the way from Hazebrouck. Doled out some medals and had Madame presented to him; took a glass of wine and drove off again.

December 3rd. We have got 6 new officers come out.

December 4th. Exercise in the morning.

December 5th. Exercise in the morning.

December 6th. Started on leave. On leave till

December 9th. Caught 1 p.m. from Victoria and after 6 hours in a motor bus reached 'home' at 12 midnight.

December 10th. Went over to La Motte to take over again.

December 11th. There is quite a sort of stir going on. All the nuts have been arriving at different times during the day but H.Q. divulge nothing.

December 12th. Handed over my job to a troop of the Bays.

December 13th. Got word to be ready to move to-morrow.

December 14th. Moved off at 7 a.m. in the direction of Bailleul and on through Bailleul for a couple of miles where we remained until about 2 p.m. At 2 p.m. we returned to billets in Bailleul. The town is absolutely stiff with troops.

December 15th. Exercised in the morning.

December 16th. Moved off at 9.30 a.m. back to our old billets which we reached about 11 a.m. Our jaunt out to Bailleul and back seems a most extraordinary affair.

December 17th. Hacked to H.Q. in the afternoon.

December 18th. We were Brigade for duty, no news of any kind.

December 19th. Roads getting absolutely under water.

December 20th. Received orders to be ready to move at a moment's notice. Later in the evening the order was cancelled.

December 23rd. Brigade route march which was ordered for to-morrow was countermanded at the last moment and we were told to be ready to move at a moments notice from to-morrow at 7 a.m.

December 24th. Turned out at 9 a.m. I thought we were going to fight but it turned into a route march in the snow. We were held up for the best part of an hour to an hour and a half while the artillery of Haig's Army went through. Back in billets by 1 p.m.

December 26th. Regimental route march.

December 29th to January 5th leave in England.

January 6th 1915. Back in billets about 10.30 p.m.

January 27th. Kaiser's birthday I think. A tremendous lot of firing during the night. We stood to with everything ready.

January 28th. Moved from our billets at Vieux Berquin to Blavingham via Merville and Thiennes and Steenbecque. We arrived at about 12 noon and spent the rest of the day getting the troops and the horses in.

January 29th. Some alterations were made in the billetting of the troops.

February 2nd. Left Steenbecque at 2 in motor bus for Ypres with 3 sergeants to billet for the regiment.

February 3rd. Started billetting at 9.30 and finished at 5. Had a pretty big job considering half the houses in our area are blown in and hardly any of them have windows.

February 4th. Inspected the Cloth Hall and Cathedral of which there is nothing left at all.

February 6th. They put no shells into Ypres last night in spite of our guns having been blazing at them most of the morning. Left for the trenches at 8.30.

February 7th. A quiet night. Returned from trenches about 12.15.

February 8th. We left Ypres at 9 p.m. and were settled in about 1 a.m.

February 9th. A very quiet day and no casualties.

February 10th. The Germans had gone on with a new forward trench and heightened it a goodish bit. Also they had been playing about in the nearest trench of all, which they had formerly used for throwing flares from only they have piled up a lot of earth in one place like a sort of redoubt. About 5.30 they put five bombs into us from their new trench. One blew in a dug-out of the 2nd troop, but none did any harm fortunately. With this exception it was a very quiet day, only a little mutual sniping.

February 11th. A very quiet night. A fair amount of shelling during the afternoon and evening.

February 13th. The 3rd Hussars arrived about 12.30 and proceeded to take over. I was left behind to show them round. About 5 a.m. I left for Ypres.

February 15th. I start for leave to-night and with any luck I shall be in London to-morrow. Really the trenches nowadays are nothing but a picnic and the nights are like the transformation scenes at the Drury Lane Pantomime with all the flares and star shells etc.

On leave till February 24th.

February 25th. Reached billets at 6 a.m.

March 11th. Moved off to La Motte and went into billets between Merville and Estaires.

March 12th. About 200 German prisoners came through in the evening.

April 23rd. Regiment moved off at 1.30 p.m. and marched just N.W. of Abeile. Our Brigade went back and billetted in Ecke.

April 24th. Moved from Ecke at 10.30 a.m. and concentrated about 2 miles S.E. of Poperinghe. We moved back and billetted in Boeschappe.

April 25th. Moved off at 9.30 a.m. and marched to cross roads about two miles North of Westoutre. They have been shelling Ypres. They were shelling Poperinghe this afternoon. At 2 p.m. we moved up North of Poperinghe and moved back early and billetted in Hootkercke. As we rode past Poperinghe the people were coming past in a huge hurry. One old woman was having a joy ride in a wheelbarrow - poor old devil.

April 26th. Concentrated in a field just east of Hootkercke at 6 a.m. At 9.30 p.m. we moved in towards Poperinghe about a couple of miles outside the town. There we tied up the horses and dismounted walked into Vlamershinghe, where we fetched up at 2 a.m.

April 27th. Very peaceful morning and afternoon and then at 5 p.m. they started shelling Vlamerhinghe and put some in the middle of the Greys' horses which were just opposite our billets. Then the fun started, ambulances, transport horses, Greys' horses and refugees all coming down the road together. We turned out and stood to. They did not shell for more than an hour and did very little damage and eventually we went back again for the night. We ought to have gone up to-day to the H in Halte.

May 3rd. At about 5 o'clock we got a sudden turn out and moved off at 6 p.m.; no one seemed to know where. We went along pretty fast through Poperinghe which rather thwarted the idea of going back to Thiennes. We eventually fetched up at our old farm, off saddled and picketed the horses and then the fun started. We set out in the direction of Ypres, skirted Vlamertinghe and kept circling round the country until we rendezvoused in a field near Ypres on the Ypres - Vlamertinghe road. We got there at 2 p.m. prepared for instant action and then lay down. We were apparently up there in support, while they were straightening and shortening a bit of the line near Zonnebeke. It was done without the Boches spotting it so we came back.

Lieutenant Leckie was killed by a shell on May 13th.

Lt.-Col. Hardwick writes (30-6-17):-

"As far as I can recollect we remained at Thiennes only
"one, possibly two nights, and we were then hurried up to
"Ypres in motor busses. We bivouacked just outside Ypres
"until the evening of the 12th May, and then marched up
"and took over the trenches during the night.

1/ Dragoons

Lt Leckie's Story
in 1914 War Diaries

allowing the sea to enter at the Nieuport locks at high tide. A second line of defence was also begun on the Loo canal, five miles behind the railway.

Sir John French, at the close of the 25th October reported that the situation was growing more favourable every hour, and his anxiety was over; and that though the casualties had been tremendous, the fighting was decreasing in intensity. He sent his Chief of the General Staff, Sir Archibald Murray, to London to report more fully. General Foch, whom he visited at Poperinghe, considered that the Belgian-French position on the Yser was also becoming much more satisfactory. He promised the British commander French reinforcements, to the extent of another regular corps, in the next two days. All appeared to be going well, and at 11.30 that night the Secretary of State for War telegraphed the thanks of the

Copy of the diary of the late Lieutenant J.H.Leckie,
1st Dragoons.
6th Cavalry Brigade 3rd Cavalry Div.

October 6th 1914. Received orders to entrain at Amesbury. Left Windmill Hill at 1 a.m. Left Amesbury at 5 a.m. and reached Southampton somewhere about 7.30. Spent all day in embarking on 'Indore'. On board there were two squadrons 2nd Life Guards, two squadrons Royal Dragoons and one squadron 1st Life Guards.

October 7th. Sailed from Southampton at 5 a.m. and stopped first off Dover and then on to Deal for sailing orders. 'Indore' not much of a boat, but being only a cattle boat one cannot expect too much.

October 8th. Arrived at Zeebrugge, just beyond Ostend, at 6 a.m. It was a real cold night and a goodish bit of wind. Took a long time disembarking the horses. Moved off from Zeebrugge about 4.30 p.m. Had a huge reception from the 'Belgies' all along the road. They rushed out with cigarettes, biscuits and drinks. Watered in Brandenberge and then on to Ostend where we arrived at 9.30 and bivouacked on the race course. Horses were tied up to the rails.

October 9th. There are a lot of aeroplanes on the race course, mostly Belgian I fancy. They are pretty clever in getting up and landing in a comparatively confined space. Left Ostend about 1 p.m. and marched to Vassanaere and billetted in a convent, horses in the open. Arrived after dark about 7 or 8.

October 10th. Left Vassanaere about noon for Thurout via Lophem. The hospitality of the 'Belgies' is really rather a nuisance. They positively hurl fruit and biscuits at you. Got very good billets in Thurout, the horses in stables, the men in Pubs. and ourselves in three houses and very comfortable.

October 11th. Went out on outpost to Lichterde. Several armoured motors came in in the evening with a few captured Uhlans in them. Received orders to remain out during the night, so pushed the horses and ourselves into a farm close by the railway. Had one post on the cross roads. As I was going round at night a shot was loosed off, must have been Belgian, as I dont fancy the Huns are anywhere near.

October 12th. Regiment moved at 8.30 and we all set off on flank guard via Costemarck and Hooglede to Oostnienkerke. Got in about noon.

October 13th. Brigade moved off in the morning to Ypres, where we waited for a long time in the market square. A very fine square with good buildings. Went on eventually to Dadizeche. I with my troop was boosted off at once on outpost to the cross roads just outside the town. Had some difficulty in getting there as it was a pitch dark night and there was a tremendous block of transport on the road. No alarms during the night except for Corporal Evans who brought in two harmless civilians, imagining, I suppose, that they were spies.

October 14th. Brigade moved off early via Ypres to a line of protection just south. Moved on to Neuve Eglise and waited just behind the firing line. Brigade was not wanted so after dark moved into billets in Wytschaete. Horses in the open.

October 15th. Brigade remained in billets in Wytschaete. The day's rest has done the horses a lot of good. They always seem to move us into billets after dark which makes it a good deal harder, but I suppose there must be something in it.

October 16th. Our Division moved early to Poelcapelle, waited for about four hours outside the village in the most fearful cold. We were waiting apparently to support the Household Cavalry Brigade, who were playing about in the Forêt d'Houthoulst

October 17th. Remained in our billets outside Zonnebeke all day.

October 18th. Received orders to move into Zonnebeke which we did at 5.30 a.m. and spent the day at the cross roads just outside the village. Moved into Moorslede late that evening. Had three troops on outpost as the woods all round were reported to be full of Huns. No alarms during the night.

October 19th. Brigade moved to St.Pieters. Two troops went on
as advanced guard by different roads. On getting to the beginning
of the village an inhabitant told me there were about 12
Uhlans feeding in a farm house. I went on a few hundred yards
when volleys of shots began. Went up with my troop and had
shots at them as they bolted from the farm to the cow-house,
where their horses were evidently. Kept on potting them whenever
they showed themselves and dropped about 6 altogether I
should say. They waved a white flag from the cow-house so we
advanced to round them up and were promptly fired on by their
people behind, so we had to retire after catching a couple of
them. Again lined the road. Grenfell and his troop advanced
parallel to the road through the roots, but were held up by
heavy fire. Rest of squadron lined out on the other side of the
road. Grenfell eventually got into the farm at the end of the
road, and the remainder got in behind a cottage on the road.
After some time retired and withdrew to St.Pieters. The Huns
were coming on across the railway in thousands. Retired back
through Moorslede and billetted in Poelcapelle.

October 20th. Brigade moved early to dig trenches and occupy a
line near Westroosebeke. Remained in the trenches until about
1 p.m. when the French, who were in Westroosebeke on our left,
retired, so we had to follow suit. Retired behind Poelcapelle
and were just going to billet by squadrons in the farm handy
when a French officer arrived to say the Huns were still advancing
and were about 1½ miles the other side of the village. They
then started shelling so the whole brigade moved back and we
billetted in St.Julien in a perfectly filthy farm. The kitchen
had just been vacated by Belgians and was inches deep in mud &
filth.

October 21st. A lot of firing during the night. "C" squadron
had a pretty sharp night attack. Went early into Ypres to
replenish supplies and forage in the square by the station. The
whole brigade moved out to Hooge in support. In the afternoon

received orders to go to Zanvoorde and occupy the trenches there and took them over from the infantry about 10 p.m. Horses were left up in the village.

October 22nd. In the supporting trenches at Zanvoorde all day. No excitement of any kind except that the horses were shelled in Zandvoorde and had to be moved down to the big wood.

October 23rd. Were relieved in the trenches by the Household Cavalry about 10 a.m. and went back to Klein Zillebeke. Spies in the houses were signalling with lamps to the Huns, so we turned them all out and marched them up.

October 24th. Remained at Klein Zillebeke all day. They had been putting 'Jack Johnsons' over us all night, pitching them just over the crest the other side of the road. To-night they got them nearer, so we had to shift after dark, only a few hundred yards away to the next farm.

October 25th. A lot of firing during the night.

October 26th. I was sent up with my troop to "A" Squadron in the Chateau of Hollebeke. Very peaceful night, practically no firing.

October 27th. Returned to Klein Zillebeke.

October 28th. Slept inside a farm cottage, first night indoors for a week.

October 29th. Saddled up and went out in support up to Zandvoorde. Back again to Klein Zillebeke after dark.

October 30th. Went into the trenches in support of Chateau early and got a fairly bad shelling, but nothing like what "A" Squadron had in the Chateau. We retired to the trenches on the edge of a wood where we remained from about 5 p.m. until 12 at night, when we were relieved by the Grenadiers. Retired to Zillebeke.

October 31st. Shelled out of our place early by 'Jack Johnsons'. Brigade moved up beyond Hooge in support. In the afternoon took up a line of trenches to cover the retirement of the 7th Division. This was unnecessary and we were soon moved out to the Division's assistance in the big woods. Bivouacked in the wood.

November 1st. Huns started shelling our wood so we had to clear out. Went back to the woods to support the Irish Guards, found they had had absolute hell in the trenches from shell fire. Took over their trenches about 3 p.m. while they reorganized themselves and were relieved by the French about 11 p.m.

November 2nd. Brigade moved off about 5 a.m. into the big wood in support. Remained there all day and got back to our bivouac about 7 p.m.

November 3rd. Back to another part of the wood at 6 a.m. Moved after a bit behind the Hooge - Ypres road. Germans were shelling the Ypres road to some tune. Bivouacked in a new farm just across the line.

November 4th. Turned out in the middle of the night on a message being sent in that the Germans had broken through; it turned out to be a false alarm.

November 5th. Was sent off with an orderly to General Cavan, 4th Guards Brigade, near Zillebeke, recalled at 3.30 p.m. as the brigade was going into trenches near Gheluvelt.

November 6th. In supporting trenches all day. Relieved at 2.30 a.m. and got back to bivouac at 4 a.m.

November 7th. Moved off at 12 noon to take place of Household Brigade. At night turned out to support Cavan, a false alarm.

November 8th. In trenches. Had a few shells over during the night.

November 9th. Regiment in trenches at Klein Zillebeke. French made an attack into the wood in front of our trenches in the evening. Regiment got back about 10 p.m.

November 10th. Turned out at 1 a.m. and went up to Zillebeke and waited until dark because the Germans were supposed to be massing for an attack. Went on into the trenches after drawing rations. Most awful block on the road caused by French cavalry.

November 11th. In firing line trenches all day. Pretty heavy shelling. Relieved and got back to our farm at 11 p.m.

November 12th. Paraded for trenches again at 5 p.m. We were in support a short way in front of Zillebeke just behind the trenches we were in before.

November 13th. In trenches all day. Heavy shelling with short bursts and lulls in between. Relieved early by the 1st Life Guards. Back to camp where we found that they had been shelling our horses pretty considerably all day. A lot of horses were hit.

November 14th. Brigade moved about 1.30 through Ypres, where the Huns had done a goodish bit of damage with 'Jack Johnsons' to new billets in some farms just the other side of Vlamertinghe. The Cathedral and Cloth Hall are still standing at Ypres.

November 15th. Stood to at 6.30 and gave the horses some exercise. Moved off at 2.30; road blocked with transport and French motor transport. Rode as far as Ypres where we left the horses. Marched from Ypres to Zillebeke along the line and then on into the firing line trenches beyond Cavan's headquarters. The Huns are within about 100 yards of us.

November 16th. Remained in the trenches all day. There was a certain amount of shooting during the morning, but on the whole it was a very quiet day

November 17th Germans made an attack all along the line lasting from 12 to 3 p.m. They failed to break through and suffered pretty severe losses. After dark a perfect fusilade started and the Huns threw up lights. We discovered afterwards that they do this when they expect a counter-attack. Later on went up to conduct the relieving party from H.Q. We started at 9 p.m. with 1st Herts. Territorials and eventually got them into the trenches and got away ourselves at 11 p.m.

November 18th. Remained in camp all day.

November 19th. According to present arrangements we go back to Hazebrouck to-morrow to rest and refit. The French seem to have taken over the whole of our line in this part of the world.

November 20th. Wagons started off at 6.30 a.m. for billeting area. Left at 3.30 p.m. Came through Poperinghe, Mont Rouge, Westoutre, Vieux Berquin. Our new billets are from Vieux Berquin through Verte Rue and on just past Candescure.

November 21st. The horses are out in the open, but the men are quite comfortable in barns and ourselves very comfortable in two farms.

November 22nd. Arms inspected in the morning.

November 23rd. Walked over to H.Q. with the letters in the morning and to Vieux Berquin in the afternoon.

November 24th. Spent all day looking for billets for horses.

November 25th. Spent the afternoon in looking for lodgings for the men.

November 26th. Started for Headquarters and found we were to go out on a reconnaissance. First went to Brigade Headquarters and then started off through Merville, Beaupré, Gorgue, Lestrem, Pont Riqual, Fosse, Vieille Chapelle, La Vert Lannot, Locon. Returned at 5 p.m.

November 27th Have received orders to go to-morrow as Corps Escort to Cavalry Corps Headquarters at La Motte.

November 28th. I started at 10.30 for La Motte and Bois and took over Cavalry Corps Escort from a troop of the 5th Lancers. The Staff are living in a magnificent chateau surrounded by Daimlers and Rolls-Royces. Every spare shed in the village is a garage.

November 29th. Sent out a patrol in the morning and afternoon through the woods to stop people shooting the pheasants with rifles and revolvers.

November 30th. A very quiet day.

December 1st. The King was driving through on his way from Merville to Hazebrouck, so I had some of my troop in the village keeping the roads clear. He came through about 4.30 a.m. Apparently to-morrow is going to be a hell of an affair.

December 2nd. Had ten men mounted along the Vieux Berquin road to keep the road clear, also a guard on each gate of the Chateau. The King arrived about 10.30 and had apparently walked most of the way from Hazebrouck. Doled out some medals and had Madame presented to him; took a glass of wine and drove off again.

December 3rd. We have got 6 new officers come out.

December 4th. Exercise in the morning.

December 5th. Exercise in the morning.

December 6th. Started on leave. On leave till

December 9th. Caught 1 p.m. from Victoria and after 6 hours in a motor bus reached 'home' at 12 midnight.

December 10th. Went over to La Motte to take over again.

December 11th. There is quite a sort of stir going on. All the nuts have been arriving at different times during the day but H.Q. divulge nothing.

December 12th. Handed over my job to a troop of the Bays.

December 13th. Got word to be ready to move to-morrow.

December 14th. Moved off at 7 a.m. in the direction of Bailleul and on through Bailleul for a couple of miles where we remained until about 2 p.m. At 2 p.m. we returned to billets in Bailleul. The town is absolutely stiff with troops.

December 15th. Exercised in the morning.

December 16th. Moved off at 9.30 a.m. back to our old billets which we reached about 11 a.m. Our jaunt out to Bailleul and back seems a most extraordinary affair.

December 17th. Hacked to H.Q. in the afternoon.

December 18th. We were Brigade for duty, no news of any kind.

December 19th. Roads getting absolutely under water.

December 20th. Received orders to be ready to move at a moment's notice. Later in the evening the order was cancelled.

December 23rd. Brigade route march which was ordered for tomorrow was countermanded at the last moment and we were told to be ready to move at a moments notice from to-morrow at 7 a.m.

December 24th. Turned out at 9 a.m. I thought we were going to fight but it turned into a route march in the snow. We were held up for the best part of an hour to an hour and a half while the artillery of Haig's Army went through. Back in billets by 1 p.m.

December 26th. Regimental route march.

December 29th to January 6th leave in England.

January 6th 1915. Back in billets about 10.30 p.m.

January 27th. Kaiser's birthday I think. A tremendous lot of firing during the night. We stood to with everything ready.

January 28th. Moved from our billets at Vieux Berquin to Blavingham via Merville and Thiennes and Steenbecque. We arrived at about 12 noon and spent the rest of the day getting the troops and the horses in.

January 29th. Some alterations were made in the billetting of the troops.

February 2nd. Left Steenbecque at 2 in motor bus for Ypres with 3 sergeants to billet for the regiment.

February 3rd. Started billetting at 9.30 and finished at 5. Had a pretty big job considering half the houses in our area are blown in and hardly any of them have windows.

February 4th. Inspected the Cloth Hall and Cathedral of which there is nothing left at all.

February 6th. They put no shells into Ypres last night in spite of our guns having been blazing at them most of the morning. Left for the trenches at 8.30.

February 7th. A quiet night. Returned from trenches about 12.15.

February 8th. We left Ypres at 9 p.m. and were settled in about 1 a.m.

February 9th. A very quiet day and no casualties.

February 10th. The Germans had gone on with a new forward trench and heightened it a goodish bit. Also they had been playing about in the nearest trench of all, which they had formerly used for throwing flares from only they have piled up a lot of earth in one place like a sort of redoubt. About 5.30 they put five bombs into us from their new trench. One blew in a dug-out of the 2nd troop, but none did any harm fortunately. With this exception it was a very quiet day, only a little mutual sniping.

February 11th. A very quiet night. A fair amount of shelling during the afternoon and evening.

February 13th. The 3rd Hussars arrived about 12.30 and proceeded to take over. I was left behind to show them round. About 5 a.m. I left for Ypres.

February 15th. I start for leave to-night and with any luck I shall be in London to-morrow. Really the trenches nowadays are nothing but a picnic and the nights are like the transformation scenes at the Drury Lane Pantomime with all the flares and star shells etc.

On leave till February 24th.

February 25th. Reached billets at 6 a.m.

March 11th. Moved off to La Motte and went into billets between Merville and Estaires.

March 12th. About 200 German prisoners came through in the evening.

April 23rd. Regiment moved off at 1.30 p.m. and marched just N.W. of Abeile. Our Brigade went back and billetted in Ecke.

April 24th. Moved from Ecke at 10.30 a.m. and concentrated about 2 miles S.E. of Poperinghe. We moved back and billetted in Boeschappe.

April 25th. Moved off at 9.30 a.m. and marched to cross
roads about two miles North of Westoutre. They have been shelling
Ypres. They were shelling Poperinghe this afternoon. At 2 p.m.
we moved up North of Poperinghe and moved back early and
billetted in Hootkercke. As we rode past Poperinghe the people
were coming past in a huge hurry. One old woman was having a
joy ride in a wheelbarrow - poor old devil.

April 26th. Concentrated in a field just east of Hootkercke at
6 a.m. At 9.30 p.m. we moved in towards Poperinghe about a
couple of miles outside the town. There we tied up the horses
and dismounted walked into Vlamershinghe, where we fetched up
at 2 a.m.

April 27th. Very peaceful morning and afternoon and then at
5 p.m. they started shelling Vlamerhinghe and put some in the
middle of the Greys' horses which were just opposite our
billets. Then the fun started, ambulances, transport horses,
Greys' horses and refugees all coming down the road together.
We turned out and stood to. They did not shell for more than
an hour and did very little damage and eventually we went
back again for the night. We ought to have gone up to-day to
the H in Halte.

May 3rd. At about 5 o'clock we got a sudden turn out and moved
off at 6 p.m.; no one seemed to know where. We went along
pretty fast through Poperinghe which rather thwarted the idea
of going back to Thiennes. We eventually fetched up at our old
farm, off saddled and picketed the horses and then the fun
started. We set out in the direction of Ypres, skirted
Vlamertinghe and kept circling round the country until we
rendezvoused in a field near Ypres on the Ypres - Vlamertinghe
road. We got there at 2 p.m. prepared for instant action and
then lay down. We were apparently up there in support, while they
were straightening and shortening a bit of the line near
Zonnebeke. It was done without the Boches spotting it so we
came back.

Lieutenant Leckie was killed by a shell on May 13th.

Lt.-Col. Hardwick writes (30-6-17):-

"As far as I can recollect we remained at Thiernes only
"one, possibly two nights, and we were then hurried up to
"Ypres in motor busses. We bivouacked just outside Ypres
"until the evening of the 12th May, and then marched up
"and took over the trenches during the night.

21st Nov - Shortage of entrenching tools

1901

121/2598

1st Royal Dragoons.

6th Cav. Brigade
3 Cav Div

Vol II. 1 — 30.11.14

Army Form C. 2118.

WAR DIARY
or
INTELLIGENCE SUMMARY.
(Erase heading not required.)

Vol. I

Instructions regarding War Diaries and Intelligence Summaries are contained in F.S. Regs., Part II. and the Staff Manual respectively. Title pages will be prepared in manuscript.

Hour, Date, Place	Summary of Events and Information	Remarks and references to Appendices
1st November 1914	We were again employed as Corps Reserve. After waiting all day we were sent up to assist the night of the 1st Brigade near KLEIN ZILLEBEKE. We found that the Irish Guards had suffered very heavily from shell fire, including that of 2 rifle guns at 500x from their trenches. Trench was that they had fallen right back and the Oxford L. Infantry's right was completely in the air. Two of our Squadrons and one of the 10th Life Guards sent us and put them back in their trenches. We had to wait till 10·30 am. When General CAVAN had got his line straightened out, French troops then took over our own trenches and we got back & bivouac near HOOGE about 11 pm. [Lieut G.A.L.F. PITT-RIVERS was wounded in leg by shrapnel. Pt COX A.L. was also wounded.]	1/ R. etc
2nd November 1914	Turned out even before as Corps Reserve. As ere time GEN CAVAN asked for help but this proved a false alarm and we returned at dusk after doing nothing.	
4th November 1914	Corps Reserve again. Nothing doing up to 2 pm. Capt LAMBERT joined 2 Troop Yesterday and took over Machine Guns. At dusk we were sent up to take trenches east of VELDHOEK. Our trenches were in support and we had little to do.	
5 November 1914	Remained in supporting trenches. 2 Troops of 'A' Sqdn were sent up to support St DRAGOON Guards in the firing line. There was no attack but fairly heavy shelling. Cap LAMBERT	
6 November 1914	was slightly wounded in the face by a bit of shrapnel and had to have it dressed. A Sqdn suffered the following casualties. Wounded 8/Sgt HORRELL STAGNALL TAYLOR 1597 HARNETT[Y?] PSMN SYMONS.	
7 November 1914	We held reserve about 10 km and returned to bivouac near HOOGE. Moved in the afternoon to farm near HALTE where we went into bivouac along the Railway. Orders received to join at Bg HdQrs during night. Lt WELSH burnt to death. Turned out on in advance.Scheme which proved to be false and returned again to camp.	
8 November 1914	Sent up dismounted and took over trenches just N of KLEINE ZILLEBEKE - ZILLE-BEKE ROAD at 8 pm. A. & C. Sqdns with M. Guns in firing line, B Sqdn in support. No French during the night attacked KLEINE ZILLEBEKE 2 ZILLEBEKE RD on our right but	

Army Form C. 2118.

WAR DIARY
or
INTELLIGENCE SUMMARY.
(Erase heading not required.)

Instructions regarding War Diaries and Intelligence Summaries are contained in F.S. Regs., Part II. and the Staff Manual respectively. Title pages will be prepared in manuscript.

Hour, Date, Place	Summary of Events and Information	Remarks and references to Appendices
8th November 1914 (Contd)	but left in again the next day. All quiet.	J.B. Egan
9th November 1914	All quiet during the day. Shell fire pretty continuous but did no damage. Relieved at 8 p.m. by 7 Cav. Brigade (no casualties). Germans advanced to destroying bridges over Canal at YPRES and then heavy gun with the idea of interrupting Communications. A Sqdn found the body of A. de Gernsberg in wood (just in front of their trenches). Lieut. Bagshawe and 150 men joined from England. This leaves us 12 men under Strength. We are now 38 riding horses short and 4 draught horses.	
9th November 1914	Remained in bivouac.	
10th November 1914	Moved up to near ZILLEBEKE in reserve to 8th Cavan but were not required at about 4.30pm. A Sqdn returned to bivouac. B & C Squadrons went into trenches to relieve 9th Cav. Bde. — [Pte FOX wounded by shrapnel in bivouac.]	
11th November 1914	Remained in bivouac till 11 a.m. at that hour received orders to "stand to" ready to move. At 5 p.m. A Sqdn went up to the trenches at KLEINE ZILLEBEKE and B Sqdn returned at 11 pm not having any very Cols. (Ptes CASTLE & STOCKWELL wounded & Pte BROWN unplaced). Our casualties to date are as follows:— Personnel — 88 (Officers 9) Killed missing wounded. 2 officers + 70 men reinforcements. Horses. 134 Casualties. 65 Reinforcements.	
12 November 1914	A & C Squadrons remained in the trenches. B Squadron turned out at 5 p.m. to go back to the trenches. C Sqdn returned to bivouac at 8 p.m. and reported the following casualties: Privately from Snipers and partly from heavy shell fire. Several of the men were practically blinded in the trenches as the shells had become very enemy to pour. And the trenches were full of water. Casualties.	

WAR DIARY
or
INTELLIGENCE SUMMARY.
(Erase heading not required.)

Army Form C. 2118.

Hour, Date, Place	Summary of Events and Information	Remarks and references to Appendices
12 November 1914 (Contd)	Casualties - Killed - 5 (See BARNETT, PTE. TAYLOR, ANDREWS, SLADE, ORR) Wounded 1 [Pte BOWMAN] The casualty list of A Sqdn is not yet in but it is reported by telephone that Capt DORINGTON has been shot (through the head by a sniper. His body is being taken to YPRES)	1 & B off. sgts
13 November 1914	We here named last night to turn out all available men at 4 A.M. this morning to be in reserve and not to take any one if required. A heavy attack was expected on the KLEINE ZILLEBEKE Road but though we saddled fell 4 A.M. there was no attack and we were sent back to bivouac. The Germans are reported to be massed in considerable force in front of YPRES and yesterday, it is said, that their Grand Division attacked the line between GHELUVELDT and ZONNEBEKE leading the line back in the form of a V. The 1st Cav Division were sent over in the night of the 11th/12th move to the 10th/Brigade. We have now had two Squadrons in the trenches for the consecutive days and it has been almost continually wet. The trenches are getting into an awful state and will not stand much more very much more in heavy falling in. Yesterday we received two new Squadrons and now have B Mackies Sqn in support orders. & C & a orders of the Inns of Court Sqn will be available for use. The N. Somerset Yeomanry have expected to join our Bge last night but did not turn up though the Gloucestershire Yeomanry arrived at 8 p.m. The report of Capt DORINGTON's death is unfortunately confirmed. He was looking out for an orchard attack upon the trenches and was shot dead through the head. He was buried in Ypres Military Cemetery. Other Casualties of A Sqdn are - Killed Sgt YEATS - Pte KNELL. Wounded 2 Sgt VICKERY - Pte TURNER (under ac of 10/11/14) A & B Squadrons returned at about 8 p.m. after having had a very bad time from the wet and steel fire. Many men were quite buried by the trenches being	

WAR DIARY
or
INTELLIGENCE SUMMARY.
(Erase heading not required.)

Army Form C. 2118.

Hour, Date, Place	Summary of Events and Information	Remarks and references to Appendices
13th November 1914 (Contd)	kept blown in. In the afternoon we had a very bad time from concentrated shell fire in our bivouac altogether 30 horses were killed and 40 severely wounded & will have to be evacuated. The enemy had evidently found us out & sprayed the casualties amongst the horses. We lost fellow N.C.O. man killed (Osborne & Pte Marshall) and also the following men wounded & injured:— Pte Read, Tyler, Mann, Janes. B.Sqn also distributed the following casualties on departure from the trenches — 3 wounded (Sgt Wilson, Cpl Philcox, L.Cpl Ford.)	1/B W.B.m
14 November 1914	During the night of 13-14 horses were again stabled, but curiously enough nothing hit the farm we were actually in. At 1.30 p.m. we moved off to a more restful position 5 miles WEST. in farm SOUTH of VLAMERTINGHE. We were told in the morning that there would be a Voluntary Church Service at our farm but as it was raining and snowing the Chaplain did not turn up. At 3.30 p.m. we started off for the trenches on L.t. Cavan's left N of KLEINE ZILLEBEKE while the 2nd Troop came from the 2nd Cav: Brigade. ½ trenches here in the wood and very close to the enemy who have in many places not more than 40 or 50 yards away. Taking over was rather a lengthy process owing to the thick undergrowth. Left A Sqn our horses at YPRES and they were sent back. We marched off from there to the trenches along the railway. Strength 300 rifles. At ZILLEBEKE rations were issued and the men got some hot tea from a "cooker" we had borrowed from the Glowester Regt a few days ago.	
16 November 1914	At 6.30 a.m. visited the firing line and found out how the trenches lay. A Sqn held 3 troops in the firing line, B. in close support. C Sqn in reserve. 50 yards behind. All trenches were dug outs holding about 2 men. 2 Squadrons of the 10 Hussars were on night in extra side were French. Snipers During	

WAR DIARY
or
INTELLIGENCE SUMMARY.

Army Form C. 2118.

(Erase heading not required.)

Hour, Date, Place	Summary of Events and Information	Remarks and references to Appendices
15 November 1914 (Cont'd)	During the day all was quiet except for sniping. On one side Sgt. McKELLAN and Cpl. KELMAN went out and shot 2 Germans out of a party of 30 whom they saw. Lt. GRENFELL with a patrol got close up to the German trenches and shot 2 through their loop-holes. Cpl. KELMAN two wounded, not seriously, in the head.	
16 November 1914	All quiet early except for sniping. Pte. BROWNE hit by a sniper in the closes. Serious but not fatal it is to be hoped. About 10.30 p.m. till 11.30 p.m. Germans shelled the trenches & ground behind our wood, very heavily, evidently trying to find out our guns. Every house in the neighbourhood was blown to pieces but CAVAN'S H.Q. & where we were down across the road and his dug outs buried the telephone ceased to work about 11-11 p.m. About 1 A.m. he heard that Germans were moving on our right front. Shortly afterwards they attacked in great force and with remarkably bravery. Said to message to our guns to shell their concentration when they did at first both success but afterwards their shells fell short in front themselves. The telephone was not in working order. A working telephone was among that the telephone was not in working order and added very much to the difficulties would have made a vast difference About 1.30 a.m. the attack was finally repulsed. In some cases the Germans got within about 20 x but they had to keep of getting further and withdrew with very heavy losses. Lord Chesham & Lt. J. Trueman counted 30 dead in front of his trench alone. Our casualties here very small about 5 men of the 10th Hussars and Cpl. Rbo shot through the knee. The 10th Hussars shot for ammunition and he unfortunately took Pte. MICHAEL Shot through the head when fetching a box from base there. Reserve. Pte. HULL was wounded and Pte. PERKS killed when taking a message.	1/R. A. D. F. a.m.

WAR DIARY
or
INTELLIGENCE SUMMARY.

(Erase heading not required.)

Army Form C. 2118.

Hour, Date, Place	Summary of Events and Information	Remarks and references to Appendices
17 November 1914 (Continued)	About 1.30 p.m. Major SHEARMAN arrived with a Squadron of the Sharks in support, but was not needed and remained at T Roads. He reports that the Germans had attacked in our right and had suffered heavy loss from the Grenadiers, N.S.Y. and 5th Dragoon Guards. At 9 p.m. the HERTS Territorials under Col. HAMPDEN arrived to relieve us. We marched back to YPRES. Got our horses and reached bivouac about 2.15 a.m.	1/R.27.gm
18th & 19 November 1914	Remained in bivouac. Col. LAMBERT sent to N.S. Yeomanry, to whom he has been lent as Adjutant for a few days. A draft of Capt. C. ANNERSLEY & 52 men joined yesterday & 16 44 horses. We also evacuated Sick Horses and about 23 horses from Remount Farm at DICKEBUSH. BEEN.	
20 November 1914	We marched off at 3.30 p.m. as Brigade. The transport started at 7 a.m. We started as far as WESTROUTRE when the road got very slippery owing to frost and we finally had to walk on our feet the remaining 12 miles (total 18) to CAPPEL ROUSSEL near VIEUX-BERQUIN where we got in rather scattered billets at 10 p.m. It was a very cold & tiring march in the snow. The transport had got stuck and we found it blocked half way by motor lorries. Eventually some of it did not get in till next afternoon. The road over MONT NOIR was very slippery owing to frost and snow.	
21st November 1914	Remained in billets. H.Q. at CAPPEL-BOOM. Men under cover but horses in open. During the day took steps to find further accommodation in the billeting area for horses. I have scattering somewhat, but in view of the cold weather is well worth it for the sake of the horses. Our billeting area stretches roughly from the Cow Roads at LA COURONNE, through COUDESCORE to ROUSSEL FARM. The area contains plenty of farm houses and houses of fairsized appear to have ample stabling. The farms, houses, and mostly full as and have roots	

WAR DIARY or INTELLIGENCE SUMMARY.

(Erase heading not required.)

Army Form C. 2118.

Hour, Date, Place	Summary of Events and Information	Remarks and references to Appendices
21 November 1914 (Continued)	roots & potatoes which makes it more difficult to dig trenches are quite frost bound and as a Cav: Regiment, we may be considered completely immobile. The Transport horses are being roughed but it takes time especially as we are short of tools. The Squadrons are all very comfortable as regards Officers mess who are all under cover and have hourly four Horses. Reg H.Qrs at CAPPER BOOM is very comfortable. The officers have a horse to themselves so has the R.Cpl. West of area lies the FORÊT de NIEPPE which contains a fair amount of game including pheasants and roe-deer. 	
22 November 1914	Horses are all practically under cover except for one troop of 'B' Squadron which Carpenters room all horses are being fitted for frost nails. This should be completed by 1st December 1914. Sanction has been given for 25% of the officers to proceed on 72 hours leave to England at one time.	
23 November 1914	S.o.C has decided that in future, mounted fours will never quarter in front of Fighting troops of the Brigade. The heavy rear the Advd Bde Brunaide stopped us on our last Trenches were drawn out and sent to be put back by Canadian Sundw.	
24 November 1914	The Cavalry Corps appears now to be concentrated in this area and has been ordered to be in readiness to move at any time. Each Division will be on duty for 48 hours at a time, 3rd Div will come in at 4 pm 28th, others men will remain in their billets and be in readiness to turn out.	
25th & 26 November 1914	Regiment remains in billets chiefly occupied cleaning saddlery. Skating continued. No special news. Casualty lists checked with Rgte Office. One dead, of Concealn to date 112.	

Army Form C. 2118.

WAR DIARY
or
INTELLIGENCE SUMMARY.
(Erase heading not required.)

(8.)

Instructions regarding War Diaries and Intelligence Summaries are contained in F.S. Regs., Part II. and the Staff Manual respectively. Title pages will be prepared in manuscript.

Hour, Date, Place	Summary of Events and Information	Remarks and references to Appendices
November 27th 1914.	The Regiment was ordered to reconnoitre a possible line of defence to the East and it was decided that in the event of attack the line to hold would be that of the Canal and River LAWE from LA GORGUE railway bridge to LA VERT LANNOWE. The country does not lend itself particularly to a line of defence, but is well connected by roads and affords good lateral communication.	1/person
November 28th – 30th.	Nothing doing. Chief occupation has been re-fitting the Regiment with clothing and picketing gear, etc. Another Tripod has been received for the Maxim Gun.	

December 2nd 1914

Hotchkiss
Hotchkiss Capt & Adjt Dragoons
Capt The Roy[al] Dragoons

6th Cavalry Brigade $\frac{121}{4197}$

1st Royal Dragoons.

Vol III 1 — 31.12.14

1st (Royal) Dragoons   Vol. III   Army Form C. 2118.

WAR DIARY
or
INTELLIGENCE SUMMARY.

(Erase heading not required.)

No. 1.

Instructions regarding War Diaries and Intelligence Summaries are contained in F.S. Regs., Part II. and the Staff Manual respectively. Title pages will be prepared in manuscript.

Hour, Date, Place	Summary of Events and Information	Remarks and references to Appendices
Appel Room, North France		
December 1st.	Nothing to report.	
" 2nd.	The Cavalry Corps was inspected by H.M. the King, who walked down the line of the 3rd Cavalry Division. The Division was formed up on either side of the HAZEBROUCK – LA MOTTE Road at 9.0 am.	
" 7th.	The General Officer Commanding 3rd Cavalry Corps inspected the men and horses of the Regiment in their Billets and congratulated the Regiment upon the general turnout.	
" 14th.	The Regiment was ordered to rendezvous at 7.15 am and move forward with the remainder of the 3rd Cavalry Division to a front N.E. of BAILLEUL. It was understood that the Cavalry were to support an Infantry attack North of NEUVE EGLISE. We could see the shells bursting on the ridge about 2 miles East of our position but after waiting for some 3 hours the Cavalry were ordered to return to Billets and were not actually employed. We heard later that the Infantry had made some ground and captured a small wood to the East of NEUVE EGLISE.	

Army Form C. 2118.

1st (Royal) Dragoons

Instructions regarding War Diaries and Intelligence
Summaries are contained in F. S. Regs., Part II.
and the Staff Manual respectively. Title pages
will be prepared in manuscript.

WAR DIARY
or
INTELLIGENCE SUMMARY.
(Erase heading not required.)

Vol: III   No. 2.

Hour, Date, Place	Summary of Events and Information	Remarks and references to Appendices
Appx Boon, N. France December 14th (contd.)	The Regiment was billeted in some "Grapeneries" at BAILLUEL, the horses being bivouacked in the open in some muddy fields.	
December 16th. — CAUDESCURE	The Regiment returned to its original Billets at CAUDESCURE	
December 16th. – 31st. —	During this period we remained in our Billets. The Cavalry Corps being divided into three reliefs. The Regiment came on duty in its turn for 4 & 8 hours, during which time Troops were confined to their Billets and were to be ready to move out at short notice. Training developed on peace lines — Route Marches, Trench-digging, Skirmishing, and practice in Sniping being the principal items. The Regiment was also refitted with warm clothing, etc., and blankets for horses were issued in addition to the usual saddle blankets. Leave was granted to Officers and Non-commissioned Officers (6 and 4 at a time) for one week in England, whilst Privates (12 at a time) were given 72 hours leave in England.	

1st (Royal) Dragoons

Army Form C. 2118.

WAR DIARY
or
INTELLIGENCE SUMMARY.
(Erase heading not required.)

Vol. III   No. 3

Hour, Date, Place	Summary of Events and Information	Remarks and references to Appendices

Upper Boom - N. France. December 16th - 31st 1914. (continued).	Our Billets have suffered from being in a very low position, and consequently the country has been waterlogged.
	There has been very little sickness, but the life naturally has been most monotonous for the Troops.
	During this period, the Regiment was made up to strength in Officers by the arrival of the undermentioned:-
	
	Captain W.C.R. Roberts (late of the Regiment)
	    " V.H. Secker
	2/Lt. J.D.L. de Wend-Fenton } 14th Hussars
	2/Lt. G. H. Bayshawe } rejoined from Hospital
	2/Lt. W.O. Berryman }
	    " A. Hopkinson } 5th Res. Regt. of Cavalry
	    " Ackeroyd }
	2/Lt. C.N.F. Browne } Gazetted from R.M.C.
	    " R.B. Hulme }
		The Hon E. Stanley Lieut. Colonel, commanded the Royal Dragoons

121/4539

6ᵗʰ Cavalry Brigade

1ˢᵗ Royal Dragoons

Vols IV & V 1.1 — 28.2.15

Feb 3ʳᵈ — Interesting description of state of Town of Ypres.

Army Form C. 2118.

WAR DIARY
or
INTELLIGENCE SUMMARY.
(Erase heading not required.)

1st. (ROYAL) DRAGOONS.

Vol. IV, Sheet I.

Hour, Date, Place	Summary of Events and Information	Remarks and references to Appendices
1915 January 1st to 26th	During the month of January, the Regiment remained in Billets and there is nothing worthy of report.	
27th	The Regiment was inspected by Field Marshall Sir John French.	
28th	The Regiment left its billets at AUDESCURE and moved to an area near AIRE; "B" Squadron at LA BELLE HOTESSE, with the other Squadrons and Regimental Headquarters near BLARINGHEM. 16 heavy draught were exchanged for the same number of light draught. This was undoubtedly an improvement as previous to this the hundred wagons had been most unsuitably horsed.	

Robson Hppard
Capt & Adjt
for Lieut. Colonel
Commanding the Royal Dragoons

5/3/15.

WAR DIARY
or
INTELLIGENCE SUMMARY
(Erase heading not required.)

1st. (ROYAL) DRAGOONS

Vol. V. Sheet I.

Army Form C. 2118.

Hour, Date, Place	Summary of Events and Information	Remarks and references to Appendices

1915 - February.

Feb. 3rd. The Regiment paraded 274 Strong at STEENBECQUE and proceeded by motor bus to YPRES; the remainder of the Regiment under Major Mr Neile with Squadron Seconds-in-Command remained to look after the horses.

Feb. 3rd – 6th. Remained in billets at YPRES. [Since we left the Town in November considerable damage had been done. When we were last there it had been shelled intermittently but now the Cloth Hall was entirely ruined and little remained except the walls, the roof had ceased to exist and the balcony over the Grand Place had been blown away. The Cathedral also had suffered terribly and appeared to be almost beyond repair. Whilst we were there this time they shelled the town occasionally but only with Shrapnel and did little damage. Curiously enough the inhabitants had returned in a large degree and probably half of the resident had regained their houses or what was left of them.

Our billets were quite comfortable and it was possible to obtain buy almost anything one wanted in the Town.

(Continued)

WAR DIARY or **INTELLIGENCE SUMMARY.**
(Erase heading not required.)

1st. (ROYAL) DRAGOONS
Vol. V. Sheet II.

Army Form C. 2118.

Hour, Date, Place	Summary of Events and Information	Remarks and references to Appendices
1915 – February – 8th ZILLEBEKE	We went up into the trenches N. of KLEINE ZILLEBEKE and slightly E. of where we had been on the 17th of November. We relieved the 1st Life Guards about midnight and had no casualties in taking over. The trenches were a great improvement on anything we have been in before. The trenches went a continuous [line] provided with loop holes and traverses with communication trenches in rear and dug-outs where men off duty could rest. There were a line of herbed wire in front and the trees which had been felled by shell fire provided an efficient protection against a surprise assault. The German trenches were situated at distances of from 120ᵡ to 50ᵡ from our lines, but there were two communication trenches which connected our line to theirs. This was due to the fact that our trenches had previously been German property. We had a very quiet time, occasional sniping, but no attack. They dropped 3 bombs just over our trenches one evening without doing any damage and we replied with rifle grenades which stopped any further offensive- ness on their part. We had occasional reports of suspicious noises (Continued)	1st R. Dgns

WAR DIARY
or
INTELLIGENCE SUMMARY.
(Erase heading not required.)

1st (Royal) DRAGOONS
Vol. II. Sheet III.

Army Form C. 2118.

Hour, Date, Place	Summary of Events and Information	Remarks and references to Appendices
1915 - February - 8th - 12th	which might have been sapping, but we came to the conclusion that this was unlikely, in view of the wet state of the ground. The worst trench was that of "C" Squadron on the left which was very wet and did not improve much in spite of much pumping. However no one was any the worse for it and at the end of our 5 days we only had one man sick.	
Feb. 13th	On this date we had our only casualty, from an un-aimed bullet:- No. 4978 Private H. MAY - shot through the stomach. The use of Periscopes with which we were provided un- doubtedly saved us from further loss, as the look out sentries were enabled to do their work without exposing themselves.	
Feb. 13th	We were relieved by the 3rd Dragoons and re- turned to YPRES, whence we were conveyed on Motor busses back to our billeting area.	
Feb. 14th - 26th	Remained in billets, chiefly occupied in trying to get the horses into hard condition. On the 22nd. we sent 3 Officers and 100 men to (continued)	

WAR DIARY
or
INTELLIGENCE SUMMARY.

1st. (Royal) DRAGOONS   Army Form C. 2118.

Vol. V. Sheet IV

(Erase heading not required.)

Hour, Date, Place	Summary of Events and Information	Remarks and references to Appendices

1915. February 14th — 26th	look after the horses of the 11th Hussars at FLETRE whilst they were in the trenches.
	
	In the London Gazette of February 17th, the following Officers, NCOs and men were mentioned as "Recommended to the Secretary of State for gallant and distinguished conduct in the field":-
	
	Lieut. Colonel G.T. Steele
	Major T.P. Dorrington (killed)
	Captain R. Stewartson
	Lt. (temporary) Hon. J.H.F. Greenfell, D.S.O.
	Lt. Hon. P. Stewart
	Lt. A.W. Waterhouse
	
	No. 6768 Sgt. J. Waldron
	    " 831 L.Cpl. R. Kelman
	    " 5768 Pte. A. Bartlett
	    " 5004 " G.W. MacDonald
	    " 3542 " J.C. Yeaman.
	
	The following announcement was made in the London Gazette of February 18th:-
	
	To be a Companion of the Order of St. Michael and St. George:-
	
	    Lieutenant Colonel G.T. Steele.
	
	The following NCOs and men have been awarded the Distinguished Conduct Medal, under authority granted by John Dunning, to the Field Marshall, C. in C.-
	(Continued)
		J.R. 8700

WAR DIARY 1st. (ROYAL) DRAGOONS. Army Form C. 2118.

or

INTELLIGENCE SUMMARY.

(Erase heading not required.)

Vol. V. Sheet V.

Hour, Date, Place	Summary of Events and Information	Remarks and references to Appendices
1915 - February - 14th - 26th -	No. 5241 Sergeant P. H. McLellan " 7995 Lance Corpl. E. Dickinson " 3364 Private (now Corpl) D. Moir " 3422 Private W. C. Shaw. The undermentioned Officer to be a Companion of the Distinguished Service Order:- Lieut. the Honble. J. H. F. Grenfell.	
5/3/1915.	Feb. 15th Fitzgerald Capto adjt for Lieut Colonel Commanding 1st Royal Dragoons	

137/4/9

6th Cavalry Brigade

1st (Royal) Dragoons

Vol VII 2 – 27. 3. 15.

N/e

ORIGINAL.

Army Form C. 2118.

WAR DIARY
or
INTELLIGENCE SUMMARY.
(Erase heading not required.)

Instructions regarding War Diaries and Intelligence Summaries are contained in F.S. Regs., Part II. and the Staff Manual respectively. Title pages will be prepared in manuscript.

Volume VI

Sheet I.

1st (Royal) Dragoons — March 1915.

Hour, Date, Place	Summary of Events and Information	Remarks and references to Appendices
Blaringhem : North France		
March 2nd 1915.	Captain Hugh Lambert and Pte. Barnes proceeded on a Machine Gun course at ST. OMER, to last for 14 days. S.Q.M.S. Goddard joined from ROUEN, and posted to M.G. Section.	
5th.	The Transport was inspected by the D.A.D.O.S. at 9 am. It was found that one of the wagons had no spare wheel, being of a different mark from the others. This wagon is to be changed at the first opportunity.	
6th.	The Colonel proceeded of on 168 hours leave.	
8th.	Horses of the Regiment were inspected "in hand" by the D.D.V.S. It was a very cold windy day, but on the whole the horses looked well. It is a pity that clipping is not allowed as with their long coats it is very difficult to get them into real hard condition.	
9th.	Brigade Route March took place.	
	(continued)	

Army Form C. 2118.

WAR DIARY
INTELLIGENCE SUMMARY
(Erase heading not required.)

Volume VI.
Sheet I.

1st (Royal) Dragoons — March 1915.

Hour, Date, Place	Summary of Events and Information	Remarks and references to Appendices
Blaringhem – N. France. March 10th 1915.	We went out and to "Stand-to" at 6 a.m. We learned that at 8 a.m. the 4th Corps assaulted and captured the enemy's front trenches at NEUVE CHAPPELLE and by noon had established themselves 1200 yards in front of the village. 750 prisoners were captured.	
11th 1915.	Reft Billet at 4.30 a.m. — "B" Echelon remained at STEENBECQUE. The Division remained concentrated near LA MOTTE till 4 p.m. The 5th Brigade, 2nd Cavalry Division had meanwhile moved close up to the front at ROUGE CROIX but were not engaged. Reached billets between MERVILLE and ESTAIRES at 6 p.m. Horses were picketted in fields, and men were under cover in barns. Infantry operations were hindered this day by mist, but the 3rd Corps captured L'EPINETTE Village.	
MERVILLE – ESTAIRES. 13th 1915.	"Stood-to" at 5.30 a.m. Sgt. Stalker and 2 men with 5 horses joined from ROUEN. Captain T. Jones and 2/Lieut. I. N. F. Browne had both gone sick on 11th. On this day the infantry failed to gain ground at PIETRE and BOIS DE BIEZ. (Continued)	

Army Form C. 2118.

WAR DIARY
or
INTELLIGENCE SUMMARY.
(Erase heading not required.)

Volume VI   1st (Royal) Dragoons — March 1915
Sheet IV

Instructions regarding War Diaries and Intelligence Summaries are contained in F.S. Regs., Part II. and the Staff Manual respectively. Title pages will be prepared in manuscript.

Hour, Date, Place	Summary of Events and Information	Remarks and references to Appendices
BLARINGHEM — N. FRANCE		
March 14th 1915	Remained in Billets. Very heavy gun fire heard about 5 p.m. in direction of YPRES. This we learnt afterwards was due to a German attack at ST. ELOI, where the enemy captured 500ˣ of our front trenches.	
" 15th "	We were "Standing-to" saddled up ready to reach Brigade Rendezvous in 30 minutes. At 4 pm the time was extended to 1½ hours. We were apparently in reserve for the ST. ELOI Section. We understood that the line was re-established there during the day.	
" 16th "	Remained "Standing-to" at 1½ hours notice.	
" 17th "	Our time for reaching the rendezvous was extended to 3½ hours.	
" 18th & 19th "	On these two days we were ordered to find 100 men for digging Reserve Trenches. These trenches were designed by the R.E. and our work was purely that of a working party.	
" 20th "	66 men were employed in digging trenches as before.	
" 22nd "	On this date we recommenced Squadron training as before under Squadron arrangement. Machine Gun Classes, Scout Classes, and Signalling Classes took place daily. Our Establishment of Draught Horses was changed as follows:— 46 light, and 24 heavy. (Continued) —	

Army Form C. 2118.

WAR DIARY
or
INTELLIGENCE SUMMARY.
(Erase heading not required.)

Instructions regarding War Diaries and Intelligence Summaries are contained in F.S. Regs., Part II. and the Staff Manual respectively. Title pages will be prepared in manuscript.

Volume VI Sheet III 1st (Royal) Dragoons — March 1915.

Hour, Date, Place	Summary of Events and Information	Remarks and references to Appendices
MERVILLE - ESTAIRES. March 12th 1915 (continued)	The 5th Cavalry Brigade were sent up at a gallop to take PIETRE, but on reaching the first line of Infantry Trenches were ordered to return. We learnt that in the operation near NEUVE CHAPPELLE about 2000 enemy prisoners were captured and their total loss was estimated at about 16000. It was understood that the operations had been successful, it was intended to push the whole of the Cavalry Corps through the German front to a point in rear of their line. The "B" Echelon arrived during the afternoon.	
March 13th	"Stood-to" at 6 a.m. The Cavalry were withdrawn during the evening, and returned to Billets at BLARINGHEM at 9.30 a.m. This was the end of an operation which might have led to big results. Mist and fog favoured the enemy, allowing them to bring up reinforcements whilst our own guns were at the same time heavily handicapped. ~~[struck through]~~ Colonel returned from leave.	

Army Form C. 2118.

WAR DIARY
OR
INTELLIGENCE SUMMARY.
(Erase heading not required.)

Volume VI
Sheet V

1st (Royal) Dragoons — March 1915.

Instructions regarding War Diaries and Intelligence Summaries are contained in F. S. Regs., Part II. and the Staff Manual respectively. Title pages will be prepared in manuscript.

Hour, Date, Place	Summary of Events and Information	Remarks and references to Appendices
BLARINGHEM — N.FRANCE		
March 22nd 1915 — (continued)	We then increased our light draught horses by 6, and reduced our heavy draught horses by the same amount.	
March 27th 1915 —	Major General the Hon. Sir J. Byng, K.C.M.G., C.B., M.V.O., Commanding 3rd Cavalry Division made a thorough inspection of the Regiment in Marching Order.	
	Casualties in Officers during March :— Captain & Quartermaster T. Jones was invalided to England on March 11th suffering from Sciatica.	

Fitzsimon Hayward
Capt & Adjt R.

April 10th 1915.

Lieut. Colonel
Commanding The Royal Dragoons

121/1408.

6th Cavalry Brigade.

1st Royal Dragoons

Vol VII 1 — 30.4.15

Army Form C. 2118

1. O Regiment

WAR DIARY The Royal Dragoons
or
INTELLIGENCE SUMMARY. APRIL 1915.
(Erase heading not required.) Volume VII - Sheet I

Instructions regarding War Diaries and Intelligence Summaries are contained in F.S. Regs., Part II. and the Staff Manual respectively. Title pages will be prepared in manuscript.

Hour, Date, Place	Summary of Events and Information	Remarks and references to Appendices
BLARINGHEM. April 1st – 12th	During this Period the Regiment remained in billets at BLARINGHEM. Training continued on these lines. Tactical schemes were practised daily. Winter clothing was gradually withdrawn – horse rugs from horses and packs from the men. On the 10th Capt. W.T. HUDSON who had been on duty at YPRES as Town Adjutant rejoined the Regiment and same of his appointment as Adjutant of the Surrey Yeomanry. He assumed command of "A" Sqn. Capt. A.H.D. CHAPMAN went to "A" as 2nd in Command. Capt. the Hon. C. ANNESLEY to "C' as 2nd in Command and Capt. C.R. TIDSWELL to same capacity to "B" Sqn.	
THIENNES April 12th – 23rd	On the 12th the new 9th Cav. Bde. was formed and in consequence our billeting area was restricted. The Regiment moved Ewito to THIENNES a small village near the Canal. We were here considerably more crowded than we had been before. Our billets were good and the horses under cover. On the 20th Capt. R. HOUSTOUN joined from England as acting Quartermaster to take over the duties of Capt. T. VAIO who was invalided last month. Peace training still continued. Squadrons did a certain amount of shell-hail - arms. On the 22nd we heard that after a 3 days battle Hill 60 had finally been taken by our troops vice 5th Div. On the 23rd a message was received from Bde HQ. timed 5.40 am stating that the French had been driven in the vicinity of LANGEMARK and of BIXSCHOOTE though their Canadians were holding on to the right. The refugees were due to as/Ihy sticking passes.	

ORIGINAL

Army Form C. 2118

1st. (Royal) Dragoons

Volume VII – Sheet II.

WAR DIARY
or
INTELLIGENCE SUMMARY.
(Erase heading not required.)

Instructions regarding War Diaries and Intelligence Summaries are contained in F. S. Regs., Part II. and the Staff Manual respectively. Title pages will be prepared in manuscript.

Hour, Date, Place	Summary of Events and Information	Remarks and references to Appendices
April 23 (cont)	The Regiment were ordered to "Stand to" ready to move at 1 hours notice. At 11 a.m. we received orders to endeavour and march with the rest of the division at 2 p.m. Reached ABEELE at 5 p.m. where we remained till dark. Then moved into billets at ECKE. The Colls. (parts of) the march into ECKE was over a very bad pavé ground. "B" Ech. & remained at THIENNES.	
April 24th	Left ECKE about 9 a.m. and moved to a position of readiness near VLAMMERTINGHE where we remained till 2 p.m. when we marched back to billets at BOESEPE & marching to VLAMMERTINGHE we had to cross the Pt. des CATS which was a very bad road for Transport and Cyclists.	
April 25	Marched at 6 a.m. to field near RENINGHELST in position of readiness. About 1 p.m. we moved just W. of POPERINGHE which was being shelled at the time to a Convent near the CHATEAU LOVIE. We stopped there about 1 hour and then returned to billets in HOUTKERQUE.	
April 26	Left HOUTKERQUE 6 a.m. and just outside village till 3 p.m. We then moved into a field just W. of POPERINGHE where we left the horses. 12 Officers and 260 men proceeded at 8 p.m. dismounted through POPERINGHE which was being shelled to VLAMERTINGHE where we billeted in a barn in the officers in houses occupied by Canadian H.Q.	

ORIGINAL

Army Form C. 2118.

1st (Royal) Dragoons
Volume VII - Sheet III

WAR DIARY
or
INTELLIGENCE SUMMARY.
(Erase heading not required.)

Instructions regarding War Diaries and Intelligence Summaries are contained in F. S. Regs., Part II. and the Staff Manual respectively. Title pages will be prepared in manuscript.

Hour, Date, Place	Summary of Events and Information	Remarks and references to Appendices
April 27 VLAMERTINGE	Remained in billets at VLAMMERTINGE. At about 3 hm the Germans started shelling the road and fields near us and shrapnel the Greys horses which were in a field close by be roused forth part of these on the road but a certain number were injured. We had 2 men Lt CRUMPTON and Lt GOODYEAR. Besides this an ambulance dropped a bomb in the garden of the park of our horse wounding 3 men of the A.S.C. At dusk we were warned to go to BRIELEN in support of the French but were not required.	
April 28	There was a little shelling chiefly H.E. in the morning. Left VLAMMERTINGE at 12.30 pm and marched to our horses then on to billets near WATOU	
April 29 - 30	Occupied billets near WATOU at night, spent the day in fields ready to move near ST JEAN TER BIEZEN.	

J.E.Otson Fitzgerald
Capt & Adjt
The Royal Dragoons.

121/5496

6/3rd Cavalry Division

1st Royal Dragoons

Vol VIII 1 — 31.5.15.

Army Form C. 2118.

WAR DIARY
~~INTELLIGENCE SUMMARY.~~

1st (Royal) Dragoons
Volume VIII - Sheet 1. - Period 1st/31st May 1915

(Erase heading not required.)

Instructions regarding War Diaries and Intelligence Summaries are contained in F. S. Regs., Part II. and the Staff Manual respectively. Title pages will be prepared in manuscript.

Hour, Date, Place	Summary of Events and Information	Remarks and References to Appendices
May 1st 1915	Same position as on April 30th 1915	APPENDIX I - Casualties of Officers of 12-14th May 1915
" 2nd "	Moved into Billets between PROVEN and HOOTKERKE where we arrived at 2½ hours later.	
May 3rd "	It was decided to reduce the Salient East of YPRES by withdrawing Troops to a line through WIELTJE Railway crossing and HOOGE later then giving up all the ground near ZONNEBEKE and E of HOOGE which we had previously occupied. The Cavalry were put behind to cover the retirement but later it was decided to move them up in position of Support just W of YPRES. Accordingly we left and drew near Pt. 35 and marched up dismounted to a position on the road about 3 mile W of YPRES. The withdrawal was effected but without any incident and we returned to our horses at dawn and then rode back to our billets near PROVEN, reaching there about 7 am on May 4th.	APPENDIX II - Honours, Rewards & Mentions 12th to 14th May 1915
		APPENDIX III - Casualties of Others 30/31 May 1915
May 4th	Remained quietly in billets near PROVEN	APPENDIX IV - Reinforcements received during May 1915
May 5th - 3.45 p.m	Paraded at 3.45 p.m. and marched with the horses to a few in a field at 11.12 c. where we left the horses from Ref. Sheet 28 BELGIUM 40,000	

WAR DIARY or INTELLIGENCE SUMMARY

Army Form C. 2118

1st (Royal) Dragoons
Volume VIII – Sheet 2 – Period 1 – 31 May 1915

Hour, Date, Place	Summary of Events and Information	Remarks and References to Appendices
May 5th (About sunset)	Three men went out to dig up line of trenches between the YPRES – COMINES Railway and the POSTE de LILLE – 17 men were employed and each man had a task of 7 feet. We dug for about 3½ hours. There was a wild shelling and Pte CLUTTERBUCK was slightly hit from 8.30 p.m.	
8.30 p.m – 9.30 p.m	till about 9.30 pm the HILL 60 was violently shelled by our guns preparing for a counter attack and the flares were extraordinarily brilliant making a wonderful display of fireworks. Reached billets	
May 6th – 5 a.m.	at PROVEN at about 5 am	
May 6th	Remained in billets at near PROVEN.	
May 7th	Received orders to return to permanent billet at THIENNES.	
– do – 3 p.m	Arrived 3 p.m. Blocked by 2nd Cav. Division and reached billet	
– do – 9 p.m	at about 9 p.m	
May 8th	Remained at THIENNES.	
May 9th 5.40 a.m	Received orders to be ready to move at 1 hour & 20 minutes	
— 11.0 a.m	notice. Ordered to turn out 300 men at once and proceed in lorries horses. There were only 111 horses and consequently	

WAR DIARY or INTELLIGENCE SUMMARY

Army Form C. 2118.

1st (Royal) Dragoons
Volume VIII - Sheet 3. - Period 1-31 May/15

(Erase heading not required.)

Instructions regarding War Diaries and Intelligence Summaries are contained in F. S. Regs., Part II. and the Staff Manual respectively. Title pages will be prepared in manuscript.

Hour, Date, Place	Summary of Events and Information	Remarks and References to Appendices
May 9th (continued)	About 30 men went out to dig-outs. Been containing officer took down and stores destroyed thoroughly.	Reference to Sheet 28 - Belgium 1/40,000 (Squares)
3 pm	Detailed at VLAMERTINGHE. Marched to dug-outs at H.11.13	
May 10th	Remained in huts. Infantry sending on in rear of huts built. There was a certain amount of shelling but we within 600x of our Camp.	
May 11th	Remained all day in huts. Marched at 8pm to take up	
8 pm	position in dug-outs East of wood in I.11.b. where we were in support of trenches occupied by Shropshire Light Infantry. Two officers wire sent off in advance to reconnoitre journey here from HOOGE road Northwards to railway. [Two men Pte. GUBB, was slightly hit by shrapnel bullet on the way up to the trenches. Drew rations at level crossing]	
May 12th	Remained in dug-outs. Nothing to report. Captain WATERHOUSE and Lieut LECKIE returned in the afternoon from reconnoitring the line to be taken over from Infantry by the 6th	

WAR DIARY
or
INTELLIGENCE SUMMARY.
(Erase heading not required.)

Army Form C. 2118.

1st. (Royal) Dragoons

Volume VIII — Sheet 4 — Period 1-31 May 15

Hour, Date, Place	Summary of Events and Information	Remarks and References to Appendices

May 12th (continued) — Canada Brigade reported that prisoners were very slack in places and that much digging required to be done. One Officer from 7th Kar. Rif. returned from reconnaissance to dug-outs close to own & shell fell on dug out killing them all and two Majors of the Shropshire Light Infantry.

— do — 9 p.m. Remainder of 6th C.B. were up about 9 p.m. to take over line from HOOGE LAKE just N of BELVARDE FARM to running 100° N of Pt. 30. Covering parties were employed to dig communication trench from our wood to trench near BELVARDE FARM. 100 of our men were sent to improve the 2nd Cav. Trenches.

190 men came up as reinforcements under 2/Lt C.N.F. BROWNE but were sent back to VLAMERTINGHE as there was no line to put them.

May 13th. 4 am. Very heavy bombardment of G.H.Q. line Rail— way. Shell but camp to HALTE nouveau. Our wood

WAR DIARY
or
INTELLIGENCE SUMMARY.
(Erase heading not required.)

Army Form C. 2118.

1st (Royal) Dragoons
Volume VIII - Sheet 5 - Period 1-31 May/15

Hour, Date, Place	Summary of Events and Information	Remarks and References to Appendices

May 13th - 4 a.m. (cont'd) — were heavily shelled and the ground all round but no damage done. The fire seemed to pour out and appears to be getting a very heavy fire. The enemy employed heavy Howitzers H.E. Shrapnel and "Whizz-bangs".

5.30/6.0 a.m. — A slight lull. Rifle fire could be heard but not very heavy. Lieut. W.H. J. St. Atkinson tried to get telephone communication between him with Shrapnel and died within half an hour.

do — 6.0 a.m. — Firing started again as heavily as ever. The General sent a message asking for news. Howitzers to be turned on DEAD MANS WOOD but we could not keep our own guns through them many have been shortly. The wire was [ILLEGIBLE] [SCATER] BOOTH had been posted as observer at the corner of communication trench but we had no news from him.

do — 7.0 a.m. — Lt. W. Smythe - Bingham arrived B.O.C.was informed the General that the Germans had broken through his line. On receipt of this information the Royals were ordered to form up to the

WAR DIARY
or
INTELLIGENCE SUMMARY.

(Erase heading not required.)

Volume VIII — Sheet 6 — Period 1-31 May 15

Army Form C. 2118.

1st (Royal) Dragoons

Hour, Date, Place	Summary of Events and Information	Remarks and References to Appendices

May 13th — 7 am (cont'd). Counter-attack. The Colonel with rest of the Regiment moved up through the wood towards the front edge. "C" Squadron on the left, "B" in centre and "A" on the Right. FITZGERALD and WATERHOUSE went on to go with remainder and cover it. flank of Regiment in moving to BILWARDE FARM and getting touch with the 3rd D.G.s there. The party of about 15 reached remainder of 3rd D.Gs. WORTHINGTON stated that they had been worse and in the wood in want of assistance. Having made certain of then it was seen left with 3rd D.Gs and FITZGERALD and WATERHOUSE returned to Regiment to report. About 8 o/am men were in the communication trench — they were told to join 3rd D.Gs or Show with them. From the communication trench it was possible to get a good view of the left front. We could see about fifty Germans dressed in khaki kilts with khaki packs on their backs moving amongst our own troops. 3rd

WAR DIARY or INTELLIGENCE SUMMARY.

Army Form C. 2118.

1st (Royal) Dragoons
Volume VIII Sheet 7 - April 1-31 January 1915

Hour, Date, Place	Summary of Events and Information	Remarks and References to Appendices

May 13th 7am (cont'd) Dragoon Guards from right to left. There were also a number of enemy groups visibly moving towards a house near the Military in I.6.c. and another farm in I.5.d.

The Regiment seemed whilst on my advance to the edge of the wood with this lot, and the riflemen and there rifle on the communication trench but I found that if we were in command others though I found a gun to their original employ. We had half succeeded when a gun to their dug-outs from which our Lewis + French guns above the dug-outs from which a good view of the situation on our left could be obtained. During this operation we had been subjected continuously to a very heavy shelling and losses had been very severe. Captain LAMBERT had been killed early whilst looking for a Machine Gun position on the left near the Railway. Lieut. LECKIE was killed near the front edge of the wood. 2/Lt. BAGSHAWE was killed after having slightly wounded on his way back to the

WAR DIARY or INTELLIGENCE SUMMARY.

Army Form C. 2118.

1st (Royal) Dragoons
Volume VIII - Sheet 8 - Period 1-31 May 15.

Hour, Date, Place	Summary of Events and Information	Remarks and References to Appendices

May 13th - 7am (contd) Trenches. These two officers were afterwards buried where they lay by the Irish Fusiliers.

Lt. WATKIN WYNN had been wounded near the 3rd. D.Gds. Trenches on his way to get touch with them. He was hit in the lower part of the chest and had to be put in a hole full of water dark enough to get him away but in the lower part of the chest and had to be put in a hole full of water dark enough to get him away.

HARDWICK was slightly wounded but did not leave his Squadron.

May 13th - 8.30 am — We now had got all our men back into the dugouts or in a trench just above them. From the left of the French the situation could be seen. We hus held by the 6th Cavalry Brigade was intact but on the left the 7th Cav. Bde. North of the railway had fallen back. Their Right i.e. the Leicestershire yeomanry were almost in line with the wood occupied by the Regiment consequently our left

Army Form C. 2118.

WAR DIARY
or
INTELLIGENCE SUMMARY.
(Erase heading not required.)

1st (Royal) Dragoons
Volume VIII - Sheet 9 - Period 1-31 May/15.

Instructions regarding War Diaries and Intelligence Summaries are contained in F. S. Regs, Part II. and the Staff Manual respectively. Title pages will be prepared in manuscript.

Hour, Date, Place	Summary of Events and Information	Remarks and References to Appendices

May 13th - 8.30 am (cont) i.e. the 3rd Dragoon Guards were in the air. The Germans appeared to be massing in the Farmhouses referred to above and a certain number of them had occupied the trenches vacated by the 9th Bde [?]. and some irregular trenches in front of these. There was a gap of over 60 yards N. of the railway, which was unoccupied. From our position we could enfilade any further German advance and selected a Machine Gun position to take them in flank. They did not, however, come in any further and the Gun did not come into action. We had an observation post at the corner of the wood and Corporal TALBOT rendered valuable service at this duty.

— do — 10.0 am. About this time Captain MILES who down in one of the dug-outs was hit by a shrapnel bullet. Although hit it was by Capt. SCRATER-BOOTH

Army Form C. 2118.

WAR DIARY
or
INTELLIGENCE SUMMARY.
(Erase heading not required.)

1st (Royal) Dragoons
Volume VIII - Sheet 10. Period 1-31 May 1915

Instructions regarding War Diaries and Intelligence Summaries are contained in F. S. Regs., Part II. and the Staff Manual respectively. Title pages will be prepared in manuscript.

Hour, Date, Place	Summary of Events and Information	Remarks and References to Appendices

May 13th - 10.0 a.m. (contd). Consequently took command of "C" Squadron. The Germans continued to concentrate in the farms referred to above and the General asked our guns to shell the farms. Then they did but without much success as most of their Shrapnel burst too high. There was no Artillery Observer with us and no telephone.

The wounded were evacuated to WITTE POORT FARM during the morning. Capt. MENZIES and L/Cpl. ALLSEBROOK were indefatigable in the performance of their duty and deserve great credit for the way in which they worked. Later the farm at WITTE POORT was shelled and the wounded were taken to dug out near the MENIN ROAD.

Pte. SHAW on a bicycle and L/Cpl. FOX both carried messages for the Brigadier with conspicuous gallantry and Sergt. MORTIMER Pte. McCANN and Cpl. PROCTOR did good work in carrying ammunition to the N.S.Y. trenches.

WAR DIARY or INTELLIGENCE SUMMARY.

Army Form C. 2118.

1st (Royal) Dragoons

Volume VIII - Sheet II. Period 1-31 May 1915

Hour, Date, Place	Summary of Events and Information	Remarks and References to Appendices
May 13th 1.30 pm	About 1.30 pm Grenfell and the Brigadier who had been observing were held up by a shell. The former severely in the head and the latter slightly in the foot. The Blues now arrived and took up a position of readiness near our dug outs. They had had orders to counter-attack along the rail.	
	road at 2.30 pm — the attack to be preceded by a bombardment of the enemy's position. At the same time the Regiment was ordered to move up to the NSY trenches as they were reported to have lost heavily in both officers and men. [The Colonel remained to report to the Brigadier who was suffering from the effects of his wounds]	
3.0 pm	(About 3 pm we arrived in the NSY trenches NW of Hooge & we soon found that they had no officer left in that part of their line and were very short of Non-Commissioned Officers. The men too were much exhausted by by no means demoralized, though they had been heavily shelled.	

WAR DIARY
or
INTELLIGENCE SUMMARY. 1st (Royal) Dragoons
(*Erase heading not required.*) Volume VIII - Sheet 12 - Period 1-31 May 1915

Hour, Date, Place	Summary of Events and Information	Remarks and References to Appendices
May 13th 3.0 pm (contd)	The trenches had been considerably damaged in places and we could not at first get into touch with the left Squadron who were BELVARDE FARM. There were several badly wounded men in the trenches and these could not at first be got out. We now took over the line with our officer and also put in about 30 of our men keeping the rest in reserve in the drive, but occupied by the K.R.R. behind the HOOGE LAKE. As soon as it got fairly dark we set to work to improve the trenches and parapets, and to dig a real trench connecting up with the left Squadron of the N.S.Y. In this were assisted by a working party of the K.R.R. We were relieved by the K.R.R. who took over from	
May 13th Midnight	us and the N.S.Y.	
May 14th	We then marched back to our original dug-out and thence to a line N. of the railway and East of the road in I.11.b, I.5.d. behind the trenches	

WAR DIARY
INTELLIGENCE SUMMARY

Army Form C. 2118.

1st (Royal) Dragoons
Volume VIII - Sheet 13 - Period 1-31 May 1915

Hour, Date, Place	Summary of Events and Information	Remarks and References to Appendices
May 14th (contd)	Shot by the 4th Hus. Bde. There therefore were mere scratches and would have afforded no protection against shell fire. Luckily except for a few "whizz bangs" there was no bombardment and our casualties were few. The Colonel was however severely wounded in the head by a high explosive shrapnel about 2 p.m. and Capt. WATERHOUSE in the back at the same time.	
2 p.m.	We reconnoitred the ground in front of our trenches for about 200 yards but saw no sign of Germans. They had evidently taken up their position in I.Barn. Beyond the wood though they undoubtedly had a few snipers in the farm about 400x in front of us. We found Lieut. HOBSON and 8 men 2nd L.Gds. in front of our trenches. There were also a certain number of dead Ger. troops belonging to some Bavarian corps. The men were very tired, hungry and thirsty as they had had no rations the night before.	

WAR DIARY or INTELLIGENCE SUMMARY.

Army Form C. 2118.

1st. (Royal) Dragoons

Volume VIII - Sheet 14 - Period 1-31 May 1915

Hour, Date, Place	Summary of Events and Information	Remarks and References to Appendices
May 14th 1915 - 9 pm to	About 9 pm we were relieved by the 12th Lancers who proceeded to dig a line about 100 yds in front of our trenches. We returned via POTIGE to our "A" Echelon at VLAMERTINGHE where we remained in reserve till May 21st when we returned in Motor Busses to	
May 21st	THIENNES	
May 23rd	BAILLEUL Hospital. The Colonel having died of his wounds at ??? Representatives of the Regiment attended the funeral at 9 am.	
May 28th	The Regiment having been ordered for the Trenches near HOOGE, 4 officers were sent up by Motor Car to take over and act as guides.	
May 29th	Regiment paraded for the trenches at 12 noon and moved up to VLAMERTINGHE in Motor Busses. Strength :- 12 officers and 280 Other Ranks, with 4 Machine Guns.	
— 4 pm	Reached VLAMERTINGHE about 4 pm	
— 7 pm	Marched from VLAMERTINGHE via Railway line to YPRES, thence	

WAR DIARY or INTELLIGENCE SUMMARY

Army Form C. 2118

1st (Royal) Dragoons

Volume VII – Sheet 15 – Period 1-31 May 1915

Hour, Date, Place	Summary of Events and Information	Remarks and References to Appendices

May 29th 7pm (contd)
Ley Avenue to SALLY PORT – a pontoon bridge just S. of MENIN

– " – 8.30 pm
BRIDGE where we met our guides at 8.30 pm. Thence by ECOLE de BIENFAISANCE to Trenches N. of ZILLEBEKE. Took over trenches

– " – 11.0 pm
from 5th Lancers as under T.13.c about 11 pm B & C Sqdns in front line with 1 troop of A Sqdn. Remainder of A Sqdn and H.Q in Support line. 50 yards in rear. W. half 2 Troops C Sqn in front line. The other 2 under Lt SWIRE were placed in Support of 3rd D.G.ds in ZOUAVE WOOD. Our Sector of the line was commanded by Major BURT 3rd D.G.ds. We connected with 3rd D.G.ds on our left and the Blues on our right.

May 30th 7.30 am
Patrols consisting of Pte Joffrey (Cpl. Bishop and Chick) went out via Old communication trench to our front to reconnoitre. They reported Germans engaged in digging 25 yds behind the crest of hill. No signs of Enemy in advance of few rounds. Enemy's moves here could be

WAR DIARY or INTELLIGENCE SUMMARY.

Army Form C. 2118.

1st (Royal) Dragoons

(Erase heading not required.) Volume VIII - Sheet 16 - Period 1-31 May, 1915

Instructions regarding War Diaries and Intelligence Summaries are contained in F. S. Regs., Part II. and the Staff Manual respectively. Title pages will be prepared in manuscript.

Hour, Date, Place	Summary of Events and Information	Remarks and References to Appendices
May 31st (Cont'd)	seen stretch N. and S. at a distance of 300 to 400 yards. The trenches we had taken over were very insufficient and we spent the morning in working hard on them, and endeavouring to improve parapets and communications.	
2 p.m.	The enemy began to shell heavily the ground in rear of 3rd D.Gds. Trenches, which were 400 yards distant on our left rear.	
3 p.m.	Bombardment continued and concentrated on the 3rd D.Gds. Trenches which we could see must have been very badly blown about. Our guns made no reply. (Stewart and Black 3rd D. Gds. were brought through our trenches wounded the former severely.)	
3.30 p.m.	Right Squadron 3rd D. Gds. were shelled out and withdrew through our left Squadron to support trench.	
4.0 p.m.	Enemy Howitzers recommenced shelling (but not so heavily) of ground behind 3rd D. Gds.	
4.30 p.m.	O.C. Detachment 4th Yorks were told to be ready to take	

Army Form C. 2118.

WAR DIARY
or
INTELLIGENCE SUMMARY.
(Erase heading not required.)

1st (Royal) Dragoons
Volume VIII - Sheet 17 Period 1.31 May 1915

Hour, Date, Place	Summary of Events and Information	Remarks and References to Appendices
May 30th 4.30 pm (contd)	take position in vacated 3rd D Gds trench in event of attack. Right Squadron 3rd D.Gds were holding right of their Original line. No touch with our left.	
4.45 pm	TIDSWELL was ordered to send a patrol to get in touch with 3rd D.Gds. left.	
5.30 pm	TIDSWELL reports touch gained with "A" Sqdn. 3rd D.Gds. who are separated by 60 x from us. "C" Sqdn. 3.DG are to try and form up and fill the gap. H.Q. LEFT SECTOR report that Lt. Squire and 2 gunners have been placed at disposal of O.C. 3.D.Gds. O.C. R.H.G. sent round a trench mortar found in their trenches. At intervals shots from a trench mortar which we could not locate made some good shooting on Germans working on trench to our front.	
7.30 pm	HOUSTON arrived from N.S.Yeo saying he had orders to	

Army Form C. 2118.

WAR DIARY
or
INTELLIGENCE SUMMARY.
(Erase heading not required.) Volume VIII - Sheet 18. Period 1-31 May 1915

1st (Royal) Dragoons

Instructions regarding War Diaries and Intelligence Summaries are contained in F. S. Regs., Part II. and the Staff Manual respectively. Title pages will be prepared in manuscript.

Hour, Date, Place	Summary of Events and Information	Remarks and References to Appendices
May 30th 7.30pm (contd)	relieve 3rd D.G. trenches at 9 pm.	
— 9.30 pm	Drew rations, sprayer for gas, and "Very" Pistols.	
— 9.30pm to	All quiet except for a certain amount of sniping	
May 31st 12.45 am		
May 31st 12.45 am —	A furious fusillade broke out from German trenches. We did not reply. Two men hit — HANDLEY and RUSSELL — presumably by Blues on our right rear. (A glorious bright moonlight night.)	
— 9 am	Enemy howitzer opened from directions of GHELUVELT, ZANDVOORDE, and ST JULIEN, directed on rear of trenches I.18-a.8.9. also N.E. corner of wood I.18-c.9.d. The shooting was wonderfully accurate. Our guns replied with a few shrapnel towards Hill 55.	
— 1 pm	Ptes. NEALE and SURTEES who had been out on a patrol brought back a good report on the enemy's trenches in front.	
— 2 pm	Enemy howitzer started shelling ground in rear of 3rd	

Army Form C. 2118.

WAR DIARY
or
INTELLIGENCE SUMMARY.
(Erase heading not required.)

1st. (Royal) Dragoons
Volume VIII - Sheet 19 - Period 1-31 May 1915.

Instructions regarding War Diaries and Intelligence Summaries are contained in F. S. Regs., Part II. and the Staff Manual respectively. Title pages will be prepared in manuscript.

Hour, Date, Place	Summary of Events and Information	Remarks and References to Appendices
May 31st 2pm (cont'd)	D Coy relieved.	
3pm	Our howitzer replied and an aeroplane appeared. Enemy stopped shelling.	
—	Artillery officer arrived to observe.	
7.30pm to midnight	Started digging operations and dug all night.	

Fitzbert Fitzgerald
Captain and
Adjutant.

1st Royal Dragoons

1st (Royal) Dragoons.

WAR DIARY
Vol. VIII

APPENDIX I

Casualties of Actions of 12th–14th May

No.	Rank	and Name	Date	No	Rank	and Name	Date
		KILLED				**MISSING – BELIEVED WOUNDED**	
	Capt.	H. McL. Lambert	13-5-15	4091	Pte.	A. Matheson	13-5-15
	"	W.H.J. St L. Atkinson	"			**WOUNDED**	
	Lieut.	J.H. Leckie	"		Major	P.E. Hardwick	13-5-15
	2/Lt.	G.H. Bagshawe	"		Capt.	W.T. Miles	"
5241	Sgt.	P.H. McLellan	"		Lt.	W. Williams Wynn	"
4253	Cpl.	A. Sandbrooke	"		2/Lt.	W. Ackroyd	"
3658	L.C.	J. Campbell	"		Capt.	A.W. Waterhouse	14-5-15
4130	Pte.	T. Boyle	"		Capt.	Fitz Glyn	13-5-15
954	"	A.E. Johnson	"	5529	Sgt.	F. Stalker	"
5920	"	H. Preston	"	5093	"	C. Sutch	"
5004	"	W. McDonald	"	4138	Cpl.	J. Gillard	"
10800	"	P. Nicoll	"	5792	"	W. Turner	"
4319	"	J. Pearce	"	7954	"	H. Treacher	"
4477	"	W. Gibbs	"	5638	"	W. Lavender	"
108	L.C.	R.J.D. Fox	"	1882	L.C.	P. Norris	"
2623	Pte.	B. Walker	"	4696	Pte.	H. Jobson	"
2867	"	R. Barker	"	7955	"	A. Woodward	"
		DIED OF WOUNDS		8712	L.C.	J. McQuillan	"
	Lt.Col.	G.F. Steele, C.M.G.	22-5-15	2644	Pte.	W. Smith	"
	Capt.	Hon. J.H.F. Grenfell, D.S.O.	26-5-15	3683	"	J. Bruce	"
	2/Lt.	C.N.F. Browne	13-5-15	5145	"	A.K. Dewar	"
				8764	"	R. Thompson	"
8075	Pte.	T. Schmude	14-5-15	3239	"	E. Shears	"
3454	"	H. Goode	13-5-15	1431	"	R. Arnott	"
3530	"	C. Sclater	23-5-15	5813	"	G. Siebert	"
1770	"	J. Waight (Surrey Yeo)	19-5-15	3348	"	W. Horne	"
3657	"	T. McGuire	13-5-15	3405	"	J. Gallagher	"
329	L.C.	D. Ryburn	25-5-15	10799	"	S. Williams	"
710	Pte.	D. Clarke	16-5-15	4897	"	A.J. Morgan	"
3442	"	W. McPherson	16-5-15	1442	"	A. Gibb	"
		MISSING – BELIEVED KILLED		6759	"	F. Howard	"
				5897	"	G. Jones	"
4782	Sgt.	F. Andrews	13-5-15	7152	"	G. King	"
3444	Pte.	H. Jennings	"	5886	"	J. Manning	"
6012	"	W. Bainbrigge	"	1948	"	F. Plumbley	"
5733	L.C.	J. Dore	"	168	S.S.	R. Bonsey	"
5726	"	F. Double	"	2060	Pte.	T. Imrie	"
5716	Pte.	T. Holland	"	8679	"	A. Torrie	"
32?	Cpl.	C. Williams	"	3439	"	J. McFarlane	"

1st. (Royal) Dragoons.

WAR DIARY - Vol. VIII - APPENDIX I (Sheet 2).

Casualties of actions of 12th - 14th May

No.	Rank	Name	Date	No.	Rank	Name	Date
		WOUNDED (Cont'd)		4557	Cpl	R. ROSE	13/5/15
				2880	"	H. V. DAVIOS	"
4195	Pte	E. A. Meacham	13.5.15	4022	"	H. J. SKILLER	"
5620	"	W. NELMES	"	2726	L.C.	P. RYAN	"
8423	"	W. SOMERVILLE	"	10798	"	A. MARGRETT	"
5316	"	F. WRIGHT	"	4264	Pte.	W. HEATH	"
5436	"	F. HELLIWELL	"	7918	"	F. FELTHAM	"
8901	"	J. MUIR	"	3351	"	W. ALDERSON	"
5160	Sgt.	H. NEWTON	"	3682	"	G. POLLOCK	"
188	"	S. HOINVILLE	"	5760	"	W. G. FLOODGATE	"
4596	Cpl.	E. A. MYNARD	"	8640	"	S. BARCLAY	"
4754	"	A. CUBITT	"	5580	"	A. E. NEWMAN	"
4374	L.C.	J. ENGLISH	"	5899	"	F. E. W. GROEGER	"
1616	Pte.	G. GRAY	"	5732	"	T. C. HULTUM	"
6673	"	J. PATTERSON	"	6006	"	W. WITHERS	"
8863	S.S.	J. MACKLIN	"	8190	"	G. BAKER	"
5153	Pte	J. PURVES	"	741	"	J. LEE	"
9238	"	T. ROY	"	979	"	J. W. PRICE	"
974	"	J. MAYNARD	"	7636	"	T. SMITH	"
8920	"	J. THOMPSON	"	3986	RSm	C. M. COOKE	"
4727	"	W. LAUDER	"	3422	Pte.	W. C. SHAW	"
2161	"	J. TURNER	"	6483	"	J. BYRNE	"
5508	"	J. CUSACK	"	4568	"	G. THOMPSON	"
5482	"	J. FORSYTHE	"	4287	"	J. MOTTRAM	"
4071	"	G. WARREN	"	5899	"	DRISCOLL	"
2854	"	A. OSBORNE	"	5465	Sgt.	H. A. BLUNDELL	"
1336	"	J. COOPER	"	911	Pte.	R. GRIZZELL	"
5781	"	C. W. WOOLLEY	"	726	"	J. SOUTHWOOD	"
8264	L.Cpl	G. CANE	"	4051	"	F. PERRY	"
3604	Pte	R. SHAW	"	3872	L.C.	D. BARNARD	"
1734	"	J. McARDLE	"	4128	Pte.	C. LEWIS †	"
8590	"	J. WORLEY	"				
5132	Sgt	A. KITE	"				
5423	"	A. SCOTT	"				

† Since reported as being INJURED, and not WOUNDED.

SUMMARY:

KILLED -	OFFICERS 4	Total 17	
	N.C.O.s & MEN 13		28
DIED of WOUNDS -	OFFICERS 3	Total 11	
	N.C.O.s & MEN 8		
WOUNDED -	OFFICERS 6	Total 100	100
	N.C.O.s & MEN 94		
MISSING -	OFFICERS nil	Total 8	8
	N.C.O.s & MEN 8		
		TOTAL	**136**

29.6.15

Capt. Adjt.
1st Royal Dragoons

1st (Royal) Dragoons

WAR DIARY
Volume VIII   APPENDIX II

Honours Awards Mentions for Good Work in the Field Dec. 12th – 12th May.

No. Rank and Name	Date	Remarks
OFFICERS		
Capt. A.W. Waterhouse	13.5.15	— name brought to notice of G.O.C. Bde.
" Hon. J.H.F. Grenfell, D.S.O.	"	— awarded the D.C.M.
" a.j. A. Menzies, R.A.M.C.	"	
OTHER RANKS:		
5001 Sq.M.S. S.J. Oxford		⎫
4294 Sergt. J. Mortimer		⎪
7110 Cpl. B. Proctor		⎪ names brought to notice
752 Pte. P. McCann		⎬ of G.O.C Brigade for
108 L.Cpl. R.J.D. Fox ×		⎪ Good Work in the Field
5500 Cpl. J.J. Talbot		⎪
6254 L.Cpl. F.J. Allsebrooke		⎪
3604 Pte. R. Shaw		⎪
7995 L.Cpl. E. Dickinson		⎪
2872 " D. Barnard		⎭

× Killed in Action

29/6/1915

Fb Wilson Fitzgerald
Capt & Adjt.
1st Royal Dragoons

1st (Royal) Dragoons

WAR DIARY
Volume VIII   APPENDIX III

Casualties of Actions of period 29-31 May, 1915

Regtl No.	Rank and Name	Date
	WOUNDED	
5258	Pte. HANDLEY, H	31-5-15
4413	" RUSSELL, J.	"
	INJURED	
7753	Pte. MITCHENER, H	31-5-15

SUMMARY:
Killed – nil
Wounded: Other ranks 2
Injured: Other ranks 1
Total 3

Robertson Fitzgerald
Capt. Adjt
The Royal Dragoons

29/6/15

1st. (Royal) Dragoons

WAR DIARY
Volume VIII

APPENDIX IV

Reinforcements joined during May, 1915

OFFICERS		OTHER RANKS		HORSES	
Rank - Name	Date	Total	Date	Total	Date
Capt. G. D'A. Edwardes	} 23/5/1915	Five	15.5.15	16 Riding & 2 L.D.	} 11.5.15
Lt. C.G.W. Swire					
2/Lt. W.P. Brown		Forty nine	23.5.15		
" H.E.F. de Trafford		Five	26.5.15		
" R.H.W. Henderson		Fifteen (M.G. Sec.)	29.5.15		
" A. Birch					
" A.W. Wingate					
2/Lt. G.A. Ripley	} 29/5/15				
" J.B. Bickersteth					
" W.H. Cubitt					
Total	10	Total	74	Total	18

29/6/15

F. Winston Fitzgerald
Capt. Adjt.
Royal Dragoons

3rd Cavalry Division

121/6341

1st Royal Dragoons

Vol IX

June 1915

WAR DIARY or INTELLIGENCE SUMMARY.

Army Form C. 2118.

1st. (Royal) Dragoons

Volume IX. Sheet 1. June 1st – 30th. 1915

Place	Date	Hour	Summary of Events and Information	Remarks and references to Appendices
N. of KILLEBEKE I.13.c.	1st.	10 a.m.	Desultory shelling early morning. Pte. GRAY slightly wounded by a sniper. 3rd D.Gds. trenches and communication trenches were heavily shelled.	Sheet 28 Belgium 1: 8000
"	"	11.30 a.m.	"C" Sqdn. Trenches, 3rd D.Gds. became untenable. Lieut. FINDLAY 3rd D.Gds. and 2 troops returned into "B" Sqdn. trench and there to support french occupied by 5th YORKS. "B" Sqdn. left troop also shelled were withdrawn to the night leaving observation posts in the trenches.	
"	"	1.45 p.m.	"B" Sqdn. re-occupied trench as shelling had somewhat subsided. My section on left was moved slightly so as to enfilade front of our left trench and the right of the 3rd D.Gds. O.C. "B" Sqdn. was ordered to endeavour to gain touch with 3rd D.Gds. on the left.	
"	"	2.0 p.m.	Enemy aircraft circled 4 times round our line entirely unmolested.	
"	"	3.0 "	Pte. McCann & Dove returned from patrolling to 3rd D.Gds. having gained touch — a good performance, as McCann was buried and had to be pulled out. The news took something in mud but made a good report.	
"	"	4.45 p.m.	A few germans reported moving from far right to left along hedge towards HOOGE Road. FINDLAY's men were ordered to re-occupy their trench. The night passed fairly quietly. 30 men of the 5th Yorks were sent up to dig for us but for all the work they did might just as well have stayed at home. The enemy were working hard on their trench during the night and appeared to be occupying it more strongly.	
"	2nd.	5 a.m.	Fairly heavy shelling commenced from all directions	
"	"	9.30 to 10.30 a.m.	Very heavy shelling.	

Army Form C. 2118.

WAR DIARY 1st (Royal) Dragoons
or
INTELLIGENCE SUMMARY.
(Erase heading not required.) Volume IX Sheet 2.

Instructions regarding War Diaries and Intelligence Summaries are contained in F. S. Regs., Part II. and the Staff Manual respectively. Title pages will be prepared in manuscript.

Place	Date	Hour	Summary of Events and Information	Remarks and references to Appendices
N. ZILLEBEKE J-13-c	2nd	10 am	"C" Sqdn. 3rd D.Gds. temporarily vacated their trench owing to shelling, and retired into supporting trench. 3 Troops "A" Sqdn. went ready to take up position on our left if required.	Sheet 28 Belgium 1:40,000 1st-31st June 1915
		11.35 a.m.	Heard that K.D.Gds. had vacated their position at or near HOOGE CHATEAU N. of MENIN road. Shelling continued steadily. 11.35 am Could see reinforcements coming up to left of 3 D.G. line. Enemy immediately opened on them with 5 inch "High Explosive" and "Crumps" which must have been very unpleasant for the reinforcement. Enemy can evidently observe the whole of the ground behind our trenches with ease.	
		10.30 "	Enemy observation balloon went up about J-16.	
		12.15 pm	Heavy shelling directed on trenches J-18 a and b. South of MENIN Road.	
		12.30 "	One of our howitzers fired 2 shots into the HOOGE CHATEAU grounds. English aeroplane appeared over and the 6th Battery gave us some support by shelling enemy's trenches and ground in rear.	
		2.35 pm	Heavy German shelling which had temporarily abated, recommenced being concentrated on ground just on our left rear.	
		2.45 pm	3rd D.Gds. had again to vacate their trenches and "B" Sqn. also had to leave some of their trenches.	
		3.15 pm	Shelling eased and on this seemed to prelude an attack on extended on our line for 70 the left if possible. The Germans evidently thought that the trenches were unoccupied and attempted to get into them down a ridge on our left front. We opened upon them with a machine gun which stopped all further offensive on their part. No doubt they meant to get a machine gun or two into our trenches but they did not seem to be inclined for a big attack and were probably not in great force. This attacking party started digging in along the ridge. Meanwhile under cover of their bombardment they had brought up a machine gun on to the ridge and we could see	

1577 Wt. W10791/1773 500,000 1/15 D. D. & L. A.D.S.S./Forms/C. 2118.

Army Form C. 2118.

WAR DIARY 1st (Royal) Dragoons
or
INTELLIGENCE SUMMARY.
(Erase heading not required.)

Volume IX - Sheet 3   1 - 31st June 1915.

Place	Date	Hour	Summary of Events and Information	Remarks and references to Appendices
N. ZILLEBEKE J.13.c	2nd	3.15pm	Men working hard at their trenches and emplacements. We probably did some fairly effective shooting at their working parties. There was a lot of sniping on both sides. 2/Lt. Berryman came up with the various parts to give "C" Sqdn. a 2nd Officer as they were somewhat shorthanded.	Sheet 28 Belgium 1:40,000
	3rd		In the morning a large German working party was observed flying away from our front and at noon found they had done a considerable amount of work during the night. The 3rd. D.Gds. had been relieved by the Lincolns and Royal Fusiliers. A quiet morning till 10 am when there was a little German shelling but nothing compared with yesterday.	
		10 am		
		12 noon	Enemy shelled ZOUAVE WOOD and then shortened on to our centre & support trenches blowing up the parapet in 2 places but little damage was done.	
		4pm	Enemy put two more shells into our trenches. 2/Lt. HOPKINSON was wounded in several places but not severely, head arm and chest.	
		4.30pm	Lt. SWIRE reported that his two Machine Guns whose centre was with the LINCOLNS had had a half time at IT DOGS, the guns and men having been known in turn and somewhat damaged, but no casualties. However the Brigade refused to relieve him. 2/Lt. RIPLEY arrived during the night from "B" Echelon to replace 2/Lt. Hopkinson. He had had no guide and consequently walked miles along the line until he found us.	
	4th.	11.30pm	Outbreak of German firing. MELVILLE. 3. LEES. 17th. Lancers came to spend a day in our trenches. Germans bombarded the LINCOLN trenches for a short time without doing much damage. German snipers active all day but we had a quiet time which we spent improving our trenches. During the night our 2 Machine Guns	

Army Form C. 2118.

WAR DIARY 1st. (Royal) Dragoons

or

INTELLIGENCE SUMMARY.

(Erase heading not required.)

Volume IX Sheet 4.   1-3th June 1915

Instructions regarding War Diaries and Intelligence Summaries are contained in F.S. Regs., Part II and the Staff Manual respectively. Title pages will be prepared in manuscript.

Place	Date	Hour	Summary of Events and Information	Remarks and references to Appendices
N. ZILLEBEKE J.13.c.	4th		With the LINCOLNS were relieved and sent back to rest in the N.S.Y. Trenches. A Major of the LINCOLNS came up to take over the line for the following night.	
	5th	1.0am	About 1am Lcpl KING "A" Sqdn. had apparently gave out on his own responsibility to bombs some Germans - He returned via Royal Fusiliers trenches who took him for a German and shot him. A most unfortunate incident but we could not fairly blame the Royal Fusiliers.	
		1.30pm	About this time our howitzers opened upon Chateau grounds to register the range. We were due to be relieved at 10.30pm but as the relieving party lost themselves 4 times they failed to turn up till about 2am on the 6th.	
	6th	2.30am	Moved out of trenches 2.30am and made a very fast pace back to VLAMMERTINGHE luckily there was a thick fog or we might have failed to get out without being seen. The Blues & Tenth failed to get out till the next night. Reached VLAMMERTINGHE about 6am and returned in busses to THIENNES at 12 noon. Leave was granted to 4 officers and 13 men to go home that night.	
		12 noon	The above period May 29 - June 6 is so far the longest consecutive period the Regiment has spent in the trenches but at the same time with the exception of one Spell in February was probably the easiest and least trying. The weather was good the whole time. The men never got wet through and we were subjected to very little shelling. Our casualties were small - 1 Officer and 30 men. The trenches were very bad when we took them over but the men deserve the greatest credit for the way they worked and by the time they were finished trenches were as good as could be made considering that it was impossible to dig deep owing to the springs in the ground. As far as our own front was concerned we felt quite confident of being able to stop any attack, Our chief anxiety was our left flank as these trenches were constantly heavy shelled and kept occupying them were always a chance of the enemy getting in with a sudden rush. Our line could have ADSS/Forms/C. 2118. been enfiladed	

Army Form C. 2118.

WAR DIARY
or
INTELLIGENCE SUMMARY.

1st (Royal) Dragoons.

Volume IX Sheet 5. 1-30th June 1915

(Erase heading not required.)

Instructions regarding War Diaries and Intelligence Summaries are contained in F. S. Regs., Part II. and the Staff Manual respectively. Title pages will be prepared in manuscript.

Hour, Date, Place	Summary of Events and Information	Remarks and References to Appendices
General	Our section of trenches would have been very considerably improved by the construction of Points d'appuis behind the line but there were neither time nor material for doing this. Further communication trenches would also have been desirable.	APPENDIX I - Casualties APPENDIX II - Reinforcements APPENDIX III - Strength December 31
June 7th - 30th THIENNES	Owing to our having received lately large reinforcements both in Officers and men, great time was devoted to the instruction of all ranks in their duties as Cavalry Soldiers. Classes of instruction in Bayonet Fighting, Bomb throwing, Trench Mortars, Scouting and Signalling were carried out. 2/Lt. W. P. Browne became Scout Master and 2/Lt. J. de W. and Teuton was appointed Pioneer Officer. All ranks are now issued with a respirator & smoke helmet. The Brigade was inspected by the Commander-in-Chief who expressed his thanks to all ranks for their conduct and conduct with the Regt. on their losses, especially of the late Colonel STEELE. Capt. F. S. Isaacs joined & assumed command of C Sqdn. Major A. D. McNeill promoted Lieut. Colonel in command of the Regiment.	

1st Royal Dragoons

1st. (Royal) Dragoons.

- W A R   D I A R Y   VOL. IX -

APPENDIX No. I.

Casualties of period 1st. to 30th. June, 1915.

Regtl.No., Rank and Name.	Sqdn.	Date.	Remarks.
KILLED:			
5808 Pte. A.Morris	B	2/6/15	Trenches nr. HOOGE.
8746 " D.Hope	B	"	"
2739 " J.Meechan	B	"	"
3448 " G.McGibbon	C	5/6/15	"
8784 " J.Hough	A	"	"
DIED OF WOUNDS:			
695 L.Cpl. L.H.P.King	A	5/6/15	"
WOUNDED:			
2/Lt. A.Hopkinson	C	3/6/15	"
5411 Sgt. E.Buck	B	1/6/15	"
9369 Pte. J.D.Gray	B	"	"
5961 " A.McKenzie	A	2/6/15	"
8491 " W.Norley	A	"	"
8620 " J.Dunnett	A	"	"
9198 Sgt. J.H.Sharpe	A	"	"
5639 Pte. J.Hingerty	A	"	"
5364 Sgt. J.Rickeard	B	"	"
4132 Pte. A.Wilson	B	"	"
6651 " G.Hocking	A	"	"
4820 Sgt. W.J.Seaton	B	"	" (slightly & at duty).
6272 Pte. W.Jess	A	3/6/15	"
8455 " G.Longden	A	"	"
688 " H.Amor	B	"	"
802 " P.James	B	"	"
5649 Sgt. T.Workman	C	"	"
6911 Pte. W.Cooper	C	"	"
8076 " H.Willmers	C	"	"
---- " A.Nairn	C	"	"
3411 " A.McDonald	B	4/6/15	"
2722 " J.F.Pocock	B	"	"
5991 A/Cpl. A.Warrilow	B	5/6/15	"

August 4th., 1915.

Capt. & Adjt.,
The Royal Dragoons.

1st. (Royal) Dragoons.

****

WAR DIARY VOL. IX.

APPENDIX No. II.

Reinforcements received during period 1st. to 30th. June/15.

Officers	Other ranks.	Horses.						Date.	Remarks.
		C.	R.	P.	H.D.	L.D.			
2/Lt.F.A.Brown	70	6	25	–	–	–		6/6/15	No.5 Base.
Capt.T.S.Irwin	1*	–	–	–	–	–		11/6/15	*Westmorld.& Cumb.Yeoy.
2/Lt.J.S.Dunville	1	1	11	–	–	–		19/6/15	No.5 Base.
-------------------	2	–	–	–	–	–		24/6/15	Prison, Harve.
-------------------	10	1	9	–	–	–		26/6/15	No.5.Base.
-------------------	1	–	–	–	–	–		29/6/15	No.5 Base.

August 4th.,1915.

[signature]
Capt.& Adjt.,
The Royal Dragoons.

1st. (Royal) Dragoons.

****

WAR DIARY. VOL' IX.

APPENDIX No. III.

Honours and Rewards, Mentions for Good Work in the Field,&c. 1st.-30th/6/15.

Regtl. No. Rank and Name.   Remarks.

NAMES BROUGHT TO NOTICE OF BRIGADIER GENERAL FOR GOOD WORK DURING OPERATIONS OF 29/5/15 to 5/6/15:-

    5001 S.Q.M.S. Oxford, S.J.
    6482 Lance Corpl. Bishop, C.W.
    3370 Lance Corpl. Chick, F.
    2624 Private McQueen, J.
    6327 Private Neal, R.J.

AWARDED THE DISTINGUISHED CONDUCT MEDAL:

    4274 Sergeant J. Mortimer.

August 4th., 1915.

                                                 Capt. & Adjt.,
                                     The Royal Dragoons.

121/6443

3rd Cavalry Division

1st Royals.
Vol I

From 1st to 31st July 1915

Army Form C. 2118.

WAR DIARY 1st. (Royal) Dragoons
or
INTELLIGENCE SUMMARY
(Erase heading not required.)

Volume X; 1st.–31st. July, 1915.
Sheet 1.

Instructions regarding War Diaries and Intelligence Summaries are contained in F. S. Regs, Part II and the Staff Manual respectively. Title pages will be prepared in manuscript.

Place	Date	Hour	Summary of Events and Information	Remarks and references to Appendices
THIENNES	1–3/7/15		During this month the Regiment as a whole remained in billets at THIENNES. Squadron and Regimental training continued. Digging parties of various strength were provided by the Regiment to assist in strengthening the line of defence immediately behind the firing line. These parties varied in strength but at no time were more than 120 away digging at the same time. At SAILLY a party worked on communication trenches immediately connecting the front line with the supporting line. Between NEUVE EGLISE and Hill 63 N.W.corner of PLOEGSTREET WOOD we provided working parties of about 70 men for about a month. The parties were able to work by day at a distance of about 1200 yds.from the Germans whose works could be easily seen towards MESSINES. There was, however, very little shelling, and we had no casualties. Another party was sent to ELVERDINGHE to construct fortified works. Here there was also a certain amount of shelling, but we had no losses.	Appendix I – Reinforcements received. Reg. Mob– Hancebtoan GA 1:100 000.
	3–7–15		Captain C.W.Turner joined from England where he had been Adjutant of the Lothian and Border Horse. He was relieved in this duty by Lieut.G.H.L.F.Pitt Rivers who was wounded on October 31st. and is still too lame for active service. Capt. Turner was posted as second in command of "B" Squadron.	
	15–7–15		2/Lt.G.A.Ripley whose eyesight was indifferent and unsuitable for cavalry work was evacuated to the Base.	
	16–7–15		Major H.A.Tomkinson, who had not been with the Regiment since 1911,rejoined from being A.P.M. 1st.Cavalry Division, and assumed command of "B" Squadron.	
	17–7–15		The following new establishment of the Machine Gun Section was ordered by the G.O.C.,6th.Cavalry Brigade:– OFFICERS: 2. SERGEANTS: 3. OTHER RANKS: 66. RIDING &PACK HORSES: 63. LIGHT DRAUGHT: 32. BICYCLES: 2. Lieut.C.G.W.Swire in Command, and Lieut.R.H.W.Henderson as second in command of the Section.	
	20–7–15 to 31–7–15		Captain C.R.Tidswell was evacuated to England vice Major Tomkinson. Lieut.& Qrmr.W.R.Lines joined as Quartermaster vice Captain T.Jones, still on the sick list. 2/Lieut.F.A.Brown being supernumerary to establishment was sent to the Base. 2/Lt.W.R.Birch proceeded to 1st.Army Trench Mortar School with intention of assuming command of a Trench Mortar Battery for 2 months. He is therefore temporarily struck off the strength of the Regiment & will be attached to whatever formation he serves with.	

Fletcher Fitzgerald
Captain & Adjt.
The Royal Dragoons.

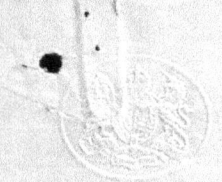

THE ROYAL DRAGOONS.

WAR DIARY - VOL. X - 1st.-31st. JULY.

APPENDIX E.

****

Reinforcements received during the month of July, 1915.

Officers	Other Ranks.	Horses. R.	C.	P.	L.D.	H.D.	Limbers.	Remarks.
Capt.C.W.Turner	9	2	-	-	16	-	4	From Base 2/7/15.
----	2	6	1	-	-	-	-	From Base 10/7/15.
Major H.A.Tomkinson	2	-	2	-	-	-	-	From 1st. Cav.Div. 15/7/15.
Lt.& Qrmr.W.R.Lines 5th.Lancers	-			-	-	-	-	From 13th. Res.Regt. 16/7/15.
----	1	1	-	-	-	-	-	From 3 C.D. HQ. 19/7/15.
-----	6	7	-	-	-	-	-	From Base 23/7/15.
2/Lieut.H.Smith	5	4	-	-	-	-	-	From Base 31/7/1915.

In the Field,

August 18th.,1915.

Capt.& Adjt.,

The Royal Dragoons.

121/6815

3rd Cavalry Division

1st (Royal) Dragoons

Vol XI

August 15.

Army Form C. 2118.

WAR DIARY 1st. (Royal) Dragoons

Vol.XI - 1/31-8-1915.
Sheet 1.

(Erase heading not required.)

Instructions regarding War Diaries and Intelligence Summaries are contained in F.S. Regs., Part II. and the Staff Manual respectively. Title pages will be prepared in manuscript.

Place	Date	Hour	Summary of Events and Information	Remarks and references to Appendices
THIENNES	1.8.15		2/Lt.H.Smith joined from the Base and was posted to "B" Squadron, vice 2/Lt.Birch.	
	2.8.15		A Billeting party was sent on to select a new Regimental billeting area.	
	3.8.15		The Regiment paraded at 8 a.m. and left THIENNES for new billets in the area AMETTES NEDON, NEDONCHELLE, FONTAINE-lez-HERMANS. The area had only just been vacated by the Indian Cavalry Corps (C.I.H. and 2nd.Lancers), so was consequently filthy dirty. However the change is an improvement as the ground is higher and more undulating while there are less houses and more opportunities for training. Brigade Headquarters moved to FEBVIN PALFART, 3rd.D.Gds. to LIETTRES, and N.S.Y. to ESTREE BLANCHE.	
AMETTES AREA	13.8.15 to		A working party of 8 officers and 200 other ranks from the Regt. proceeded to ARMENTIERES by Motor bus as part of a digging party found by the 3rd.Cav.Div. for strengthening the defences of the town. Lt.Col.McNeile was in command of the detachment from the 6th.Cav.Bde. N.C.Os.& men were billeted in warehouses in the Rue de la Gare, Officers at 10 Rue Denis Pepin and 12 Rue de Montin.	
ARMENTIERES	31.8.15		The section allotted to the Regiment was from the level crossing just N.of the Farm DESJARDINS (I.2.b) to a point on the railway line just E.of NOUVELLE HOUPLINES church (C.26.d). The line of defence did not follow the railway line but formed a half moon bulging N.W.with its two points resting on the railway. The trenches were generally so sited as to bring fire to bear on an enemy attacking the one next to it Six separate defensive works were constructed numbering from right to left, with communicating trenches leading to dug-outs or cellars of neighbouring houses. In order to get sufficient "command" it was only possible in most cases to dig down about 1 ft. 6ins. whilst the parapet and parades had to be built up 3 ft.with sand bags - a very tedious job. "A" Sqdn.were unfortunate enough to have a house collapse on top of one of their communication trenches which had been built to close to the foundations. However, luckily nobody was near it at the moment. The fire bays generally averaged 5½ yds.with traverses of 9 ft.wide. "B" Squadron worked in a market garden and here most of the work had to be done at night as the enemy shelled this portion of the line (only 1200 yds.in rear of the firing line and in full view of the PERENCHY ridge) at frequent intervals. In every case low wire entanglements from 2 ft. to 1 ft.high were constructed in front of the trenches 35 yds.from them and 18 ft.wide. These were flanked by machine gun emplacements constructed by 10 of our Machine Gunners. On an average, each man of the working party did about 6 hours work per day. The work done differed from that of previous working parties found furnished by the Regiment in that we were given a definite job to	Sheet 36 40.0.0 Belgium & France.

The trenches were supplied at each end with communication trenches which led into fortified dug-out 60 yds.in rear.

Army Form C. 2118.

WAR DIARY 1st.(Royal) Dragoons.

INTELLIGENCE SUMMARY. Vol.XI - 1/31-8-1915.
Sheet 2.

(Erase heading not required.)

Place	Date	Hour	Summary of Events and Information	Remarks and references to Appendices
ARMEN-TIERES.	13.8.15 to 31.8.15		to carry through from start to finish, and we were not merely completing work already half done by somebody else. The men worked extremely well and complimentary letters were received from all quarters, including one from the G.O.C. 2nd.Army. The chief difficulty was scarcity of materials which delayed the work. Concrete especially did not arrive until the end and consequently could not be used as much as one would have wished. The floors of the trenches were drained with broken bricks. It is interesting to note that in the works constructed by the 3rd.Cavalry Division 3,000,000 sand bags were used. We were lucky in having no casualties whatever. Unfortunately 2/Lieut. Theodore Smith, R.E., who was supervising the work of the Brigade section, was killed by a shrapnel bullet. The party returned to permanent billets on September 4th. During the period referred to above the remainder of the Regiment remained in billets near AMETTES and were occupied only in grooming and exercising the horses.	Appendix I "Honours & Awards" Appendix II "Reinforcements received".

15-9-1915.

[signature]
Capt.& Adjt.,
The Royal Dragoons.

THE ROYAL DRAGOONS.

* * * * * * * *

WAR DIARY, VOLUME XI, 1st.31st.August, 1915.

APPENDIX I.   "HONOURS AND REWARDS"

The following Russian Decorations have been conferred on the N.C.Os. and Men named below. (London Gazette, 25/8/15):-

CROSS OF THE ORDER OF ST.GEORGE, 4th.CLASS:

    7995 Corporal E.Dickinson
    3542 Lance Corporal J.C.Yeaman.

MEDAL OF ST. GEORGE, 3rd.CLASS:

    5768 Private A.Bartlett
    5004 Private G.W.McDonald   (Killed in action 13/5/1915).

In the Field,   Capt.& Adjt.,
September 15th.,1915.   The Royal Dragoons.

THE ROYAL DRAGOONS.

* * * * * * * *

WAR DIARY, VOLUME XI, 1st.-31st.AUGUST, 1915.

APPENDIX II.   REINFORCEMENTS RECEIVED.

Officers.	Other Ranks.	Horses.	Date joined & from whence.
2/Lieut.H.Smith	6	4	No.5 Gen.Base, 1/8/15.
---	2	-	Divnl.H.Q.& R.F.C. 8/8/15.
---	12	5	No.5 Gen.Base, 27/8/15.
---	1	-	30/8/15.

In the Field,
September 15th.,1915.

Capt.& Adjt.,
The Royal Dragoons.

6th Cav. Bde.
3rd Cav. Div.

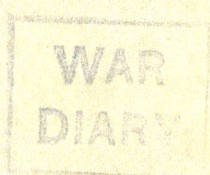

1st (ROYAL) DRAGOONS.

SEPTEMBER

1915

Attached:

Appendices I, II & III

Army Form C. 2118.

SECRET. WAR DIARY. 1st.(Royal) Dragoons.
or
INTELLIGENCE SUMMARY.
(Erase heading not required.) VOLUME XII - SHEET 1 - 30/9/15.

Instructions regarding War Diaries and Intelligence Summaries are contained in F.S. Regs., Part II. and the Staff Manual respectively. Title pages will be prepared in manuscript.

Place	Date	Hour	Summary of Events and Information	Remarks and references to Appendices
	September 1st - 20th		The Digging Party having returned from ARMENTIERES, the Regiment was once again able to do some Cavalry Training, and the first work over open country since leaving South Africa was undertaken. This was possible, owing to the fact that the harvest had all been got in and the light ploughs and stubbles were in most cases passable for troops without fear of damaging crops. Both officers and men, many of whom had little or no cavalry training, were greatly in need of work of this kind. Training was necessarily hurried but progressive. Section work was the ground work and subsequently Squadron, Regimental and Brigade Training was carried out - the latter being in the form of a combined field day against the 7th. and 8th. Cavalry Brigades. In order that, in the event of a rapid forward move, Cavalry should be independent of "B" Echelon and Supply Lorries, practice took place in loading the limbers with extra rations. It was found that by transferring all tools, machine guns and belt boxes to pack horses, 2 days corn (at 8 lbs) per horse could be carried; whilst on the horse and man 8 lbs. of corn and 3 days iron ration for the men could be carried for emergency.	
	9th.		An expert from G.H.Q. arrived and gave the Brigade a demonstration of Gas. A proportion of the Regiment put on their Smoke Helmets and walked through a trench filled with gas - the intention being to give the men confidence and prove the efficacy of the helmets. During this period the vicinity of our billets was full of British Infantry chiefly 1st. Division, who were resting and preparing for the coming offensive. Curiously enough there appeared to be no attempt whatever to keep the secret, if it was one, and long before we received any orders on the subject, we learned from outside information that full and detailed preparation had been made for an attack by the First Army.	
	19th. 20th		We received orders to be ready to move. Orders were received about 11 a.m. that the Brigade less "B" Echelon would rendezvous at 6.30 p.m. Meanwhile billeting officers of the Guards Division arrived to reconnoitre our area with the intention of occupying it on the following day. H.R.H. the Prince of Wales accompanied this party. The Brigade moved off about 7.30 p.m., having been delayed by the late arrival (Continued) ---	

1577 Wt.W10791/1773 500,000 1/15 D.D.&L. A.D.S.S./Forms/C. 2118.

Army Form C. 2118.

Instructions regarding War Diaries and Intelligence Summaries are contained in F.S. Regs., Part II. and the Staff Manual respectively. Title pages will be prepared in manuscript.

WAR DIARY 1st.(Royal) Dragoons
or
INTELLIGENCE SUMMARY.

(Erase heading not required.) VOLUME XII: 1 – 30/9/15.

Sheet 2.

Place	Date	Hour	Summary of Events and Information	Remarks and references to Appendices
	September		of the 3rd.D.Gds.billeting party. We marched via AUCHEL and MARLES – LEZ – MINES to the BOIS des DAMES which we reached about 11 p.m. We bivouacked in this wood and had orders to keep horses and men under cover in order that they might escape the notice of aircraft.	
	21st.		Remained in the wood. The men were completed with 3 days iron rations. 2 days extra corn for horses i.e. 16 lbs. was drawn and packed on limbers.	
	22nd/23rd.		Two Officers per Regiment were sent out to reconnoitre the ground between VERMELLES and GRENAY with a view to a possible forward movement of the Cavalry in that direction. From various points a good deal of the ground towards LOOS and HULLUCH could be seen. The terrain was open and undulating and except for the trenches of both sides appeared to provide no serious obstacle to a Cavalry advance between LOOS and HULLUCH. Of course one could see nothing beyond the first line of German trenches. Our guns were heavily bombarding the German lines – the enemy made little or no reply. Observation was difficult owing to the clouds of dust and smoke.	
	24th.		Six officers per regiment were sent out to reconnoitre the approaches which had been constructed by the R.E. up to our first line; 8 roads had been made, all clearly marked. These officers were to be ready to act as guides.	
	25th.		Two officers were sent out at dawn with a patrol to picquet one of the routes mentioned above. About 4 a.m. we heard a very heavy bombardment and later dead silence. It afterwards transpired that our infantry had attacked about 5.20 a.m. aided by gas and smoke, and captured the first German line from the Quarries to LENS road with little opposition. The right was reported to have pushed on through LOOS to Hill 70. About 300 Germans were however holding out at LONE TREE. About 7.30 a.m. the Brigade received orders to move to VAUDRICOURT. We remained there till about 11 a.m. and then pushed on at a fast pace in column of sections to CORONS de RUTOIRE where we halted and remained in mass under cover of some houses. Luckily the weather was foggy and we did not get shelled. It was understood that orders had been received to push the 6th. and 8th. Cav. Bdes. through the "Gap" to the canal and occupy the crossings about PONT a VENDIN. As, however, patrols sent out failed to discover the Gap in question, the G.O.C.	

Army Form C. 2118.

WAR DIARY 1st.(Royal) Dragoons.
or
INTELLIGENCE SUMMARY.
VOLUME XII; 1 – 30/9/15.

Sheet 3.

(Erase heading not required.)

Place	Date	Hour	Summary of Events and Information	Remarks and references to Appendices
	26th Sept.		Division decided to keep us where we were. We remained in this position all day and obtained a good view of our immediate front. Infantry and guns could be seen moving about all day in the open. Further attacks appeared to be taking place in the direction of HULLUCH apparently without success. Officers patrols were continually sent out to report progress but from reports sent in, there was no opportunity for Cavalry action. We spent an uncomfortable night as it was wet and cold, and very few of the men could get shelter. Till 12 noon our position was unaltered. Our infantry continued to attack towards HULLUCH without gaining ground. Later somewhat alarming reports came in. We could see bodies of British infantry retiring from the direction of LOOS and guns and transport were retiring under hostile shell fire. The LENS road was heavily shelled, and crowded as it was with transport a considerable amount of damage was done. Before 1 p.m. the Royals and 3rd.D.Gds. received orders to move up dismounted and consolidate the first line of German trenches taken on the 25th. We moved up in column of sections extended under slight shell fire and occupied a section of about 600 yards from the LOOS – VERMELLE road half way to the LENS road, our right being in touch with the 3rd.Dragoon Guards. On our left there were no troops in position though large numbers of infantry from 21st.Division were retiring past us saying they had had orders to retire. These troops were disorganized and appeared to have no one in charge of them. The trenches we occupied were not greatly damaged. They were provided with dug outs about 20 feet deep. The wire had all been well cut by our artillery fire. We started to work hard and induced some of the infantry to prolong our left, however, after being there about 3 hours we received orders to advance at once and occupy LOOS which was to be held at all costs; the 3rd.D.Gds. South of the dump and the Royals to the North of it. No one seemed to know at the time whether the village was in German or British hands. East of LOOS just clear of the crest of Hill 70 could be seen yellow flags which were supposed to belong to the 15th. Division but it afterwards turned out these had been abandoned. In spite of considerable shell fire, we had so far suffered no casualties, and we reached the village without having a man hit. On arrival at the outskirts of LOOS various bodies of British infantry were encountered who all said they had orders to retire. The Colonel told them they were mistaken and induced a proportion who with Captain Robinson and Lt. A.B.S.Holland C.A.S. held the place. (continued) –	

Army Form C. 2118.

WAR DIARY 1st.(Royal) Dragoons.
INTELLIGENCE SUMMARY.

Sheet 4.   VOLUME XII; 1 - 30/9/15.

(Erase heading not required.)

Place	Date	Hour	Summary of Events and Information	Remarks and references to Appendices
	27th.		We had a large front to hold, and the strength of the Regiment was only 250 men with 4 machine guns. Our dispositions with reference to the map 36c,N.W.Sheet 3, 1:20000, were as follows:-	
			"A" Sqdn.from pt.58 to Pt.53; "B" Sqdn.pt.53 to the windmill; from this point a company of the 9th.Gordon Highlanders (Pioneers) held a short section of trench and the northern line of houses to pt.48 where about 50 Camerons occupied a trench facing S.E. Slightly in front of the latter with their right on the dump were about 250 Argyle and Sutherland Highlanders with 2 troops of "C" Squadron in support behind them in houses. A patrol from these 2 troops was sent out to the top of the dump to connect with the 3rd.D.Gds. The remaining 2 troops of "C" were in reserve at Regimental Headquarters near pt.27.	Appx. III
			Two machine guns were allotted to "B" Sqdn.section and the other 2 were kept in reserve - a position on the dump being selected for the day time.	
			During the night one Squadron of the 3rd.D.Gds. (47 men) relieved the A.& S. Highlanders who retired into cellars and "C" Squadron relieved the Camerons.	
			The enemy had displayed no activity whatever and evidently had no intention of counter attacking - his line being behind the crest of Hill 70. Things were quite quiet except for a certain amount of desultory unaimed fire which came over the line without doing any damage.	
			The village was full of dead and wounded - chiefly British. As there were no infantry stretcher bearers or doctors the whole of this work devolved upon Captain Menzies, who was indefatigable in his efforts to cope with the wounded. We could, unfortunately, do little for them, as we had no men to spare, and many of these could not be got away till the following night.	
			Before dawn the 8th.Cavalry Brigade came up and also the N.S.Y. This lengthened our line considerably, as we were able to put "C" Sqdn.entirely in reserve whilst "A" Squadron handed over to the N.S.Y.and took over half the "B" Sqdn.line. The Gordons were at the same time relieved by the 3rd.D.Gds. whilst the Blues took over what was originally the right of our line to the dump.	
			When it became light, we were able to reconnoitre the position more thoroughly. The line ran from the dump about 200 yards S.E.of LOOS in a N.E.direction up to hill 70; the other end of this trench being held by the enemy. Thence the line ran along the perimeter of the village to FORT GLATZ whence a communication trench ran up to the old German line at the LOOS road redoubt. This trench was now occupied by the Grenadiers. We were not holding a continuous line but a series	

Army Form C. 2118.

WAR DIARY 1st.(Royal) Dragoons.
or
INTELLIGENCE SUMMARY.

(Erase heading not required.)   VOLUME XII. 1 - 30/9/15.

Sheet 5.

Place	Date	Hour	Summary of Events and Information	Remarks and references to Appendices

of detached posts in houses with cover in the cellars for men not actually on duty. Slightly in advance of the rest of the line 2/Lt.Dunville's Troop held a farm at pt.53. 800 yards to our left front was the Chalk Pit wood and to the right of that was Puits No.14 bis. 2/Lt.Wingate with a patrol of 3 men was sent out to reconnoitre the latter. He worked through the Chalk Pit wood and to within 50 yards of the PUITS when he was fired on. In connection with this patrol 2/Lt.Wingate and Cpl.Butler did valuable service at considerable risk to themselves in clearing up an obscure situation.   *Appx III*

As a result of this reconnaisance a Brigade of the Guards (General Ponsonby) was sent up at 2.30 p.m. to attack the Puits and wood behind it. There was little artillery preparation. The attack advanced in perfect order across the open from the old German first line and reached the Puits. It, then, disappeared over the crest where it came under heavy machine gun fire and had to retire under the crest of the hill and dig in by the Chalk Pit with supports along the line of the LOOS - HULLUCH road.

Meanwhile another Guards Brigade advanced through LOOS and took up a position to the left of the BLUES where they dug in below the crest of Hill 70.   *Appx I*

We took no part in the attack though we had to put on our smoke helmets for about 20 minutes owing to a heavy fire from hostile gas shells. Our machine Guns endeavoured to support the attack by indirect fire on the BOIS HUGO. The Regiment suffered a great loss during the afternoon in the death of Captain CHAPMAN who was killed whilst watching the attack by a burst of shrapnel. He was in command of "A" Squadron at the time. In action throughout the Campaign, he had proved himself full of resource and energy in every emergency. He had always displayed the utmost coolness and had set a great example to all under him. His body was removed and buried at NOEUX-LEZ-MINES.   *Appx III*

The enemy shelled LOOS heavily throughout the afternoon and evening, but our casualties were extraordinary few owing to good cover provided by cellars.

About dawn a patrol under 2/Lt.Berryman was sent out to clear up the situation. He worked along the line from right to left and returned about 12 noon with a considerable amount of very useful information, shewing the positions held by the various units of the Guards Brigades. It appeared that there was a gap of about 1000 yards which was not joined up. In connection with this patrol Private Duff did a great deal of good work, whilst the sketch made by 2/Lt.Berryman was very   *Appx III*

Army Form C. 2118.

WAR DIARY
or
INTELLIGENCE SUMMARY.

1st. (Royal) Dragoons.

Sheet 5. VOLUME XII; 1 - 30/9/15.

(Erase heading not required.)

Instructions regarding War Diaries and Intelligence Summaries are contained in F. S. Regs., Part II. and the Staff Manual respectively. Title pages will be prepared in manuscript.

Place	Date	Hour	Summary of Events and Information	Remarks and references to Appendices
			useful. About 3.30 p.m. after a short and ineffective artillery preparation supported by our machine guns, 2 companies of the Guards again attacked in the Puits from the Chalk Pit wood with the same result as yesterday. They again successfully reached the crest but then came under heavy machine gun fire and were forced to return to their original position. In the evening about 10 p.m. we were relieved by the 2nd.Suffolks, 2nd.Division who in their turn had been relieved by the 28th.Division. The relief was carried out without incident and the Regiment rejoined its horses in the vicinity of MAZINGARBE about 1 a.m. on 29th.	Appendix I Casualties Appendix II Reinforcement Appendix III Honours & Rewards
	24/3.30		Marched back to the BOIS des DAMES where we reoccupied our old bivouac, where we remained until October 3rd.	

Robertson Fitzgerald
Captain and Adjutant,
The Royal Dragoons.

APPENDICES

I, II & III.

THE ROYAL DRAGOONS.

****

WAR DIARY - VOLUME XII - 1 - 30th. SEPTEMBER, 1915.

APPENDIX I: CASUALTIES.

Regtl.No.Rank and Name.	Sqdn.	Casualty.	Date.	Remarks.
KILLED:				
Captain A.H.D.Chapman	A	Killed	27/9/15	Buried at NOUEX-les-MINES.
3452 Pte.W.Emuss	A	"	"	" "
6938 " G.Hartley	B	"	"	
WOUNDED:				
1610 Pte.G.Milton	M.G.	Wounded	26/9/15	
3224 " H.James	"	"	"	
4560 " G.Thompson	C	"	"	
4934 L/Cpl.J.Styles	B	"	"	
4107 Pte.W.Mitchell	B	"	"	
4459 " T.M.Maguire	B	"	"	
3731 " C.Ingram	B	"	"	
9126 " R.Motion	B	"	"	
11834 " J.Hogarth	B	"	"	
8994 " E.Comline	B	"	"	
4635 " C.E.Tait	C	"	"	
5781 " W.H.Lacey	C	"	"	
6254 Cpl.F.J.Allsebrooke	H.Q.	"	27/9/15.	
1764 Pte.A.Tott	A	"	"	
2054 Cpl.T.Butler	A	"	28/9/15	
1505 L/Cpl.A.R.Davison	C	"	"	
10261 Pte.D.Alexander	C	"	"	
5500 Cpl.J.J.Talbot	C	"	"	
5117 Pte.T.Reeve	C	"	"	
7312 " S.Kerr	C	"	"	
7354 " D.McKenzie	M.G.	"	"	
3649 Cpl.E.Edwards	B	"	"	
8821 Pte.J.Bolton *	M.G.	"	"	
6181 " F.Brown	M.G.	"	"	
5754 " W.E.Westcott	M.G.	"	"	
INJURED:				
5529 Pte.J.C.Wilson	B	Injured	28/9/15.	

SUMMARY:
  Killed   (Officers   1
           (Other Ranks   2   Total - 3.

  Wounded (Officers   nil.
           (Other ranks   25   Total - 25

  Injured (Other ranks   1   Total - 1

Total Casualties. 29.

*Remained at duty until 1/10/15.

F.C.Wilson Fitzherald Capt.& Adjt.,
3/11/15.   The Royal Dragoons.

THE ROYAL DRAGOONS.

WAR DIARY - VOLUME XII - 1st./30th. September, 1915.

APPENDIX II - REINFORCEMENTS.

Officers.	Other ranks.	Date.	Remarks.
-	7	3/9/15	From Base.
2/Lt. J.S. Parr " W. Newcombe	9	14/9/15	"

F.D.W. Ison Fitzgerald
Capt. & Adjt.,
The Royal Dragoons.

3/11/1915.

THE ROYAL DRAGOONS.

WAR DIARY - VOLUME XII - SEPTEMBER 1st./30th., 1915.

APPENDIX III - HONOUR & REWARDS.

Regtl.No., Rank and Name.	Remarks.
7995 Corporal E. Dickinson	Awarded the Cross of the Order of St. George, 4th. Class. London Gazette, dated 25/8/15.
3542 Lance Corporal J.C. Yeaman	
5768 Private A. Bartlett	Awarded the Medal of St. George, 3rd. Class. London Gazette, dated 25/8/1915.
5004 Private G.W. McDonald *	
*Killed in action 13th. May, 1915.	
Captain A.J.A. Menzies, R.A.M.C. (attached 1st. Dragoons)	To be Companion of the Distinguished Service Order.
Temp. 2/Lieut. W.O. Berryman	Awarded the Military Cross
2/Lieut. A.W. Wingate	Awarded the Military Cross.
8093 Pte. W. Duff	Awarded the Distinguished Conduct Medal.

3/11/1915.

F.W. Wilson Fitzgerald

Capt. & Adjt.,
The Royal Dragoons.

3rd Cavalry Division

1st (Royal) Dragoons

Dec. 1915

Vol XIII

Army Form C. 2118.

WAR DIARY 1st. (Royal) Dragoons
or
INTELLIGENCE SUMMARY. Volume XIII - Sheet 1.
October, 1915.

(Erase heading not required.)

Place	Date	Hour	Summary of Events and Information	Remarks and references to Appendices
BRUAY	1st 3rd		The Regiment remained in the BOIS des DAMES. The men all got a hot bath in the BRUAY MINES.	Appx. "A" - Reinforcements joined. Appx. "B" - Summary of Operations.
CAUCHY-A-LA-TOUR	3rd		We moved to CAUCHY-A-LA-TOUR about 4 miles further West. Here we got very comfortable billets for the men. The horses were in fields. Our "B" Echelon here rejoined us from the neighbourhood of AIRE. We had been separated from it since leaving our billet at FONTAINE.	
"	7th		2/Lieut. NEWCOMBE rejoined from the Base where he had been sent as supernumerary a month ago before. Our Regimental Serjeant Major C.M.COOKE obtained a commission in the Carabineers. Lieut.H.M.P.Hewett rejoined from York after having been wounded at HOLLEBEKE CHATEAU, Oct.30th., 1914. R.Q.M.S. Edwards was appointed R.S.M. in succession to R.S.M.Cooke.	
"	8th 19th		The Brigade left its billets and proceeded to the neighbourhood of LAIRES with the North Somerset Yeomanry. The Regiment left LAIRES and proceeded to occupy billets near LIGNY-lez-AIRE. "A" Sqdn., Headquarters and Machine Gun went to LIGNY-lez-AIRE, "B" Sqdn. to LE TIRNAND and PIPPLEMONT, with "C" Sqdn.at RELY. Later it was found that the "B" Sqdn. Troop at PIPPLEMONT was too far away and consequently was moved to LIGNY-lez-AIRE. Also owing to overcrowding at LE TIRNAND another troop of "B" Sqdn. was moved to CHEMIN RELY.	
"	19th to 31st		The Billets generally were fairly good and the men were well off for shelter and in most cases satisfactory arrangements were made for messing. A lot of trouble was taken to improve the stabling and standings for horses, and hundreds of cart loads of clinker and cinders were got from the mines to put down on the floorings. A trench was dug between RELY and LIGNY for the use of Bombers. Arrangements were also made for a musketry range near LIERES.	
"	16th		The Leave season had now reopened and the numbers allotted to the Regiment were 7 of all ranks on Mondays and Fridays. Each man was allowed four clear days in England, and an extra day to Ireland or Scotland.	

S.Q.M.S. F.B. Ratcliffe was granted a commission in the Royal Dragoons, and posted for duty to the North Somerset Yeomanry as their Machine Gun Officer.

F.B. [signature]
Captain & Adjt.
The Royal Dragoons.

1st. (ROYAL) DRAGOONS.

APPENDIX A.   War Diary, Vol. XIII, October, 1915.

REINFORCEMENTS JOINED.

Detail of Personnel.				Remarks.
Officers.	O.R.	Horses.		
		R.	D.	
	4	–	–	4/10/15.
2/Lt. W. Newcombe	23			7/10/15
	7	5	–	10/10/15
	14	7	1	17/10/15
2/Lt. O.B. Scott				
" O. Birkbeck	100	–	–	21/10/15
	11	1	2	30/10/15.
Lt. Ion. P. Hewett				7.10.15.

Capt. & Adjt.,
The Royal Dragoons.

29/11/15.

1st. (ROYAL) DRAGOONS.

****

APPENDIX B.   War Diary, Vol. XIII, October 1915.

HONOURS AND DECORATIONS.

Rank and Name.	Remarks.
To be Companion of the Distinguished Service Order:	
Captain A.J.A. Menzies, R.A.M.C.	Attached 1st. Dragoons.*
Awarded to Military Cross:	
Temp. 2/Lieut. W.O. Berryman	*
Temp. 2/Lieut. A.W. Wingate	*
Awarded the Distinguished Conduct Medal:	
No. 9593 Private (now Lance Corporal) W. Duff. *	
*Divnl. Routine Order 777, d/16-10-15.	

Novr. 29th., 1915.

Capt. & Adjt.,
The Royal Dragoons.

3rd Cavalry Division

1st (Royal) Dragoons.
Nov. 1915
Vol XIV

WO
171/9

Army Form C. 2118.

SECRET

ORIGINAL

THE ROYAL DRAGOONS

WAR DIARY
or
INTELLIGENCE SUMMARY

The Royal Dragoons.

Vol. XIV. Sheet 1.

November, 1915.

(Erase heading not required.)

Instructions regarding War Diaries and Intelligence Summaries are contained in F.S. Regs., Part II. and the Staff Manual respectively. Title pages will be prepared in manuscript.

Place	Date	Hour	Summary of Events and Information	Remarks and references to Appendices
LIGNY-LES-AIRE.	1st.		A party under Major Hardwick was sent up to SERCUS to dig a line of trenches and dug-outs as a defensive position but returned after 3 or 4 days as the billets which they occupied were required by units of the Indian Corps.	
	9th.		A party of 3 officers and 164 other ranks proceeded to OUDERDOM for duty in improving communication trenches in the YPRES salient, near ZILLEBEKE lake. Captain Turner was i/c this party until relieved by Captain & Brevet Major Cosens who rejoined from England on the 13th. This officer had been absent from the Regiment since 1913 when he was seconded for service with the Egyptian Army. When War broke out in August 1914 he was doing Political work in the SOUDAN. He went on the Intelligence Staff in Egypt and later became Military Secretary to General Maxwell, Commanding the Troops in Egypt. He, then, went to the Dardanelles on a special mission to disembark guns and transport animals at SUVLA BAY. He subsequently became G.S.O.3 to the Welsh Division and was later invalided home with dysentery where he remained until rejoining the Regiment.	Appx. I
			2/Lieut. R.F. Heyworth-Savage joined from England and was posted to "B" Sqdn.	
CREQUY	10th. 16th.		The Regiment moved with the rest of the Brigade from their billets to a new area near FRUGES. H.Qrs., M.G.Sec. and "A" & "B" Squadrons to CREQUY, "C" Squadron to TORCY. Brigade Headquarters were situated at ROYON; North Somerset Yeomanry at LEBIEZ, and the 3rd. Dragoon Guards at LOISON. The change of billets from the point of view of the men was not an improvement. Accomodation was bad, the area was full of refugees and very dirty. In many cases men had to be put in places whence sheep had just been cleared. The stream of the river CREQUOISE however, provided ample water for the horses and in this respect we were better off than we had been before.	Appx. I
	22nd.		The Digging Party which had been up at OUDERDOM was sent back and another party were sent up the next day to take their places. Major Cosens remained at OUDERDOM and was not relieved.	
			Owing to an epidemic of "itch" which appears to have originated in the huts at OUDERDOM, all men returning from the digging party had to be medically inspected regularly by the Medical Officer.	
			The work on which this Digging Party were engaged appears to have consisted chiefly in draining communication trenches near ZILLEBEKE LAKE. Unfortunately we had several casualties but the majority occurred from a single shell. The work proceeded in the day-time usually from 7 a.m. to about 1 p.m. when the men would return to their huts at OUDERDOM.	Appx. III
			(Continued)	

WAR DIARY

Army Form C. 2118.

The Royal Dragoons.
Vol. XIV. Sheet 2.
November, 1915.

Instructions regarding War Diaries and Intelligence Summaries are contained in F.S. Regs., Part II. and the Staff Manual respectively. Title pages will be prepared in manuscript.

Place	Date	Hour	Summary of Events and Information	Remarks and references to Appendices
CREQUY	23rd-26th		2/Lieut. A.R. Cooper joined from England (York) and was posted to the Machine Gun Section for duty. S.S.M. Coe, S.S.M. Reynolds, and Sergeant Loader, who had been waiting commissions for some time, received orders to report to the Base at once. Their Commissions in the R.F.A. were dated 29/10/15. S.Q.M.S. Elmes succeeded S.S.M. Reynolds as S.S.M. of "B" Squadron, whilst Sergt. Angus did the duties of S.S.M. in "C" Squadron, vice Coe. Sergt. Farrell succeeded Elmes as acting S.Q.M.S. of "A" Squadron. 2/Lieut. C.T. O'Callaghan was posted to the Regiment from the North Somerset Yeomanry, his regular commission being dated 22/11/15. It was, however, arranged for him to remain with the N.S.Y. until the conclusion of the present War. Owing to the absence of a large number of men Digging, training was confined chiefly to Machine Gunners and Bombers. There are now 30 Regimental Bombers and 24 Squadron Bombers. More are being trained.	Appx. I
"	to			APPENDIX I - REINFORCEMENTS
"	30th			" II - HONOURS & REWARDS
LIGNY-LES-AIRE.	3rd.		Lt. A.W. WINGATE appointed A.D.C. to G.O.C. 6th. Cav. Bde. (Brig. Gen. O.M. CAMPBELL). J.O.L. deWEND FENTON- Orders were received for this officer to report at W.O. preparatory to proceeding to join his Unit - 14th. Hussars. 2/Lt. W.R. BIRCH rejoined Regiment from command of 18th Trench Mortar Battery, 1st. Army. Capt. G.O'A. EDWARDES was ordered to proceed home and report to W.O. to take up the appointment of 2nd in Command of an Infantry Battalion of the New Army. He was subsequently appointed to the 13th (Ser. Bn.) WELCH Regiment with the rank of Major.	III - CASUALTIES.
"	11th.			

In the Field,
December 24th., 1915.

[signature]
Capt. & Adjt.,
The Royal Dragoons.

The Royal Dragoons.
****

WAR DIARY   Vol. XIV.
APPENDIX I.   November, 1915.
                              REINFORCEMENTS.

Officers.	Other Ranks.	Remarks.		
		----------England----------		
2/Lt.R.F.Heyworth-Savage	-	From ######		10/11/15
Capt.& Bt.Major G.P.L.Cosens	2	"	"	13/11/15
2/Lieut.A.R.Cooper	-	"	"	24/11/15.
	11	"	Base	30/10/15
	10	"	"	8/11/15
	3	"	"	21/11/15
	4	"	"	27/11/15.

(signed) F.W.H. von Fitzgerald
Capt.& Adjt.,

December 24th., 1915.   The Royal Dragoons.

The Royal Dragoons.

WAR DIARY.
APPENDIX II.

HONOURS AND REWARDS.

Vol. XIV.
November, 1915.

Rank and Name.	Remarks.
Lieutenant (Temporary Captain, A.S.C) R.F. Glyn (Reserve of Officers, The Royal Dragoons)	Awarded the Croix de Chevalier, 5th. Class.

December 24th., 1915.

Capt. & Adjt.,
The Royal Dragoons.

The Royal Dragoons.
****

WAR DIARY.
APPENDIX III.

CASUALTIES.

Vol. XIV;
November, 1915.

Regtl.No.Rank and Name.	Sqdn.	Date of Casualty & remarks.
KILLED:		
985 Pte.S.W.Tyler	A	20/11/15, nr.ZILLEBEKE.
WOUNDED:		
9518 Pte.G.Wood	A	" " S.w.thigh(sev
9267 " E.Stark	A	" " "
2971 " E.Barge	A	" " B.w.leg.
8821 " J.Bolton	A	" " slightly; at duty.
DIED OF WOUNDS:		
2809 Lce.Cpl.W.Compton	A	" " G.s.w.leg,right.
6862 Pte.J.Addison	A	21/11/15 " " back.(wound 20/11/15).
9155 " J.Goring	C	" " " thigh,left. (wounded 20/11/15)

December 24th.,1915.

                                              & Adjt.
                                         The Royal Dragoons.

Royal Dragoons
Dec 1915
Vol XV

SECRET. ORIGINAL. Army Form C. 2118.

Instructions regarding War Diaries and Intelligence Summaries are contained in F.S. Regs., Part II. and the Staff Manual respectively. Title pages will be prepared in manuscript.

WAR DIARY
or
INTELLIGENCE SUMMARY.
(Erase heading not required.)

The Royal Dragoons.
Volume XV.
December 1915.

Sheet 1.

Place	Date	Hour	Summary of Events and Information	Remarks and references to Appendices
CREQUY, North France	1-12-15		The Digging Party from OUDERDOM returned arriving at MARESQUEL station at 6p.m. They had travelled via HAZEBROUCK, ST.OMER, CALAIS, BOULOGNE, and ETAPLES. It was surprising that PARIS was not included in the tour but presumably the engine driver had run short of coal. A new Dismounted organization for the Cavalry Corps has been produced. The Corps is to be re-modelled on the lines of an Infantry Division. Each Cavalry Division is organized as an Infantry Brigade, and each Cavalry Brigade as an Infantry Battalion. The Regiment is thus called upon to provide a Company consisting of 8 officers and 300 men. In turn each Regiment of the Brigade provides the Battalion Headquarters, and for the month of December we are on duty. This means that we provide all the Battalion Staff.	
''	7-12-15		Parties of 30 men per Squadron attended a Gas Demonstration which took place at Brigade Headquarters.	
''	10-12-15		A digging party of 72 men proceeded to LYNDE for work on a reserve line of trenches. Major P.E.Hardwick was in charge of the Brigade Working party, and Capt. C.W.Turner i/c of the Regimental Party. Lieut.H.P.M.Hewett and Sergeant T.Elliott proceeded on a course of Bombing at 44th.Bde.,15th.Division Bombing School.	
''	14-12-15		2/Lt.C.B.Scott proceeded to Divisional Headquarters for a short signal course.	
''	17-12-15		All horses in the Regiment were malleined.	
''	20-12-15		Lieutenant Colonel H. D. McNeile who had commanded the Regiment since the death of Lieutenant Colonel G. F. Steele, C.M.G., in May last, was accidentally killed by a fall from his horse. It was a most extraordinary accident as he fell on very soft ground and clear of his horse. The fatal nature of the injury must have been entirely due to the angle at which he fell.	
''	24-12-15		The Digging Party from LYNDE returned to billets. 40 horses which were picked out as unsuitable were cast. Captain A.J.A.Menzies, D.S.O., R.A.M.C., was posted to the 7th.Cavalry Field Ambulance and was succeeded as Medical Officer of the Regiment by Captain J.Biggam,R.A.M.C., from the 7th.Cavalry Field Ambulance.	
''	25-12-15		Christmas Day passed off quietly. The final of the Troop Football Competition which had been played during the last fortnight took place and resulted, after a good game, in the victory of the 2nd.Troop of "A" Squadron over the 4th.Troop of "C" Squadron.	
''	27-12-15		The Digging Party started off again for LYNDE but had not got 4 miles from (continued)—	

SECRET

ORIGINAL

Army Form C. 2118.

Instructions regarding War Diaries and Intelligence
Summaries are contained in F.S. Regs., Part II.
and the Staff Manual respectively. Title pages
will be prepared in manuscript.

WAR DIARY
or
INTELLIGENCE SUMMARY

(Erase heading not required.)

The Royal Dragoons.

Volume XV.

December, 1915.

Sheet 2.

Place	Date	Hour	Summary of Events and Information	Remarks and references to Appendices
CREQUY, N. FRANCE	26.12.15		billets when they were recalled. At the same time the Dismounted Division was ordered to be concentrated in its billets by 6 p.m. on the 28th. A parade of the Dismounted Company was held. The men carried improvised packs. The Company was organized into 7 platoons - 2 from each Squadron each of 45 men & 1 of 30 Bombers. The platoons of "A" Squadron are now known as Nos.1 & 2, those of "B" as Nos.3 & 4, and those of "C" as Nos.5 & 6 Platoons. It was now understood that the Dismounted Division of the Cavalry Corps would be required to take over a line of Trenches relieving the 47th. Division in th line in the vicinity of the HOHENZOLLERN REDOUBT and HULLUCH.	Appx. 1.
"	30.12.15		Captain A.W. Waterhouse who had been wounded May 14th. rejoined the Regiment from England and was posted to "C" Squadron. The following officers were detailed for duty with the Dismounted Company:- Captain T.S.Irwin (Commanding), Capt.A.W.Waterhouse (2nd.in.Command), Lieut.W.P. Browne and 2/Lieuts.O.Birkbeck, J.B.Bickersteth, H.Smith, W.H.Cubitt.(Platoon Leaders), Lieuts.C.G.W.Swire and R.H.W.Henderson (Machine Gun Section), 2/Lieut. S.J.Parr (Bombing Officer), and 2/Lieut.W.R.Birch (Trench Mortar Battery). Battalion Headquarters was taken over by the 3rd.Dragoon Guards so that we were not required to find this establishment.	
"	1st to 31st Dec.		TRAINING DURING THE MONTH. Owing to the absence of a large number of men on digging parties no Squadron work on a large scale could be attempted. Bombers received daily practice and instruction. The Machine Gun Section also got through a good deal of training. A small rifle range was constructed and every man available was put through a short course. Once per week there were tactical tours for young officers.	APPENDIX 1. Reinforcements received.

6/1/1916.

[signature]
Captain and Adjutant,
The Royal Dragoons.

WAR DIARY.
The Royal Dragoons.

Volume XV.
December, 1915.   Reinforcements Received.   APPENDIX 1.

Officers.	Other Ranks.	Horses.	Date joined and from Whence.
	3	16.	Base 4/12/15
	19	-	" 4/12/15
	7	2	" 11/12/15
	6	-	" 12/12/15
Captain A.W.Waterhouse	-	-	England 31/12/15
	10	-	Base 31/12/15,

January 10th., 1916.

Capt. & Adjt.,
The Royal Dragoons.

Army Form C. 2118.

WAR DIARY
or
INTELLIGENCE SUMMARY
(Erase heading not required.)

The Royal Dragoons.
Volume XVI.
January, 1916.   Sheet 1

Place	Date	Hour	Summary of Events and Information	Remarks and references to Appendices
	Jan. 1st.			
	3rd.		The Dismounted Company was to have left but at the last moment their departure was postponed until the 3rd. The Machine Gun Section consisting of 2 officers 2 Sergeants and 26 Gunners with 6 limbers and 12 drivers entrained at MARESQUEL at 10 a.m.	1.
	9th 12th		The Dismounted Company paraded mounted at 5.30 a.m. and proceeded to MARESQUEL Station where they entrained at 8.15 a.m. News received from Dismounted Company that 3 men of "A" Squadron were injured by Bombs which had been left ready detonated by the last occupants of their billets. Captain A.W.Waterhouse was killed by a shell when walking up a communication trench. No.1625 Sgt.S.W.Futcher & No.4180 Private R.Bowie were also killed this day. Capt.E.W.T.Miles who had been wounded through the calves of both legs rejoined from England. The following casualties also occurred- KILLED "A" Sqdn. 3 other ranks, "C" Sqdn. 1. WOUNDED "A" Sqdn. 6 other ranks. Regimental Headquarters proceeded to take over command of the 6th.Dismounted Battalion.	
	18th.		Regimental Headquarters proceeded to take over command of the 3rd. Dragoon Guards. Battalion which had been found since January by the 3rd. Dragoon Guards. The party including officers and regimental staff proceeded by the train from MARESQUEL at 10 a.m. and reached BETHUNE at 1.30 p.m. Batt. Hd. Qrs. were established close to the EGLISE DU PERROY. All men of the Battalion were housed at the ORPHANAGE - a very fine building for troops if it had been cleaner. There was, however, no proper cook-house which was a considerable advantage. The building having been previously used by infantry,this want had not been felt as they were in possession of Field Cookers. The Battalion found working parties daily whilst in reserve at BETHUNE --the chief item being a party of 200 men which went daily to VERMELLES by lorry for the purpose of carrying stores. The Battalion moved from BETHUNE at 7.0 a.m.by road,being played out of the town by the band of the 3rd. D.Gds.	
	21st		Coys. were distributed in local reserve as follows :- 3rd. D.Gds and Battalion Transport at SAILLY - LABOURSE in billets - Royals in cellars at VERMELLES - N.S.Y. and Battalion Head Quarters in North Lancashire Trenches. Battalion H.Qrs. relieved the 3rd. D.Gds. Lancashire Trench was on the whole in good condition the floor was boarded and the men had comfortable dug-outs,washing places etc. The relief was completed by 11.0 a.m. The following working parties were found during	

Army Form C. 2118.

Instructions regarding War Diaries and Intelligence Summaries are contained in F. S. Regs., Part II. and the Staff Manual respectively. Title pages will be prepared in manuscript.

WAR DIARY
or
INTELLIGENCE SUMMARY
(Erase heading not required.)

The Royal Dragoons   Volume XVI
                      January 1916
                      Sheet 2

Hour, Date, Place	Summary of Events and Information	Remarks and References to Appendices
Jany. 22nd	during the day:-	
	N.S.Y., 1 officer, 150 men, cross roads VERMELLES 3.30 p.m. work on D.1.	
	Royals, 1 officer, 150 men CLARKES KEEP 3.30 p.m. work on D.2.	
	Royals 60 men CLARKES KEEP 5.0 p.m. work in the 155th. Coy R.E.	
	N.S.Y., 14 men M.G.Cellars Brewery 4.0 p.m.	
	3rd.D.Gds. 1 N.C.O. and 6 men at H.Q. C.R.E. satily SAILLY at 8.0 a.m.	
	3rd. D.Gds., 75 men work with 180th. Tunnelling Coy.	
	"B" Sqdn.	
	The Royals reported one casualty namely 306 Pte. H.Tilley who was killed on fatigue.	
	Working parties were found as under:-	
	N.S.Y. 1 officer, 150 men work on D 1 3.30 p.m.	
	Royals 1 officer 150 men work on D 2 3.30 p.m.	
	Royals 60 men work under 155th. Coy. R.E. 5.0 p.m.	
	3rd. D.Gds., 75 men under 180th. Tunnelling Coy. 8.30 a.m.	
	" " ; 10 men M.G. emplacements 5.0 p.m.	
	N.S.Y., 1 N.C.O. and 27 men salvage work at 12 noon at Brewery VERMELLES	
	N.S.Y. 10 men M.G. emplacements at 5.0 p.m.	
	3rd. D.Gds., 10 men at 10.0 a.m. salvage work VERMELLES.	
	During the morning the sector D.1 was reconnoitred by C.O. and Adjutant but the line being very intricate, a cursory inspection was really insufficient to get anything but a very vague idea of the line.	
	During the morning the enemy shelled VERMELLES with small Crumps also NOYELLES and SAILLY but did little or no damage.	Appx. 1.
	Orders were received late at night to the effect that owing to a defensive mine having been exploded in the vicinity of the KINK reliefs would be postponed until the afternoon as there was a certain amount of hostile activity.	
	Capt. G.W.Turner having returned from leave assumed command	

SECRET

The Royal Dragoons

WAR DIARY
or
INTELLIGENCE SUMMARY
(Erase heading not required.)

Volume XVI
January 1916
Sheet 3

Army Form C. 2118.

Instructions regarding War Diaries and Intelligence Summaries are contained in F. S. Regs., Part II. and the Staff Manual respectively. Title pages will be prepared in manuscript.

Hour, Date, Place	Summary of Events and Information	Remarks and References to Appendices

Jany 3rd.

of the Royals Company with Capt. the Hon. C. Annesley as his Second in command. Interpreter Bonnet also arrived from CREQUY and joined the Transport at SAILLY.
All the men's feet were rubbed with anti-frostbite grease.
The relief of the 7th. Dismounted Battalion was effected during the afternoon and the 6th. Dismounted Battalion was distributed as under:-
Royals Coy. relieved 2nd. L.G. in KAISERIN, BIGGERWILLIE and the KINK, 3 platoons.
2 Platoons in support in VIGO STREET.
1 Platoon in support in GORDON ALLEY.
3rd. D. Gds. Coy. relieved Lieicestershire Yeomanry in ALEXANDRA TRENCH with 4 platoons. 2 platoons being in support in CROWN TRENCH.
N.S.Y. Coy. relieved 1st. L.G. as follows:- 1 platoon at JUNCTION KEEP remainder in South Lancashire Trench.
The platoons in Lancashire Trench were responsible for bringing up from VERMELLES all rations and stores required in the front line.
Battalion H. Qrs. relieved Lt. Col. Robertson of the Liecestershire Yeomanry.
The relief was necessary slow but was carried out without incident.
During the night the Royals and 3rd. D. Gds. repaired and improved their parapets. Sap 6 was dug out and overhead cover was erected. Parapetsin Sap 1 and 2 were improved.
Enemy Trench Mortars were active during the night, we replied with rifle grenades which were effective but we were handicapped by an insufficient quantity of these missiles.
The enemy also annoyed us with rifle grenades in the vicinity of Saps 6 and 7, from the direction of the new Crater.
Enemy working parties were heard in the new trench opposite RIFLEMANSalley and in the new crater where they put up iron loophole plates.

Jany 4th. 2.30 a.m. Our Trench Mortars opened on the New Crater assisted by

The Royal Dragoons **WAR DIARY** Volume XVI
or
INTELLIGENCE SUMMARY. January 1916
(Erase heading not required.) Sheet 4.

Hour, Date, Place	Summary of Events and Information	Remarks and References to Appendices
	by fire from the 2 forward guns of "C" Battery at LE RUTOIRE. This stopped their grenades but does not seem to have interfered very much with their work. About 12 noon enemy shelled CROWN TRENCH, VIGO STREET and HULLUCH ALLEY. Our guns replied with effect. About 5.0 p.m. a small enemy mine was exploded close under their own parapet opposite Sap 8. It was nearly dusk and in spite of rifle fire, they occupied the crater. Enemy at the same time opened heavy fire with big mortars for 5 minutes on support trenches without any result. There was also a rifle grenade duel opposite Saps 5,6,7. These saps were again bombarded with rifle grenades and bombs from the new crater about 6.30 p.m. At 8-45 p.m. our trench mortars opened on the crater with good effect and stopped the bombing. Later two officers patrols reconnoitred the new crater and pulled down the loophole plates. About 5 dead Germans were found in the crater. It was also discovered that a covered passage apparently led from the crater to the German front line Trench by means of which it was possible for them to enter and leave it without being seen. Another patrol under L.Cpl.Margrett of the Royals went out from Sap 5 and reconnoitred round the rear of the crater toward the German Trenches and reported that the rear edge of the crater was apparently linked up by a trench with their front line. Casualties :-	
	3rd. D.Gds. 3 O.R. wounded by grenades Royals 2 O.R. wounded by grenades N.S.Y. 2 O.R. wounded by grenades 2nd.L.G.M.G.Sec. One O.R. killed by grenade	
Jany 25th	8.30 a.m. The enemy started bombing Saps 6 and 7 from the CRATER. The Trench Mortars were turned on but did not stop the bombing which unfortunately caused a considerable number of casualties to our bombers. The reason being that whilst the enemy could freely throw their long handled bombs from the crater, we	appx I

Army Form C. 2118.

The Royal Dragoons

WAR DIARY
or
INTELLIGENCE SUMMARY.
(Erase heading not required.)

Volume XVI
January 1916
Sheet 5

Place	Date	Hour	Summary of Events and Information	Remarks and references to Appendices
			we were obliged to operate from the confined space of Sap 6 and 5.	
		9.0 a.m.	Enemy shelled ALEXANDRA and CROWN TRENCHES especially in the neighbourhood of RIFLEMAN'S ALLEY.	
		9.30 a.m.	asked for artillery co-operation but our batteries were unable to open owing to the presence of a large number of hostile xxxxxxxxxxxxxxxxxxxxaircroraft. At one time there were 5 up and hostile bombardment had evidently been initiated with the object of drawing our batteries and so locati/png them.	
		10.0 a.m.	The heavies opened but the enemy continued to shell CROWN TRENCH. There was a considerable amount of bombing at Saps 6 and 7.	
		11.0 a.m.	Situation much quieter though hostile shelling continued on RIFLEMAN'S ALLEY though not so heavy. Enemy were employing a certain amount of 5.9 several of which were blind.	
		11.30 a.m.	The shelling had practically ceased.	
		12.0 noon	Our horse batteries shelled the New Crater opposite Sap 6 with effect.	
		Afternoon	enemy shelled GORDON and HULLUCH ALLEYS also CROWN TRENCH. The 3rd. D.Gds. filled in Farmers Hole with wire and loose earth during the night.	
			A considerable amount of work on the parapets and trenches were done during the night and fresh wire was put up. A gap made in KAISERIN @ by a trench mortar was repaired.	
			A fatigue party under the R.E. started digging emplacements for West spring guns but these guns will be no use to us until the guns are adapted for Mill's grenades.	
			JUNCTION KEEP was strengthened with sandbags.	
			Casualties:-	
			3rd. D.Gds. 2 O.R. killed, shell fire	
			3 O.R. wounded " "	
			Royals. 1 O.R. killed, grenade	
			1 O.R. wounded, rifle	
			3 O.R. " Grenades	
			3 O.R. " shell	
			N.S.Y. 1 O.R. killed, grenade	
			7 O.R. wounded, "	Appx I
			2 O.R. " Shell.	

The Royal Dragoons

WAR DIARY or INTELLIGENCE SUMMARY.

(Erase heading not required.)

Army Form C. 2118.

Volume XVI
January 1916
Sheet 6.

Place	Date	Hour	Summary of Events and Information	Remarks and references to Appendices
in Sap 6.	Jan 2nd		1st L.G.(M.G.Sec.) 2/Lieut. O.S.Portal, wounded shell. R.H.G. M.G. Sec. with Lewis gun killed an enemy sniper approach	
		6.45 a.m.		
		8.30 a.m.	Enemy bombarded KAISERIN TRENCH with mortars from the direction of the DUMP TRENCH. On our guns replying the mortars ceased. At the same time they started shelling HULLUCH and GORDON ALLEYS also SACKVILLE STREET reaching a maximum at 10.0 a.m. The shelling died down about 11.0 a.m.	
		11.45 a.m.	Enemy heavily shelled communication trenches and dug-outs from the direction of BENIFONTAINE. The early part of the afternoon was quiet but at 4.0 p.m. the enemy started a heavy concentrated bombardment of four front line especially KAISERIN and ALEXANDRA also communication trenches and dug-outs. The shelling ceased completely about 5.5 p.m. Our artillery replied effectively and no doubt as a result of this the enemy showed no signs of life in their front line on completion of their bombardment with the exception of 2 isolated and feeble attacks on Saps 4 and 2. In the former case 1 German reached the parapet and was shot by Sergt. Elliott, Royal Dragoons with his revolver whilst 3 others were also accounted for close to the sap. In the latter case 10 Germans came out but were reported to have been obliterated by a shell. A considerable amount of damage was done to our sector. KAISERIN was blown in in two places and in one place there was a gap of 15 yards which was completely exposed. Curiously enough in spite of working parties being constantly exposed, the enemy did not open either rifle or machine gun fire and the only feasible deduction is that he was not manning his front line at the time. ALEXANDRA TRENCH, CROWN TRENCH, SACKVILLE STREET and GORDON ALLEY were considerably knocked about and the latter blown in in two places on either side of Battalion Headquarters. During the bombardment all telephone communication was as usual cut but we managed to get a message through by wireless and others by runner. In consequence of the bombardment supports were sent up by Brigade 180 men of the F.F.G. were places in close support close to the O.B. Line. 2 Machine guns which had been damaged were also replaced. During the night a large amount of work had to be done on the parapets and trenches at which the N.S. Yeomanry were employed.	

Army Form C. 2118.

The Royal Dragoons. **WAR DIARY** Volume XVI.
or January 1916
INTELLIGENCE SUMMARY. sheet 4.
(Erase heading not required.)

Place	Date	Hour	Summary of Events and Information	Remarks and references to Appendices
	Jan 24th		Casualties:-	

3rd.D.Gds 4 O.R.Killed, shell fire
                11 O.R.Wounded   "   "
                 1 O.R.Wounded Grenade
Royals   3 O.R.Killed, Shell Fire
                12 O.R.Wounded "   "
                 1 O.R.M Killed Shell Fire
N.S.Y.   1 O.R.Wounded, Shell fire
6th. Signal Troop 4 O.R.Killed Shell Fire
M.G.Sec. 9th.Batt. 1 O.R.Wounded

There were also some other casualties to Machine Gun Section 1st.Batt. but these were not ascertained before the Battalion was relieved.
The Battalion was relieved by the 1st. Dismounted Battalion Lt.Colonel Winwood D.S.O. 5th. D.Gds. The relief was completed by 10.30 a.m. and the Battalion proceeded to its old billets in BETHUNE.
Lorries were to have been provided at NOYELLES but these failed to appear and consequently we walked arriving at the ORPHANAGE about 7.0 P.M.
During the second period in the trenches the Battalion had 64 casualties in action. These were with 2 exceptions all caused either by shell fire or grenades, the latter including rifle grenades and bombs. There were also 7 casualties to Machine Gunners attached to our sector.
The majority of the casualties from shell fire occurred in the right sector on the 26th. there 15 casualties from this fire in the KAISERIN and communication trenches..
The various saps were responsible for the large number of men hit by hand bombs though men in the fire trench were knocked over by rifle grenades. The wounds received from grenades of all kinds were very severe and several of these casualties subsequently died of wounds.
As regards the comfort of the trenches this was on the whole good as the floors were wonderfully dry and the parapets bullet proof. There was, however, a much felt want of dug-outs for the men in the support line and many casualties might have been saved by the provision of good overhead cover.
The enemy throughout showed considerable activity with grenades and mortars of all sorts but sniping and machine gun fire was curiously infrequent, in fact we never had a single man sniped during the whole time we were in the trenches.

Appx 1

The Royal Dragoons

WAR DIARY
INTELLIGENCE SUMMARY.
(Erase heading not required.)

Army Form C. 2118.

Volume XVI
January 1916
Sheet 8.

Place	Date	Hour	Summary of Events and Information	Remarks and references to Appendices
	Jan 28/29.		Telephone communication with Brigade Headquarters was fairly good but that with companies was continually breaking down. Artillery support was very good. Medical arrangements were not good. The Medical Officer was too far off and was handicapped by want of space in his dressing station. Stretcher bearers and stretchers were both insufficient and double the establishment might well have been provided. Ration arrangements on the whole worked well and there was plenty of water in the trenches for drinking purposes. The Battalion remained in billets at BETHUNE and found fatigue parties as before the only alteration being that the parties were now found by platoons complete with Officers N.C.Os. and men. Officers were sent out to reconnoitre for the BETHUNE defence scheme. This included the routes to be used in marching East and the locality of the various keeps etc. which were to be occupied by the battalion in case of emergency. Permanent garrison of 1 N.C.O. and 3 men were provided by the Battalion for these Keeps. Whilst out on reconnaissance 2/Lieut. HUISHE N'.S.Y. was slightly wounded by shell fire near VERMELLES. On January 29th. Headquarters were relieved by those of the North Somerset Yeomanry.	

WAR DIARY
or
INTELLIGENCE SUMMARY

Volume XVI
January 1916

(Erase heading not required.)

Army Form C. 2118.

Summary of Events and Information

EXTRACTED FROM "G" SQDN. DIARY

Captain T.S. Irwin, Commanding Royals Company.
Royals Dismounted Company.

Jan.3rd. - Jan.18th.
The Dismounted Company proceeded to BETHUNE forming part of the 6th. Dismounted Battalion under Lieut. Colonel Burt, 3rd. Dragoon Guards. The men were all billeted in the ORPHANAGE RUE DE PERROY.

Jan.4th.
Company marched to SAILLY - LA BOURSE which was an even filthier billet than BETHUNE.

Jan.5th.
Remained at LA BOURSE. Lieut. W.P. Browne reconnoitred route to MAZINGARBE.

Jan.6th.
Returned to ORPHANAGE at BETHUNE.

Jan.7th.
Fatigue party of 200 men by lorry to VERMELLES carrying stores to trenches

Jan.8th.
Remained in billets at BETHUNE.

Jan.9th.
Royals Coy. went into old billets at SAILLY. 10.30 a.m. L.Cpl.Jones, Ptes. Baker, and Cossins, all of "A" Sqdn. were wounded in the legs as a result of a bomb accident. Apparently they had been playing with some bombs which had been left behind by previous occupants of their billet.

Jan.10th.
Fatigue party of 200 men went to VERMELLES for carrying stores and another 40 in the afternoon. Irwin and Waterhouse went up to reconnoitre sector of 2nd.L.G. which we take over tomorrow.

Jan.11th.
Paraded at 7.15 a.m. at SAILLY - LA BOURSE and marched by platoons to VERMELLES entering the front line trenches by GORDON ALLEY. Relief of 2nd.L.G. complete by 10.30 a.m. Spent the day in cleaning up trenches, making ammunition reserves etc. A quiet day.

Jan.12th.
6.0 a.m.. Order from 10th.Hussars passed down to put on Gas Helmets

Continued.

Army Form C. 2118.

WAR DIARY
or
INTELLIGENCE SUMMARY.

The Royal Dragoons   Volume XVI   January 1916

Place	Date	Hour	Summary of Events and Information	Remarks and references to Appendices

but cancelled after 20 minutes.
7.0 a.m. Boots taken off and feet rubbed with anti-frostbite grease.
7.30 a.m. Front line visited by 3 generals.
9.0 a.m. Captain Waterhouse, Sgt.Futcher and Pte. Bowie all killed by Whiz Bang which burst in parapet of BIGGER WILLIE.
7.15 p.m. Lieut. Parr organised a bomb attack from head of Sap 5 against enemy sniper. Enemy retaliated with mortars and one pitched full on a box of bombs lying at foot of sap exploding it and killing L.Cpl.Goodyear and Ptes.Walker Burt and McLean, Wallace wounded. These men buried in G 4 d 04.

Jan.13th.
1.45 a.m. Trench mortar wounded Cpl. Styles and Ptes.Cox Dunnet and Morgan.
Artillery retaliation from our guns lessened enemy mortars.
12.30 p.m. Bickersteth and 10 men attended Waterhouse's funeral at VERMELLES. Quiet day.

Jan.14th.
6 - 7 a.m. Enemy trench mortars active.
12.45 p.m. Order passed from Right to Left to "Stand to" - nothing happened.
8.0 p.m. 2/Lieut. Birch arranged a mortar and artillery bombardment of enemy lines. Considerable damage to hostile parapets. Enemy replied with little effect.

Jan.15th.
10.30 a.m. Relieved by 9th. Lancers.
2.30 p.m. Company reached BETHUNE.

Jan.16th.17th.
Remained in BETHUNE.

Jan.18th.
Our headquarters relieved 3rd.Dragoon Guards.

END OF "C" SQUADRON EXTRACT

Army Form C. 2118.

WAR DIARY

The Royal Dragoons Volume XVI
INTELLIGENCE SUMMARY.
January 1916

(*Erase heading not required.*)

Jan. 30th.
Head Quarters of the Regiment return to billets at CREQUY with the exception of Major Hardwick who had to stay at BETHUNE till the arrival of Lt. Colonel Burt who was on leave.
Captain Miles also remained temporary in charge of Royals Coy till relieved by Major H.A. Tomkinson.

Jan. 31st.
Major Hardwick returned to billets.

[signed]
Captain & Adjt
The Roy. Dragoons

The Royal Dragoons.
* * * * * * * *
APPENDIX I - WAR DIARY.

Volume XVI.   January, 1916

CASUALTIES.

KILLED IN ACTION:

    5767 Pte.J.Grigglestone   Declared "Killed in Action 19/10/14" (previously reported "Missing") W.O.letter E/15762/C.2.C.(P.M) dated 18-12-15.

    ~~Captain A.W.Waterhouse~~
    Captain A.W.Waterhouse   12/1/1916
    1625 Sergeant S.W.Futcher   "
    3693 Lance Corporal H.Goodyear   "
    4180 Private R.Bowie   "
    5930 Private R.Burt   "
    8899 Private W.Walker   "
    3906 Private D.McLean   "
    906 Private H.Tilley   21/1/1916
    5368 Private J.H.Bray   24/1/16
    2901 Private J.Robertson   25/1/16
    4274 Sergeant J.Mortimer   26/1/1916
    1736 Private C.Kille   "
    11878 Private D.Marquis   "

DIED OF WOUNDS:
    3620 Private J.Dunnett   20/1/1916   (Wounded 12/1/1916)
    7942 Private J.S.Pritchard   25/1/1916   (Wounded 24/1/1916)

WOUNDED:
    5897 Lance Corporal G.Jones   9/1/1916   (Accidentally)
    9121 Private E.H.Baker   "   "
    5070 Private F.J.Cossins   "   "
    2547 Private A.G.Wallace   12/1/1916
    4934 Lance Corporal J.Styles   "
    6646 Private C.Cox   "
    4897 Private A.J.Morgan   "
    8300 Private W.Mitchell   "
    6650 Lance Corporal R.Buckham   14/1/1916
    7735 Lance Corporal F.Kettle   "
    12315 Private F.Macklin   "
    188 Sergeant S.Hoinville   25/1/1916
    2880 Sergeant H.V.Davids   "   (Shock)
    6073 Private J.Keegan   "
    3846 Private W.Orr   "
    5867 Private W.Robson   "
    5630 Private M.Francis   "
    6554 Private J.Lavery   "
    2304 Sergeant A.D.Philpot   26/1/1916
    1395 Lance Corporal L.A.Young   "
    8764 Private F.Thompson   "
    12654 Private E.Lewis   "
    8309 Private E.Bull   "
    3353 Private W.Crombie   "
    5226 Private A.McDonald   "
    9122 Private J.Forsythe   "
    15019 Private T.C.Parkinson   "
    5271 Lance Corporal C.Crowhurst   "   (Shock)
    4192 Trumpeter W.Goodbody   "   "
    15001 Private J.W.Townsend   "   "
    6665 Private C.Heath   24/1/1916.

                                                        Capt.& Adjt.,

February   1916.   The Royal Dragoons.

Secret

The Royal Dragoons.
* * * * * *

APPENDIX II - WAR DIARY.

Volume XVI.   January, 1916.

HONOURS AND REWARDS.

Lieutenant Colonel H. D. McNeile)	"Mentioned in Despatches" for
Major the Hon.C.H.C.Guest)	Gallant and Distinguished
Major P. E. Hardwick)	Service in the Field.
Captain A.H.D.Chapman*)	(London Gazette. Dated 1/1/16)
Captain W.T.Hodgson)	
Captain F.W.Wilson Fitzgerald)	
Captain A.W.Waterhouse*)	
Lieutenant (Temp.Capt.A.S.C.)R.F.Glyn)	
(Res.of Offrs.))	
T/2/Lt.W.O.Berryman)	
2/Lt.A.W.Wingate)	
2/Lieut.C.T.O'Callaghan (attd.N.S.Y))	
2054 Corporal T.Butler)	
7110 Corporal B.Proctor)	
6254 Corporal F.J.Allsebrooke)	
752 Private P.McCann)	
3604 Private R.Shaw)	
317 Lance Corporal R.Durnin)	

*Since Killed in Action.

Qrmr.& Hon.Capt.J.Crowley (Leicester Yeoy.T.F)R.M.& Hon.Lt.Res.Offrs.R.Dns)	To be Honorary Major. Lond. Gaz.dated 13/1/16.
Major P.E.Hardwick) Temp.Capt.R.F.Glyn,A.S.C.(Res.Offrs.) Royal Dns.)	To be Companions of the Distinguished Service Order. Lond.Gaz.dated 13/1/16.
Captain W.T.Hodgson) Captain A.W.Waterhouse)	Awarded the Military Cross. Lond.Gaz. dated 13/1/16.

GGGG

February 1916.

Captain & Adjt.,
The Royal Dragoons.

Secret

The Royal Dragoons.

* * * * *

APPENDIX III   —   WAR DIARY.

Volume XVI.   January, 1916.

REINFORCEMENTS RECEIVED.

Captain E.W.T. Miles	Joined	12/1/1916
3 light draught horses	"	15/1/1916
3 other ranks & 23 riding horses	"	22/1/1916
24 riding horses	"	29/1/1916

February 1916.

F. Robertson Fitzgerald
Capt. & Adjt.,
The Royal Dragoons.

Army Form C. 2118.

THE ROYAL DRAGOONS **WAR DIARY** **Volume XVII**
or
INTELLIGENCE SUMMARY. **February 1916**
(Erase heading not required.)

Instructions regarding War Diaries and Intelligence Summaries are contained in F. S. Regs., Part II. and the Staff Manual respectively. Title pages will be prepared in manuscript.

ORIGINAL

SECRET

Place	Date	Hour	Summary of Events and Information	Remarks and references to Appendices
			February 1st. Major Tomkinson relieved Captain Miles i/c of Royals Company, the latter returned to CREQUY.	
			February 2nd. Royals Company paraded at 4.0 a.m.and marched to VERMELLES where they took over cellars from 18th. Hussars. 5.0 p.m.found working party of 150 men. 10.30 p.m. All available men turned out to carry bombs to front line. Could only muster 30.	
			February 3rd. Quiet day found small working parties. February 4th. Relieved 2nd. L.G. in front line. 5.0 a.m.Relief complete. Same trenches and dispositions as before. Very quiet except for rifle grenades.Cpls.Procter and Greenwood wounded by these,former believed to have lost his leg. During the night built up parapet and wired in front of KAISERIN. One man hit in the arm.	
			February 5th. Quiet day. 7.0 p.m.The N.S.Y. bombers reconnoitred the crater in front of saps 6 & 7. One man hit. These saps then bombed by enemy,trench mortars then shelled crater which stopped bombing. Remainder of night quiet. Pte. Keenan accidentally blew off his finger whilst cleaning his rifle.	
			February 6th. Very quiet except for rifle grenades,2 signallers hit by these,not badly. 8.0 p.m. Lieut.Browne and Corporal Margrett,went out on patrol to Bill's Bluff. They lay in a shell hole for about 40 minutes,20 yards from enemy parapet, saw one sentry but heard little or no movement. Returned at 10.0 p.m. Put up more wire in front of KAISERIN and built up parados of BIGGER WILLIE.	
			February 7th. Quiet day. 5.0 p.m. Heavily bombarded by rifle grenades for half an hour. This was stopped by our guns. Helme hit in the foot by the fuse of one of our shells. His boot was cut and foot badly bruised and he had to be evacuated. Quiet night.Thoroughly cleaned up all the trenches.	
			February 8th. Relieved by 9th.Lancers. 9.0 a.m.Relief complete.Busses and lorries conveyed us from NOYELLES to BETHUNE.	
			February 18th. Royals Company returned to billets at CREQUY. This ended the tour of duty in B. Sector of the 6th. Dismounted Battalion.	

Army Form C. 2118.

THE ROYAL DRAGOONS.   **WAR DIARY** or **INTELLIGENCE SUMMARY.**
Volume XVII
February 1916
Sheet 2

(Erase heading not required.)

Instructions regarding War Diaries and Intelligence Summaries are contained in F. S. Regs., Part II. and the Staff Manual respectively. Title pages will be prepared in manuscript.

Place	Date	Hour	Summary of Events and Information	Remarks and references to Appendices

			During the period from January 3rd.- February 11th. the casualties sustained by the Royals Coy. were as follows:-
			     Captain A.W.Waterhouse Killed
			     2/Lieut. R.B.Helme Slightly wounded
			     11 Other ranks Killed
			     4 " " Wounded accidentally,
			     40 " " *Wounded
			 *Of these 5 subsequently were reported as having died of their wounds. D.H.WATSON.	

	February 12th.		2/Lieuts.S.J.Dumbreck,P.H.Davies-Cooke,D'A.F.H.Harris joined from York on the 5th. inst.and were posted to Squadrons for training being supernumery to establishment.	
	February 15th.		Sergeant Newton who had rejoined the Regiment after having been wounded in May was promoted S.S.M. in "C" Squadron. Sergt. Angus had been acting S.S.M. since S.S.M.Coe received his commission in the R.A. 2/Lieut. Helme rejoined the regiment on the 13th. having recovered from his slight wound.	
	February 17th.		Lieut.Colonel F.W.Wormald D.S.O. who was promoted to command the Regiment from the 8th. Hussars reported at Regimental Head Quarters and then proceeded on a weeks leave. Sergeant Wischnhusen was appointed Acting S.Q.M.S. in "A" Squadron.	
	February 20th.		Instructions were received that the Regiment would find a digging party of 1 officer and 37 other ranks for work on the old line at LA BELLE HOTESSE.	
	February 21st.		A bioscope entertainment provided by the chaplain to the 3rd. cavalry Division gave a performance to the Regiment in the Schoolhouse UREQUY. News was received that the Germans had commenced a heavy attack on the line North of VERDUN.	
	February 25th.		All leave stopped except for special cases.	
	February 27th.		Lieut.Colonel F.W.Wormald D.S.O. joined the Regiment and took over command.	
	February 28th.		The party detailed to go digging was ordered to stand fast owing to bad weather. 2/Lieut.O.Birkbeck who was on leave in England reported sick and struck off the strength.	

1577 Wt.W10791/1773 500,000 1/15 D. D. & L.   A.D.S.S./Forms/C. 2118.

THE ROYAL DRAGOONS   Volume XVII
                                      February 1916

            W A R   D I A R Y

            Summary of events.

February 29th. The Regimental Machine Gun Section was broken up and the
majority of the personnel, horses and equipment transferred to No.6
Machine Gun Squadron which was formed in the Brigade under command
of Captain Sartorius, 6th.Cavalry.
        2/Lieut. Bickersteth and 2/Lieut.Cooper,66 Other ranks,94
horses and 2 bicycles were transferred from this Regiment with the
4 Regimental Machine Guns. In addition Corpl.S.S.Welsh went as
farrier and Sergeant Walker as S.S.M. to the Squadron.

                                          [signature]
                                          Capt & Adjt
                                          The Royal Dragoons

THE ROYAL DRAGOONS.

WAR DIARY.　　　　　　　　　　　　　　　　　　　　APPENDIX I
VOLUME XVII.　　　　　　　　　　　　　　　　　　　　FEBRUARY, 1916.
　　　　　　　　　　　Reinforcements Received.

Officers.	Other ranks.	Horses.	Date joined & from whence.
2/Lt. S.J. Dumbreck	–	–	4/2/16 from England.
" D.H. Watson	–	–	"
" P.R. Davies-Cooke	–	–	"
" D'A.F.H. Harris	–	–	"
	23	3 R.	5/2/16 from Base
	–	1 R.	12/2/16 "
	15	18 R, 1 L.D	19/2/16 "
		3 R	" from 8th. Hussars.
	12	–	27/2/16.

26/3/16.　　　　　　　　　　　　F Johnston FitzGerald
　　　　　　　　　　　　　　　　　　　　　　　　　　　Capt. & Adjt.,
　　　　　　　　　　　　　　　　　　　　　　　　　　The Royal Dragoons.

THE ROYAL DRAGOONS.

WAR DIARY.　　　　　　　　　　　　　　　　　　　　APPENDIX II
VOLUME XVII.　　　　　　　　　　　　　　　　　　　　FEBRUARY, 1916.
　　　　　　　　　　　Honours and Rewards.

Regtl. No. Rank and Name.	Remarks.
4226 R.S.M. S.J. Lawrence (attached Surrey Yeomanry)	Mentioned in Despatches; Lond. Gazette, d/28-1-16. (Meditt. Exped. Force.)

26/3/16.　　　　　　　　　　　　F Johnston FitzGerald
　　　　　　　　　　　　　　　　　　　　　　　　　　　Capt. & Adjt.,
　　　　　　　　　　　　　　　　　　　　　　　　　　The Royal Dragoons.

THE ROYAL DRAGOONS.

WAR DIARY.   APPENDIX III.
VOLUME XVII.   FEBRUARY, 1916.

Casualties.

Regtl.No., Rank and Name.	Sqdn.	Nature of casualty and date.
6974 Pte. A. Williamson	B	Wounded 4/2/16
7110 Cpl. B. Proctor	B	Wounded 5/2/16
819 L/Cpl. J. Greenwood	B	" "
8501 Pte. T. H. Reece	A	" "
2/Lieut. R. B. Helme	B	Wounded 7/2/16
5413 Cpl. C. E. Murkett	A	" "
6573 Pte. R. Gilchrist	A	" "
6478 " F. Field	A	" "
5713 L/Cpl. H. Elliott	C	" "
●38 Pte. H. Drury	C	" "
12120 Pte. W. C. Keenan		Wounded-accidentally-self inflicted 5/2/16
7109 Pte. A. W. Birkholtz	C	Wounded 6/2/16.

26/3/16.

Capt. & Adjt.,
The Royal Dragoons.

Original

SECRET

The Royal Dragoons · Army Form C. 2118

WAR DIARY or **INTELLIGENCE SUMMARY**

Volume XVIII — March, 1916.

Sheet 1.

(Erase heading not required.)

Place	Date March	Hour	Summary of Events and Information	Remarks and references to Appendices
CREQUY, N.France	3.3.16		Orders were received to send billeting parties to take over from 1st.Cav.Bde Brigade owing to the break up of Cavalry Corps and consequent distribution of Cavalry Divisions to Armies.	Reinforcements Appx. I
	4th		Above order was cancelled and we were informed that this move would not take place.	
	6th		2/Lieut.W.Newcombe went to the 8th.S.Lancashire Regiment as Adjutant, and is seconded.	Casualties Appx. IV
	7th		2/Lieut.C.B.Scott proceeded to 15th.Division near LOOS for a Signal Course in the trenches to last about a fortnight.	
	9th		The G.O.C.Brigade inspected Squadrons in marching order. Weather cold; snow but fine.	
	10th		With a view to the issue of Hotchkiss Rifles to Regiments in the near future, some types of packsaddles were sent to us for trial. The trial was not altogether successful.	Honours & Rewards Appx. III
	12th		L/Cpl.Elliott.(C) proceed on a Signal Course to 3rd.Cavalry Division.	
	13th		Sergeant Monkhouse went on a Boyonet Course to FLIXECOURT.	
	14th		Cpl.Clarke to MONTREUIL on duty for a month at the Divisional Rest Billet.	
	16th		Lieut.R.H.W.Henderson was placed under arrest by order of the A.G. for forwarding a Secret Map through the post under cover of a private letter.	
	17th		A Divisional Training School was started at TRAMECOURT. The following were sent from this Regiment as Instructors: Major P.E.Hardwick - Commandant; Lieut.W.P.Browne - Adjutant; Lieut.C.G.W.Swire - Instructor in Hotchkiss Rifle, and also L/Cpl.Smith.	
	18th		R.S.M.Edwards went on leave with a view to being attached to the N.S.Y. as soon as his Commission appeared in the Gazette.	
	20th		3 Officers and 7 other ranks went to TRAMECOURT for instruction in Sniping Bombing, Pioneering and Hotchkiss Rifle.	
	23rd		2/Lieut.Hilton Green who had lately joined from Base developed German meazles and was sent away to MALAISIE. All "A" Squadron were consequently placed in quarantine.	
	24th	9 p.m.	About 9 p.m. the farm of M.BEUGNY at PREHEDRE was struck by lightning and caught fire. The outbuildings were burnt to the ground but largely owing to the assistance of the men of "A" Squadron the farmhouse itself was saved.	
	25th		2nd.Course for Officers & N.C.Os.at Div.T.School commenced.	
	29th		A second case of meazles broke out in "A" Squadron.	

(continued)

Army Form C. 2118

WAR DIARY
or
INTELLIGENCE SUMMARY

The Royal Dragoons
Volume XVIII, March, 1916
Sheet 2.

(Erase heading not required.)

Place	Date	Hour	Summary of Events and Information	Remarks and references to Appendices
CREQUY N. France	General 1-30th		During the month the Regiment was trained strenuously both on foot and in mounted duties. A field was obtained in PREHEDRE and a certain amount of Troop Drill could be done here. In many cases this was the first opportunity which the men had had since the beginning of the War. Jumps and dummies were put up and men were given some practice in the use of the sword. 　　Bombers, Scouts, and Signallers also had daily classes. 　　Classes were started in the Hotchkiss Rifle, of which 5 were issued to the Regiment. (eventually we shall be equipped with 12 - one per Troop.)	

[signature]
Capt. & Adjt.,
The Royal Dragoons.

May 8th., 1916.

Original

Appendix I
Vol. XVIII.

WAR DIARY * THE ROYAL DRAGOONS.

Reinforcements.

March, 1916.

Details.	Remarks.
Other ranks 2	Ex Base 4/3/16
2/Lt. C.C.H. Hilton Green)	
Other ranks 8)	do 11/3/16
" 3	do 19/3/16
" 1, riding horses 3	do 21/3/16
" 1	Ex England 22/3/16
Riding horses 48, Pack 9,)	
Light draught 1)	Ex Base Remount Depot 25/3/16.

May 8th., 1916.

Capt. & Adjt.,
The Royal Dragoons.

Original

WAR DIARY * THE ROYAL DRAGOONS.

Appendix II
Volume XVIII   Casualties.   March, 1916.

No. Rank and Name.	Remarks.
5318 Sgt. A.B. Marlow	Previously reported "Missing and Wounded, 30/X/14" Now declared to have been "Killed in Action - 30/10/14" (W.O. letter No.E/196473/1, dated 18-3-16.)

May 8th., 1916.

Capt. ~ Adjt.,
The Royal Dragoons.

Original

* WAR DIARY * THE ROYAL DRAGOONS.

Appendix III.
Vol. XVIII.   Honours and Rewards.   March, 1916.

No. Rank and Name.	Remarks.
4226 Sqdn.Sgt.Maj.S.J.Lawrence (attached Permt.Staff, Surrey Yeomanry)	Awarded the "Medaille Militaire". Lond.Gaz.Supplement, dated 30/3/16.

May 8th., 1916

Capt. & Adjt.,
The Royal Dragoons.

SECRET • **The Royal Dragoons** Army Form C. 2118

WAR DIARY or INTELLIGENCE SUMMARY
Volume XIX — April 1916.
Sheet 1.
(Erase heading not required.)

Original
Instructions regarding War Diaries and Intelligence Summaries are contained in F.S. Regs., Part II. and the Staff Manual respectively. Title Pages will be prepared in manuscript.

Place	Date April	Hour	Summary of Events and Information	Remarks and references to Appendices
CREQUY, N. France.	10th.		Lieut. H.M.P. Hewett was sent to G.H.Qrs. as Instructor in Light Trench Mortar (Stokes) Gun. Protests were unavailing. 2/Lt. Scott was accordingly transferred from "A" Sqdn. and placed on H.Q.s Signalling Officer i/c Headquarters Details. 2/Lt. Parr assumed the duties of Pioneer and Bombing Officer. 2/Lieut. Wingfield Digby who had joined us from the R.F.C. was posted to "C" Sqdn He had belonged to the Special Reserve of the Regiment but had not previously been out with the Regiment in France.	appx 1. Reinforcement
	14th.		L/Cpl. D.F. Barnard rejoined from a course of wireless telegraphy at Cav. Corps Signals.	
	16th.		An Officers' Mess Meeting was held, and it was decided, among other things to pay off the debt on the Band account and restore the Mess Plate and pictures which were badly in need of repair. This money was to be borrowed from the Sporting Fund for the purpose. All officers not already subscribing were asked to subscribe £1 per month to this Fund.	
	18th.		All ranks were recalled from leave and further leave cancelled for the present.	
	19th.		2/Lieut. O'Callaghan joined from the N.Somerset Yeomanry and was posted to "C" Squadron.	
	24th.		Divisional Boxing Tournament took place. 3 competitors from the Regiment McCann, Porter, and Bartlett, but none of them reached the finals.	
	29th.		Major G.P.L.Cosens became D.A.A.& Q.M.G., 3rd.Cavalry Division, and was consequently struck off the effective strength. Leave recommenced.	
General 1-30.			A considerable amount of time was devoted to the individual training of man and horse in the sword. Field training was largely devoted to the instruction of Protective Detachments. All Hotchkiss Rifles were fired on the range. All men were trained in use of the Bayonet on the latest lines. Wiring Drill by day and night was also practised. Signallers, who had done little Field work previously, did schemes twice weekly.	

Forster Littlefield
Capt. & Adjt.,
The Royal Dragoons.

May 8th., 1916.

Original

Appendix I.
Vol.XIX.

WAR DIARY * THE ROYAL DRAGOONS
++++++++++++++++++

April, 1916.

Reinforcements.

Details.	Remarks.
2/Lt.J.F.Wingfield Digby	Ex R.F.C. 7/4/16
1 Other rank	" Base 17/4/16
2/Lieut.C.T.O'Callaghan	" N.S.Yeomanry 18/4/16
5 other ranks, 24 riding, & 7 chargers	" Base 28/4/16
5 other ranks	" Base 30/4/16.

F.W. ten Hundy
Capt.& Adjt.,
The Royal Dragoons.

8th.May, 1916.

Appendix I   Part I

WAR DIARY
or
INTELLIGENCE SUMMARY

Army Form C. 2118

The Royal Dragoons
Volume XX May 1916

Place	Date	Hour	Summary of Events and Information	Remarks and references to Appendices
Inks Hotel May	6th		Regimental assault at arms.	
"	8th		Officers Staff Ride.	
"	9th		Squadron Leaders proceed to Division School at TRAMECOURT on a 2 days course.	
"	11th		Second-in-command of Squadrons proceed to Division School on a 2 days course.	
"	14th		Division Training School begin to up. In consequence Major Hardwick and Lieutenants Muir & Brown return to the Regiment	
"	15th		The whole of the 3rd Cav Division proceed to the area of St. RIQUIER for training. Marched at 6am. reached billets at MAISON ROLLAND and COULONVILLERS about 3pm. H.Qrs. and 'B' Sqdn at the former; 'C' Sqdn and 'D' Sqdn at the latter. Distance 32 miles.	
"	16		The training ground was about 4 miles square and was allotted in divisions to Regiments for 4 hours at a time. Practice took place in reconnoitring and seizing a hill feature as a tactical objection.	
"	17th		Same as Yesterday with the addition of practice of crossing lines of trenches at previous crossings in half sections and then rapidly into line of troop columns.	
"	18th		Regimental work. Practice in mounted attack on Infantry.	
"	20th		Divisional day under General Vaughan.	

Appendix I

Sheet II

WAR DIARY
or
INTELLIGENCE SUMMARY
(Erase heading not required.)

Army Form C. 2118

1st Royal Dragoons
Volume XX
May 1916.

Instructions regarding War Diaries and Intelligence Summaries are contained in F. S. Regs., Part II. and the Staff Manual respectively. Title Pages will be prepared in manuscript.

Place	Date	Hour	Summary of Events and Information	Remarks and references to Appendices
In the Field	21		Returned under Regimental arrangements to billets at CREQUY via HESDIN FRESSIN. Started 4-15 am arrived 12 noon — distance 32 miles.	
	22		Horse inspection. For almost the first time during the war a number of sore backs were found.	
	26		Stokes gun demonstration at HESDIN by light French Mortar School. Moral effect would be very great but damage to trenches and wire negligible.	
	27		Moved billets to FRESSIN — with Headquarters at house of M. BERNANOS. The whole regiment in one village.	
	29		Major P.K. Hardwick appointed to Command 10th Hussars (temp) vice Colonel Wickham to K.D. Gds.	

J.H.H. Tufnell
Capt & Adjt

1875 Wt. W593/826 1,000,000 4/15 J.B.C. & A. A.D.S.S./Forms/C. 2118.

Sheet III

WAR DIARY
or
INTELLIGENCE SUMMARY

Army Form C. 2118

1st Royal Dragoons.
Volume XX May 916.

Place	Date	Hour	Summary of Events and Information	Remarks and references to Appendices
In the field	30th		Appendix II Honours & Rewards. Attached L./Sh. Lawrence awarded "Medaille Militaire". London Gazette Supplement d/ 30/3/16.	
"	9th		Appendix III Reinforcements. 11 other ranks joined from Base and taken on strength of Regiment 9-5-16.	
"	20th		1 other rank " " " " " " 20-5-16.	
"	31st		4 other ranks " " " " " " 31-5-16.	

John Robert Attwood
Captain & Adjt.,
The Royal Dragoons.

WAR DIARY
1st The Royal Dragoons

Army Form C. 2118

(1 Cav Bde XI Corps June 1916)

Place	Date	Hour	Summary of Events and Information	Remarks and references to Appendices
	11th		Major Ph. Hardwick proceeded to ABERLIMONT to take over command of Brit. troops	
			Arrived at 6pm. The Regiment proceeded to train to take over temporary Paris Platform 3.9 Dragon Gds.	
			Regiment arrived at FRESSIN at 11.30am and marched to Camp, the training about two miles. On 3rd Sqn Gds Huss. left their camp being too small.	
	12th		Lieut. S.R. Littow joined from England. Regimental Distribution.	
	13th		Regimental Rest. Divisional Staff not near ESTREE.	
	14th		Regimental Rest.	
	9.10		Returned to FRESSIN to rendezvous against 9th Dragoon G. Exhibition & drowned new Bit Khaki in camp. Reached FRESSIN 1pm – a set march.	
	12.15		At 5pm orders were received cancelling rendezvous march Evening 9th Div. Daylight saving. B.W. came into force in FRANCE at same time as in ENGLAND. Arrived Khakimas.	
	15th		Inspection of horses proposed for easting by G.O.C and D.A.A.R. – 11 Passed Regiment marched fresh Camp near PARIS PAGE when the picked about 12pm 1 Cav. Bde - close in Jackson.	

Army Form C. 2118

WAR DIARY
or
INTELLIGENCE SUMMARY
(Erase heading not required.)

1st Royal Dragoons

Volume XXI June 1916

Appendix I

Instructions regarding War Diaries and Intelligence Summaries are contained in F. S. Regs., Part II. and the Staff Manual respectively. Title Pages will be prepared in manuscript.

Place	Date	Hour	Summary of Events and Information	Remarks and references to Appendices
	1916		Regimental Drill	
	18		Regimental Drill in squads. A.O.C. Division present	
	19		Regiment on Parade	
			Appendix I Training Grade	
			Just received 13 Normans & 50 Royal Dragoons transferred on Reserves (No Officer lost this month)	

F W Fitzwilliam

WAR DIARY or INTELLIGENCE SUMMARY

Army Form C. 2118

(Erase heading not required.)

Instructions regarding War Diaries and Intelligence Summaries are contained in F.S. Regs., Part II. and the Staff Manual respectively. Title Pages will be prepared in manuscript.

Place	Date	Hour	Summary of Events and Information	Remarks and references to Appendices
	22nd		Regiment came up to FRESSIN at 12.45 pm arrived at 3.15 pm. The whole of 19th Division Camp held to stand and laid in bivouac in the Rural roads. Billets and Bivouac at Rally area 1st Divnd for the purpose 2 Divns were also placed at our disposal to assist. Lieut Brown was ordered to report to 10th Reserve Army HQ. General reconnaissance was made previous to TRAMECOURT at 8am.	
	23rd		Marched 15km as a Brigade to RUIPAS and BRAMONT at about 2.30 pm arrived 4.30 pm in RUIPAS. Billets at RALLY area 10th. Bivouac placed 1st Divnd (to be advanced upon a few hours) billets - one at Forkes area marching out stage — beginning to go out mark 8. 12.3 divns.	
	24th		Brigade to SUPPLY 19 Regiments — 1 Corps. 3 hour fall in bivouac at PRINSIN. Spent the day in the field at BROXLEY and work in field. Notes made to move in new alarm. 6th Guards tried to get further. Evening PERNOIS went 2 km, arrived the next day. Battery marry out at 4 am	
	25th		Regiments of officers and 2nd Lt had arrived by train. Regiment arrived at 9pm. Lost men, 1 mg. by Russians but 1 mg. by Germans. Had the 2nd march ALBERT & BOUZINCY & PUZEELES and QUINCUX & — at 12pm to BOUZINCY. By reviewed day. Regiment marched at 9pm. Lost men came on temporary bivouac but went sleep. Now woke. Regiment moved into bivouac before daybreak.	
	26th		Received orders to proceed at 7.30 am — Brigade was advance on temporary bivouac but kept filing Moving with River line having been entrained in Bois du FRENOY at ALBERT.	
	29th		Received orders at 7.30 am to march to ALBERT from Bois du FRENOY. Marched with 4 Brigade from ALBERT & left ground behind Germans line, had billets arrived for us to go in.	
	30th		Remained in bivouac again. Lost two battn known as Refuges, the bivouac chosen by Major K 17th Bgtn (Ben Bridge). There has been few shell fire and some stragglers arriving from advance and were returned to unit.	

Th. Fogherty Capt & Adjt
The Royal Dragoons

Duplicate

Instructions regarding War Diaries and Intelligence Summaries are contained in F. S. Regs., Part II. and the Staff Manual respectively. Title Pages will be prepared in manuscript.

Sheet III

WAR DIARY
or
~~INTELLIGENCE SUMMARY~~
(Erase heading not required.)

The Royal Dragoons

Army Form C. 2118

Appendix III Honours & Awards. Volume XXI June 1916

Place	Date	Hour	Summary of Events and Information	Remarks and references to Appendices
[illegible]	June 1916 3rd		Extract from London Gazette 3-6-16. — Lt G.J. Pa[illegible] awarded Military Cross for good work in January.	
			752 Pte R. [illegible] awarded Distinguished Conduct Medal.	
			1760 Lcpl J. Elliot awarded Military Medal.	
			911 L/Cpl R. Grizzell awarded Military Medal	
			Appendix III Reinforcements	
	7th		2/Lt D.P. Lithgow } joined from Base and taken on strength of Regiment [illegible] 2 Other ranks }	
	20th		9 O.Ranks joined from Base and taken on strength of Regiment [illegible]	
	27th		2/Lt O. [illegible] } " " " " [illegible] 1 other Rank }	

F.W. [illegible]

Captain & Adjt.
The Royal Dragoons

1875 Wt. W593/826 1,000,000 4/15 J.B.C. & A. A.D.S.S./Forms/C. 2118.

Original • SECRET

WARDIARY or INTELLIGENCE SUMMARY

Army Form C. 2118

Volume XIII.

(Erase heading not required.)

Sheet 1.

Place	Date	Hour	Summary of Events and Information	Remarks and references to Appendices
Bonnay.	July 1916 1st		The Allied offensive between the Ancre and the Somme commenced at 7.30am. The Division consequently "stood to" in its bivouac at ½ an hours notice. In the afternoon this became 2 hours and later 4 Hours. The offensive started well but the left was held up at BEAUMONT, THIEPVAL and OVILLERS.	
	2nd		"A" Sqdn. rejoined the Regiment during the evening as their services were no longer required. Remained standing to at 4 hours notice. OVILLERS and LA BOISSELLE frequently changed hands. Line from MONTAUBAN to CURLU consolidated.	
	3rd		Still "standing to". OVILLERS taken but lost again from enfilade Machine Gun fire. FRICOURT taken with little opposition. Received orders that Regiment was to be ready to move West to-morrow at 5am. Lieut. Henderson returned from liaison work with 21st.Division.	
	4th		Marched out of bivouac at 5am. Dismounted Party marched to MERRICOURT and thence by train to LONGPRE and route march to ALLERY. 2/Lieut.Cubitt joined this party on return from leave. Regiment marched via AMIENS, PICQUIGNY, SOUES, AIRAINES to ALLERY where horses were bivouacked and men billetted. March about 32 miles, 12 hours on the road, watered and fed at AILLY-SUR-SOMME. Passed 8th.Division who had suffered heavily at OVILLERS and had just come back to SOUES.	
Allery	5.6.6(?) 7th. 8th		Remained at ALLERY - general wash and clean up. The billets were good - most of the population weavers of sacks. Water Moderate. Brigade Headquarters were at MERELI ESSART. Division at HEILENCOURT. Left ALLERY at 1.30pm. Watered at SOUES. Long halt at PICQUIGNY, via AMIENS, CAMONT?, DAOURS to CORBIE where the whole Division was concentrated for the night in one swampy field. Our brigade arrived at 2.15am. after a very tedious march, distance about 30 miles. 2/Lieut.Cubitt was evacuated from ALLERY.	
	9th		Dismounted Party arrived by road from HEILLY losing two men on the way. Brigade moved to VAUX in the afternoon about 2½ miles, a much pleasanter bivouac.	

Army Form C. 2118

Original · SECRET

WAR DIARY
or
INTELLIGENCE SUMMARY

(Erase heading not required.)

Sheet 2. Volume XXIII.

Instructions regarding War Diaries and Intelligence Summaries are contained in F. S. Regs., Part II. and the Staff Manual respectively. Title Pages will be prepared in manuscript.

Place	Date	Hour	Summary of Events and Information	Remarks and references to Appendices
VAUX-SUR-SOMME	10th		VAUX-SUR-SOMME. About 30 tents had been allotted to the Regiment, and men and horses were very comfortable. Good shade, excellent bathing and good grazing for horses.	
VAUX.	11th		Dismounted party arrived by 'bus from CORBIE. S.S.M.Elmes having received a commission was attached to 6th.Machine Gun Squadron for duty. (S.Q.M.S.) Smallwood became acting S.S.M. (B. Sqdn.) and Sergt.Rogers acting S.Q.M.S. (B.Sqdn.)	
	14th		The XV and XIII Corps in co-operation with French attacked German 2nd.Line at 3.25am The Regiment "stood to " at 2 am hours notice. XIII Corps reported to have captured LONGUEVILLE and DELVILLE Wood and villages of BAZENTIN-le-PETIT and BAZENTIN-le-Grand. One Brigade Indian Cavalry advanced mounted and occupied a portion of HIGH Wood. One Squadron 7th.D.Gds. and some DECCAN Horse charged some Germans S. of HIGH Wood with/success.	
	15th		Notice extended to 4 hours.	
	17th		Major G.D.A.Edwards attached 13th.Welsh reported missing from 9th.instant. 2/Lieut.	
	18th		Newcombe attached as Adjutant 8th.South Lancs, reported killed in action.	
	19th		2/Lieut.S.G.Goddard who received a commission in the Sussex Regiment was reported killed in action. 2/Lieut.D.H.Watson and 56 other ranks attached to 7th.Division for Salvage duty work were relieved by a similar party under 2/Lieut.D.P.Lithgow. This party were working near MAMETZ.	
	20th		2pm. Brigade moved to LA NEUVILLE, a suburb of CORBIE.	
LA NEUVILLE			Regiment was bivouacked near BONNAY road. Good dry standing for horses, but roads were continually blocked with troops and transport. Men were all under cover in a large empty farm, and there was a large Y.M.C.A. tent which provided the men with refreshments.	
	23rd		Lieut.W.P.Browne proceeded to BECORDEL as Adjutant to 3rd.Cavalry Division Dismounted party vice Lieut.Herbert, R.H.G.	
	24th		State of readiness at 4 hours cancelled.	
	25th		The 3rd.Cavalry Division sent up a dismounted party to work under 3rd.Corps for digging trenches and wiring between MAMETZ Wood and CONTALMAISON.Lt.-Colonel F.W.Wormald,D.S.O. was in charge of this party. The Regiment found 2 Officers and 85 other ranks.* They were bivouacked near BECOURT. *Subsequently reinforced by 2 officers and 95 o.R	
	27th		2/Lieut.D.F.Lithgow and 53 other ranks rejoined from 7th Division, also Lieut.W.P. Browne.	
	28th		Lance-Corporal Morgan (C.Squadron) gazetted 2/Lieut. 12th.Battn.Middlesex Regt.???? (8/6/16)	

Original
SECRET

WAR DIARY
or
INTELLIGENCE SUMMARY
(Erase heading not required.)

Army Form C. 2118

Sheet 3. Volume XXII

Instructions regarding War Diaries and Intelligence Summaries are contained in F.S. Regs., Part II. and the Staff Manual respectively. Title Pages will be prepared in manuscript.

Place	Date	Hour	Summary of Events and Information	Remarks and references to Appendices
LANEUVILLE	1916. July. 31st		The working party under Lieut.-Colonel F.W.Wormald, D.S.O. rejoined from BECOURT to-day. Orders received that the Division would move West to-morrow.	
VAUX.	15th (Cont)		S.Q.M.S.Rankin R.G. having arrived from the Base became S.S.M. "B" Sqdn. This Non-Commissioned Officer had been to EGYPT and the DARDANELLES as R.S.M. to FIFE and FORFAR Yeomanry.	

John Fitzgerald
Captain & Adjt.,
The Royal Dragoons.

APPENDIX I

Army Form C. 2118

Original
SECRET

WAR DIARY
or
INTELLIGENCE SUMMARY
(Erase heading not required.)

Instructions regarding War Diaries and Intelligence Summaries are contained in F.S. Regs., Part II. and the Staff Manual respectively. Title Pages will be prepared in manuscript.

Place	Date 1916 July	Hour	Summary of Events and Information	Remarks and references to Appendices
			Sheet 1. Volume XXII.	
			Reinforcements	
	2nd		3 Other Ranks arrived from Base as re-inforcements	
	9th		4 " " " " " " " "	
	14th		4 " " " " " " " "	
	15th		4426 S.S.M.Rapkin " " " " " "	
	14th		3 Other Ranks arrived " " " " "	
	24th		3 " " " " " " " "	
	28th		2 " " " " " " " "	
BONNAY	30th		8377 Pte.W.Noble rejoined from Prison 30/7/16. as re-inforcement.	
			Casualties	
	1st		6892 Pte.Gertree (C) Wounded, accidentally, (Self-inflicted)	
	9th		" " Reported Died from Wounds, thigh, left, amputated, (Hospital)	
	10th		8617 " Jackson A.W. (B) Wounded accidentally, (attached XV Corps.)	
			6275 " Kemp A. (B) " " (working party)	
30-10-14	26th		843 " Henderson W.F. (previously reported missing) officially reported Killed.	
			5805 " German A. (A) Wounded.	
			6724 " Thorne A.M. (B) "	
	3rd		5525 " Wilson J.C. (B) "	
	30		9235 " McGerthy W. (C) "	
			4415 " Ward F. (A) "	

F.H.Attfield
Captain & Adjt.,
The Royal Dragoons.

Aug 1916

ORIGINAL

VOLUME XIII.

1 Royal Dragoons No 3 2 3

WAR DIARY
or
INTELLIGENCE-SUMMARY
(Erase heading not required.)

Army Form C. 2118

Instructions regarding War Diaries and Intelligence Summaries are contained in F.S. Regs., Part II. and the Staff Manual respectively. Title Pages will be prepared in manuscript.

Place	Date	Hour	Summary of Events and Information	Remarks and references to Appendices
BRESLE	1st		The Brigade marched out from LA NEUVILLE at 6.am. Watered near ARGOEUVES on the SOMME CANAL. Reached LAMESCH bivouac near LAMESCH at 2.30.pm. - about 18 miles. F.Q.M.S. YOUNG who sprained his ankle badly last night had to be evacuated.	
NEUF MOULIN	2nd		Left LAMESCH about 4.30.am. a very slow march to NEUF MOULIN which we reached at 1.45.pm. - 18 miles. Halted at PONT REMY for 2 hours and watered in the SOMME. At NEUF MOULIN we bivouacked near the SCARTON brook. - Ground very dirty. Dismounted Squadron rejoined from CORBIE.	
MONTENAY	3rd		Spend the day in bivouac and commenced preparations for a month's stay.	
MAINTENAY	4th		Left bivouac at 4.15am. arriving MAINTENAY at 11.am. where we had a most comfortable bivouac by the AUTHIE river. - Distance about 19 miles.	
FRESSIN	5th		Returned to permanent billets - about 19 miles, arriving about 10.30.am.	
	6th		Sergt.Waghorn and Corpl.Griffin who had been at the Cadet School received commissions in Royal Fusiliers and Middlesex Regt. respectively.	
	8th		2/Lieut.D.H.Watson and 3 snipers were lent to the 21st.Division.	
	9th		Brigade Headquarters moved from ROUEN to AMBNY.	
	11th		The names of 8 N.C.Os. were submitted for transfer to Infantry and to receive as step in promotion. Owing to 3rd.Field Squadron sending a detachment up to the trenches, 14 other ranks of the Regiment were out of good their horses. A new interpreter, Paul ABB joined the Regiment in succession to GARDEN who proceeded to the 5th Dragoon Guards "Aonti or Aieison"	
	13th		2/Lieut.J.H.Melrs and 69 other ranks proceeded to 2nd Corps. for work in laying cables and improving roads in trench areas. Locality - OVILLERS.	
	14th		2/Lieut.B.Parsons together a 2/Montgom, acted as Billeting Officer with 21st.Div.	

Army Form C. 2118

WAR DIARY
or
INTELLIGENCE SUMMARY

(Erase heading not required.)

Vol. XXIII.

Instructions regarding War Diaries and Intelligence Summaries are contained in F. S. Regs., Part II. and the Staff Manual respectively. Title Pages will be prepared in manuscript.

Place	Date	Hour	Summary of Events and Information	Remarks and references to Appendices
FRESSIN	1/6		Lieut. O. Birkbeck was appointed Regimental Transport Officer.	
	23"		Orders were received that the Brigade might expect to leave its present billets on 25th. This order was, however, soon cancelled. TRAINING. After the return of the Regiment from CORBIE area, a few days were devoted to inspection of equipment and general cleaning up. Training was then devoted to - (a) Musketry, especially Rapid Fire. (b) Hotchkiss detachments and instruction of every N.C.O. and man in the firing of the Automatic rifles. (c) Individual training of the horse and man. (d) Swordsmanship. (e) Bombers. (f) Signallers. Towards the end of the month a great number of crops had been cut and there was an opportunity of working across country.	

F. B. MontAffleck
Capt. Adjt.
1st Royal Dragoons

8.V.16

Army Form C. 2118

Original

SECRET

Instructions regarding War Diaries and Intelligence Summaries are contained in F.S. Regs., Part II. and the Staff Manual respectively. Title Pages will be prepared in manuscript.

WAR DIARY or INTELLIGENCE SUMMARY

(Erase heading not required.)

THE ROYAL DRAGOONS. VOLUME XXIV.

SEPTEMBER 1916.

(Sheet 1.)

Vol 24

Place	Date	Hour	Summary of Events and Information	Remarks and references to Appendices
FRESSIN	1st		The Working Party attached to II.Corps. returned to billets under Lieut.R.E.HELME. Their total casualties were seven all from shrapnel. This Party was chiefly employed in digging communication trenches and burying cable.	
"	5th		3 snipers were sent to relieve those already with 21st.Division.	
"	6th		2/Lieut.S.J.PARR was evacuated to ENGLAND sick.	
"	7th		Yorkshire Dragoons attached return to XIII.Corps. 2/Lieut.P.R.DAVIES-COOKE transferred from "B" to "C" Sqdn. Lieut.W.P.BROWNE and snipers returned from the ARRAS front. The total Germans accounts for by the Bde.party were 17 certain and 10 others which could not be verified.	
DOMINOIS	8th		Division was ordered to be ready to move.	
"	10th	9.a.m.	left FRESSIN 9.a.m., marched to DOMINOIS on river AUTHIE - about 15 miles. Good billets by the river. Fairly good bivouac.	
DRUCAT	11th		left DOMINOIS 2pm. Marched to DRUCAT - about 15 miles. Dismounted Party by road to BEAURAINVILLE.	
LA CHAUSSEE	12th		2/Lieut.J.R.WINGFIELD-DIGBY went sick with internal complaint. Marched to LA CHAUSSEE via VAUCHELLE and FLIXECOURT - about 21 miles.	
"	13th		Remained at LA CHAUSSEE. Lieut.H.M.P.HEWETT and Capt.Hon.C.A.J.ANNESLEY were detailed to remain with dismounted Party after reaching concentration area.	
BUSSY-LES-DAOURS	14th		Moved to bivouac just North of BUSSY-LES-DAOURS - about 15 miles, where the Division was concentrated.	
W. of BONNAY	15th		Moved to position of readiness just W. of BONNAY at ½ an hour's notice. The whole of the Cavalry Corps were so placed as to be ready to exploit any success which might be achieved by the 4th.Army in their attack on FLERS, LES-BOEUFS and MORVAL. Reports showed that FLERS, MARTINPUICH and COURCELETTE were captured but the attack on the right was held up by the QUADRILATERAL near LEUZE Wood. The "Tanks" were used in this attack for the first time, and proved of great value. No opportunity for use of Cavalry having occurred, we moved back to bivouac near PONT-NOYELLES.	
PONT NOYELLES	17th		2/Lieut.J.F.HOUSTOUN-BOSWALL joined the Regiment from ROUEN and was posted to "B" Sqdn., to fill vacancy created by 2/Lieut.W.R.BIRCH having been invalided home.	
"	18th		19 men from the Dismounted Party rejoined from duty with 2nd. Field Sqdn. who were making a road to FLERS. Lieut.H.M.P.HEWETT proceeded to G.H.Q. in connection with a Court of Inquiry on damages caused by Trench Mortar School. Lance-Corpl.MARGRETT "C" Sqdn. and Lance-Corpl.MC.KENZIE "B" Sqdn. were despatched to 21st.Division with a view to Transfer.	

1875 Wt. W593/826 1,000,000 4/15 J.B.C. & A. A.D.S.S./Forms/C. 2118.

Army Form C. 2118

WAR DIARY
or
INTELLIGENCE SUMMARY (Sheet 2.) VOLUME XXIV.
(Erase heading not required.)

THE ROYAL DRAGOONS.
SEPTEMBER 1916.

Instructions regarding War Diaries and Intelligence Summaries are contained in F.S. Regs., Part II. and the Staff Manual respectively. Title Pages will be prepared in manuscript.

Place	Date	Hour	Summary of Events and Information	Remarks and references to Appendices
PONT-NOYELLES	19th		Four Sergeants and four Corporals, supernumery to establishment arrived from Base for duty with Dismounted Squadron.	
" "	20th		7 other ranks rejoined from Dismounted Squadron. The weather from 17th. to 20th. was very wet.	
LE-MESGE	21st		Left camp about 12 noon and marched via AMIENS to LE-MESGE - about 23 miles. Spent the night in the same bivouac as we had used when last in that neighbourhood.	
BEAUVOIR RIVIERE	22nd		Moved about 8. am. and marched to BEAUVOIR RIVIERE near AUCHI-LE-CHATEAU - about 20 miles.	
RAYE	23rd		Marched at 6. am. to HAVE-EN-AUTHIE and went into billets. Horses on stubble fields. Accommodation for men arranged but majority slept out. 2/Lieut. D.H. WATSON and 36 other ranks rejoined from Dismounted Party where they had been working under 2nd. Field Squadron.	
RAYE	25th			
ST. JOSSE.	26th		Marched at 11. am. to new billeting area - about 19 miles. Headquarters and "B" Squadron at ST.JOSSE, "C" Squadron at LE-MOULINEL and LE-LOT, "A" Squadron at ST-AUBIN	

In the Field,
Oct. 8th. 1916.

[signature]
Capt. & Adjt.,
The Royal Dragoons.

SECRET
ORIGINAL

Army Form C. 2118

Instructions regarding War Diaries and Intelligence Summaries are contained in F. S. Regs., Part II. and the Staff Manual respectively. Title Pages will be prepared in manuscript.

WAR DIARY
or
INTELLIGENCE SUMMARY
(Erase heading not required.)

THE ROYAL DRAGOONS.
VOLUME XXIV
SEPTEMBER 1916.

APPENDIX I. - CASUALTIES DURING MONTH.

3348 Pte. HORNE W. (A) Died of Wounds 1/9/16 (Previously reported wounded. 31/8/16)
6685 " PUNTON J. (A)   "   "   20/9/16.   "   "   "   "

APPENDIX II. - HONOURS AND REWARDS.

APPENDIX III. - REINFORCEMENTS RECEIVED DURING MONTH.

1 other rank from Base 1/9/16.
4 Sergts. taken on as supernumery to establishment - from Base 19/9/16.
4 Corpls.   "   "   "   "   "   "   "   "   19/9/16.
8 other ranks joined Dismounted Sqdn. - direct from Base 16/9/16.
1   "   "   "   Joined Regt. from Base 21/9/16.
3   "   "   "   "   "   "   " 26/9/16.

In the Field,
October 8th. 1916.

Capt. & Adjt.,
The Royal Dragoons.

ORIGINAL

Army Form C. 2118

WAR DIARY
VOLUME XXIII.
or
INTELLIGENCE SUMMARY

APPENDIX I* (CASUALTIES) *(Erase heading not required.)*

Place	Date	Hour	Summary of Events and Information	Remarks and references to Appendices
OVILLERS	31.8.16		8639 Pte. Barbour G. "A" Sqdn. Wounded 31/8/16.	
			3482 " Breeze J. " " "	
			8908 " Ferguson A.T. " " "	
			3348 " Horne W. " " "	
			6685 " Punton J. " " "	
			6889 " Sanders A. " " "	
			8309 " Bull E. "B" " "	

F.H. Newton Thwaite
Capt & Adjt
The Royal Dragoons

8.IX.16.

Army Form C. 2118

ORIGINAL

WAR DIARY
VOLUME XIII.
or
INTELLIGENCE SUMMARY
(Erase heading not required.)

(APPENDIX III.)

Instructions regarding War Diaries and Intelligence Summaries are contained in F. S. Regs., Part II. and the Staff Manual respectively. Title Pages will be prepared in manuscript.

Place	Date	Hour	Summary of Events and Information	Remarks and references to Appendices
	7-8-16		6 Other ranks joined from Base 7/8/16.	
	13-8-16		8 " " " " " 13/8/16.	
	22-8-16		7 " " " " " 22/8/16.	
	26-8-16		8 " " " " " 26/8/16.	

F. W. Wentworth
Capt. & Adjt.
1st Royal Dragoons.

8-9-16

Army Form C. 2118

THE ROYAL DRAGOONS. WAR DIARY
VOLUME XXV.
October 1916.

(Sheet 1.) (Erase heading not required.)

Place	Date	Hour	Summary of Events and Information	Remarks and references to Appendices
	2nd.		A working party of 26 other ranks under Lieut.O.BIRKBECK proceeded to Reserve Army area for work under II.Corps.	
	7th.		2/Lieut.P.WAGHORN, Royal Fusiliers, late Orderly Room Clerk to the Regiment was reported killed in action on the SOMME.	
	3rd.		L/Cpl.KIRKBY K.T. proceeded to ENGLAND with a view to attending at Cadet School for Artillery.	
	8th.		2/Lieut.D'A.F.H.HARRIS was invalided to ENGLAND with a dislocated shoulder.	
	13th.		Capt.Hon.C.A.J.ANNESLEY rejoined the Regiment from Machine Gun School at CAMIERS where he had been undergoing a course of instruction.	
	14th.		Corpl.(L/Sergt) GROOM C. was transferred to Durham Light Infantry a/Company Sergt-Major from 4/7/16. Lieut.G.R.PITT-RIVERS was seconded as A.D.C. from 1/9/16. 2/Lieut.F.B.RATCLIFFE appointed temp.Lieutenant from 20/9/16.	
	19.		Owing to the inclemency of the weather and in consequence of the fact that the Division was not likely to be required for mounted work in the Battle of the Somme, arrangements were now made to get all horses and men under cover.	
	20.		Lieut.C.W.G.SWIRE, 2/Lieut.R.F.HEYWORTH-SAVAGE and 70 other ranks proceeded to Reserve Army area on relief. The former party under Lieut.O.BIRKBECK returning the next day. This party had been employed in road making, unloading shells, salvage operations and digging cable trenches. Their work took place chiefly in the neighbourhood of THIEPVAL and MOUQUET FARM. In the former place all dugouts were thoroughly searched and large quantities of enemy stores discovered. Lieut.BIRCKBECK, however stated that he could find no traces of the Machine Gun hoists which the enemy were said to have used in this neighbourhood. We were lucky enough to have only one man wounded in this party.	
	22nd.		Capt.Hon J.L.R.SCLATER-BOOTH rejoined from ENGLAND where he had been resting since the Summer of 1915.	
	31st.		Major H.A.TOMKINSON was appointed Commandant of a Divisional Training School which was to open in November at MERLIMONT PLAGE. Capt.Hon.C.A.J.ANNESLEY was appointed Adjutant of this School.	
TRAINING.			During the early part of the month a considerable amount of Cavalry work was done across country till the crops prevented it. After October 18th, our energies were chiefly devoted to improvement of existing stabling and billets. The weather throughout the month was uncertain and towards the end vile.	

Army Form C. 2118

SECRET

WAR DIARY or INTELLIGENCE SUMMARY. DUPLICATE

(Erase heading not required.)

THE ROYAL DRAGOONS.
VOLUME XXV.
October 1916.

(Sheet 2.)

Place	Date	Hour	Summary of Events and Information	Remarks and references to Appendices
			APPENDIX I (Casualties)	
	25/9/16		No.10007 L/Cpl.McKenzie D.A. (Attached 10th.K.O.Y.L.I.) - Killed - previously reported "Missing". 25/9/16.	
	15/10/16		No.9080 Pte.Timson A. Wounded 15/10/16.	
	7/10/16		2/Lieut.P.W.Waghorn, Killed 7/10/16.	
			————————	
			APPENDIX II. (Honours and Rewards.)	
			————————	
			APPENDIX III. (Reinforcements Received)	
	8/10/16.		6 other ranks from Base.	
	9/10/16.		2 " " " "	
	22/10/16.		Capt.Hon.J.L.R.Sclater-Booth from Base.	
			2 other ranks from Base.	
	31/10/16.		9 " " " "	
			————————	

J.Tippetts
Captain & Adjt.
The Royal Dragoons.

Army Form C. 2118

WAR DIARY or INTELLIGENCE SUMMARY

(Erase heading not required.)

THE ROYAL DRAGOONS.

NOVEMBER 1916.   VOLUME XXVI.   (SHEET I)

Instructions regarding War Diaries and Intelligence Summaries are contained in F.S. Regs., Part II. and the Staff Manual respectively. Title Pages will be prepared in manuscript.

ORIGINAL

Place	Date	Hour	Summary of Events and Information	Remarks and references to Appendices
	6th		Sergts. HEWITT, KELSEY, PHILPOT, and CHICK went to G.H.Q. Cadet School.	
	7th		Divisional Training School opened with a Course for all Squadron Leaders.	
	11th		Lieut. C.W.G. SWIRE, 2/Lieut. R.F. HEYWORTH-SAVAGE and Working Party rejoined from Reserve Army. Sergt. HEWITT returned from Cadet School.	
	12th		S.S.M. H. NEWTON goes for a 5 days Course to Divisional Anti-Gas School, where he qualifies as Troop Gas N.C.O.	
	19th		Squadron Leaders return from School. Football Match - the Officers V "A" Squadron, 1-3.	
	20th		Lieuts. SWIRE, HENDERSON, and CUBITT proceeded to Divisional School for 4 months Course.	
	26th		Major H.A. TOMKINSON to be Temp-Lieut-Colonel whilst Commandant of Divisional Training School.	
	29th		Lieut-Colonel F.W. WORMALD, D.S.O., proceeded to YORK for 2½ months to assist in Training Reserve Regiment. Captain F.W. WILSON FITZGERALD went to take over Command of Corps School, XIII Corps, with rank of Major whilst so employed. Captain T.S. IRWIN assumes command of Regiment in the Colonel's absence. Lieut. W.P. BROWNE become a/Adjutant.	

Lieut & Adjt.
The Royal Dragoons

Army Form C. 2118

ORIGINAL

THE ROYAL DRAGOONS. WAR DIARY or INTELLIGENCE SUMMARY. VOLUME XXVI (SHEET II)

NOVEMBER 1916.

(Erase heading not required.)

SUMMARY OF THE MONTH'S WORK.

Surprisingly little rain was experienced and Training, which recommenced after November 5th. suffered few interruptions. Up to November 29th. Squadrons usually had 2 schemes a week over the open country towards WAILLY and BAHOT - the other days being devoted to Training Hotchkiss Detachments, Despatch Riders and Ground Scouts.
During the latter part of the month the "going" was not so good, but we did Troop Drill on the Sands twice a week. We also practised crossing a system of trenches which has been dug E. of the BOIS de VERTON. By November 29th. the Regiment was comfortably settled in to billets for the winter.

APPENDIX I - CASUALTIES DURING MONTH.

- NIL -

APPENDIX II. - HONOURS AND REWARDS.

APPENDIX III. - REINFORCEMENTS.

2 other ranks from Base 11/11/16.
7 "   "   "   "   20/11/16.

Lt. & Adjt.
The Royal Dragoons.

SECRET

DUPLICATE

Army Form C. 2118

WAR DIARY
or
INTELLIGENCE SUMMARY

THE ROYAL DRAGOONS. VOLUME XXVII

(Erase heading not required.)

Instructions regarding War Diaries and Intelligence Summaries are contained in F.S. Regs., Part II. and the Staff Manual respectively. Title Pages will be prepared in manuscript.

Vol 27

Part II. DECEMBER 1916.

Place	Date	Hour	Summary of Events and Information	Remarks and references to Appendices
ST. JOSSE	2nd		2/Lieut. D.P. Lithgow had an accident while drilling on the sands, and ran his sword through his arm, and was invalided to England.	
ST. JOSSE	3rd		Major-General J. Vaughan, C.B., D.S.O., came to Church and inspected the billets.	
ST. JOSSE	15th		The final of the Regimental Inter-Troop Football was played. The 3rd. Troop of "A" Sqdn. - 2/Lieut. Wingfield-Digby's Troop, beat the 4th. Troop of "B" Sqdn. - 2/Lieut. Helme's Troop, by 4 - 0.	
"	"		The Headquarters Interpreter, M. Bonnett left the Regiment for the French Flying Corps.	
VERTON	16.		A Brigade Horse Show was held to decide on the Troop which had the best conditioned horses. The result was:- 1st. 3rd. D.Gds. 2nd.Royals(1st.Troop "B" - 2/Lt.Smith.)	
	17.		2/Lieut. C.B.Scott left the Regiment to serve with the Cavalry Corps Signals.	
	17.		2/Lieut. Hon.G.R.D.Browne joined the Regiment from the Base.	
ST. JOSSE	18.		Sergt. S.T.M. Abel E.O. died suddenly from heart failure whilst cycling.	
	20.		A Pioneer Company left the Regiment to go digging, consisting of 8 Officers and 262 other ranks. Captain Hon.Sclater-Booth, Commanding, and Lieuts. deTrafford, Henderson, Cubitt. 2/Lieuts. Dumbreck, Milton-Green, Houstoun-Boswall, were the Officers.	
	22.		The Regiment marched to a new billeting area - AUBIN-ST. VAAST, BOUIN and PLUMOISON.	
PLUMOISON	27.		2/Lieut. J.S. Dunville joined the Regiment from the Base.	
	27.		Lieuts. Browne, Hewett, Birkbeck and 2/Lieut. O'Callaghan went for a month's course at the Divisional Training School. Major Wilson-Fitzgerald went as an instructor.	
	30.		Lieut. Henderson was recalled from the Pioneer Battalion to take over the duties of Adjutant, and 2/Lieut. Hon.G.R.D. Browne went up to join the Pioneer Battalion in his place.	

Lieut. & a/Adjt.,
The Royal Dragoons.

SECRET DUPLICATE

Army Form C. 2118.

WAR DIARY
or
INTELLIGENCE SUMMARY

THE ROYAL DRAGOONS. VOLUME XXVII.

(Erase heading not required.)

DECEMBER 1916.

Sheet 2.

Place	Date	Hour	Summary of Events and Information	Remarks and references to Appendices
	17.		APPENDIX I. – CASUALTIES DURING MONTH.	
	27.			
	11.		APPENDIX II. – HONOURS AND REWARDS.	
	18.			
	18.		APPENDIX III. – REINFORCEMENTS RECEIVED.	
	22.		2/Lieut. Hon. G.R.D. BROWNE from Base 17/12/16.	
	27.		2/Lieut. J.S. OURVILLE " " 27/12/16.	
			8 other ranks from Base 11/12/16.	
			2 " " released from Prison 18/12/16.	
			2 " " from Base 18/12/16.	
			9 " " " " 22/12/16.	
			1 " " " " 27/12/16.	

[signature] Lieut. & a/Adjt.,
The Royal Dragoons.

Army Form C. 2118.
DUPLICATE

Vol 28

WAR DIARY or INTELLIGENCE SUMMARY

THE ROYAL DRAGOONS VOLUME XXVIII JANUARY 1917.

(Erase heading not required.) (Sheet 1.)

Place	Date	Hour	Summary of Events and Information	Remarks and references to Appendices
PLUMOISON	1.		Lieut. R.H.W.Henderson assumed duties of Adjutant.	
	1.		Capt. T.S.Irwin appointed Temp.Major whilst 2nd.in-Command of Regiment.	
	3.		Lieut. H.B.Helme to Divisional Anti-Gas School.	
	3.		Major T.S.Irwin leave to United Kingdom - Captain C.W.Turner assumes Command of the Regiment.	
	6.		2/Lieut. E.St.G.Stedall joined Regiment from Base.	
	12.		Captain W.T.Miles returned from Leave and assumed Command of the Regiment	
	13.		Captain J.L.R.Sclater-Booth returned from Pioneer Battalion to go on 2 month's Signal Course.	
	13.		Lieut. G.W.G.Swire to England to be attached to R.F.C. as Special Observer.	
	14.		2/Lieut. S.C.Dumbreck and 2/Lieut. Hon G.R.D.Browne returned from Pioneer Batt'n.	
	16.		Major T.S.Irwin returned from Leave and resumed Command of the Regiment.	
	19.		Lt-Colonel F.W.Wormald, D.S.O., rejoined Regiment and resumed Command.	
	22.		Following reliefs carried out with Pioneer Battalion. 2/Lieuts. Wingfield-Digby, Hon.G.R.D.Browne, and W/St.G.Stedall relieves Lieut. H.E.F.deTrafford, J.F. Houstoun-Boswall and 2/Lieut C.C.H.Hilton-Green.	
	23.		Capt. Hon.J.L.R.Sclater-Booth to England to be Signalling Officer to 2/1st. Northumberland Hussars.	
	27.		Lieut.H.M.P.Hewett, Lieut. W.P.Browne, Lieut.O.Birkbeck and 2/Lt.C.T.O'Callaghan rejoined from Divnl. Training School.	
	"		Lieuts. Hewett and Henderson proceeded on leave to U.K.	
	28.		Lieut. W.P.Browne takes over duties of Adjutant.	
	31.		Lieuts. deTrafford, Helme, and 2/Lts. Dunville and Smith to Divnl. Training School.	
	31.		2/Lieut. C.C.H.Hilton-Green rejoined from Pioneer Battalion.	

C. O'Callaghan 2/Lieut. @ a/Adjt.,
The Royal Dragoons.

Army Form C. 2118.
DUPLICATE

SECRET

WAR DIARY
or
INTELLIGENCE SUMMARY

THE ROYAL DRAGOONS VOLUME XXVIII JANUARY 1917.

(Erase heading not required.) (Sheet 2.)

Instructions regarding War Diaries and Intelligence Summaries are contained in F.S. Regs., Part II. and the Staff Manual respectively. Title Pages will be prepared in manuscript.

Place	Date	Hour	Summary of Events and Information	Remarks and references to Appendices

APPENDIX I - CASUALTIES.

— nil —

APPENDIX II - HONOURS AND REWARDS.

Major F.W.Wilson-Fitzgerald awarded The Military Cross. (Lon. Gaz. Sup. 1/1/17.)
Lieut. W.P.Browne,
Lt.& QMr. W.R.Lines
2/Lt. A.W.Wingate,M.C.   } Mentioned in Despatches dated War Office
5327 R.Q.M.S.W.Alliott   } Jany. 2nd. 1917.
Bt.Major G.P.L.Cosens
5454 a/R.Q.M.S. Hobbs A.

6254 L/Sergt. Allsebrook, H.J. } Awarded Meritorious Service Medal.(Lon. Gaz.
5054 Cpl.   Butler, T.H.   } d/- 4/1/17.)
5500 "   Talbot, J.
6650 L/Cpl. Buckham, P.   } Awarded the Military Medal (London
631   "   Kelman, R.   } Gazette, d/- 22/1/17.)
3604 Pte.   Shaw, R.
3405 "   Gallagher, J.H.

APPENDIX III - REINFORCEMENTS RECEIVED.

2/Lieut. E.St.G. STEDALL, from Base 6/1/17.
5649 Sergt. WORKMAN T, from Base 7/1/17.
4762 S.S.M. R.R.JEFFREY S.L. from Base 27/1/17.

Co Cullajan
2/Lieut. & a/Adjt.,
The Royal Dragoons.

Army Form C. 2118.

SECRET

WAR DIARY
or
INTELLIGENCE SUMMARY

(Erase heading not required.)

The Royal Dragoons
February 1917.
VOLUME XXIX

Vol 29

Instructions regarding War Diaries and Intelligence Summaries are contained in F. S. Regs., Part II. and the Staff Manual respectively. Title Pages will be prepared in manuscript.

Place	Date	Hour	Summary of Events and Information	Remarks and references to Appendices
LUCHEUSSE	1		Lieut. F.H.W.HENDERSON proceeded on Leave to U.K. to get married.	
	2		Cavalry Squadron R.F.C. arrives at LAMBUS.	
	3		2/Lieut. D.H.WATSON returned from Divnl.Signalling Course.	
	4		Lieut. W.P.BROWNE proceeded on Leave to U.K. 2/Lieut. C.T.O'CALLAGHAN takes over duties of Adjutant.	
	7		Corpl. Neil,E. to HQtrs. 4th.Army on Intelligence Course. Forage ration dropped from 12lbs. of Oats to 9lbs.	
	8		Lieut. J.F.HOUSTOUN-BOSWALL proceeded to Cavalry Corps Hqtrs. to undergo Course of Intelligence.	
	9		Relief of Signallers at DOULLENS.	
	10		Capt.H.McCOLL-JOHNSTON(A.V.C.) to PARIS for Pastuer Treatment.	
	11		Major T.S.IRWIN to Divnl.Anti-Gas School.	
	13		Lieuts.HEWETT, HENDERSON, and DAVIES-COOKE to Pioneer Battalion to relieve Lieuts. CUBITT, STEDALL and BROWNE.	
	14		Cpl. Powell,E.C.(R.A.M.C.) to England for Commission.	
	15		2/Lieuts.C.C.H.HILTON-GREEN and S.C.DUMBRECK to 12th.Div, VI Corps.for instruction in trenches.	
	16		Lieut. J.F.HOUSTOUN-BOSWALL rejoined from Cav.Corps.	
	17		Inspection of Signallers by O.C.Cav.Corps Signals.	
	18		A War Game for all Officers at HQ Mess. G.O.C.present.	
	19		2/Lieut. R.F.HEYWORTH-SAVAGE to Cav.Corps Hqtrs. for Signal Course. Boxing at Bde.HQ. Ptes. Bartlett, Board, McCarthy qualify for Cav.Corps Tournament at ABBEVILLE.	
	21		Arrival of 500 men of 261st.French Territorial Infy.in Regimental Area for work on the Railway.	
	22		Interpreter M.D.lde VILLIE VILLLIE reported for duty with Regiment. Inspection of Signallers by O.C.1rd.Field Sqdn.	
	24		Inspection of "A" Sqdn. horses by General VAUGHAN.	
	26		Lieut-Colonel F.W.TOTBALD,D.S.O., proceeded to DOULLENS on a visit to Pioneer Battalion.	
	27		Lieuts. C.C.H.HILTON-GREEN and S.C.DUMBRECK returned from trenches.	

C/O O'Callaghan
2/Lieut. & a/Adjt.,
The Royal Dragoons.

Army Form C. 2118.

Duplicate

SECRET

WAR DIARY
or
INTELLIGENCE-SUMMARY

(Erase heading not required.)

The Royal Dragoons

February 1917.

VOLUME XXIX

Sheet II.

Place	Date	Hour	Summary of Events and Information	Remarks and references to Appendices
LUDWSON	27/23		APPENDIX I. – CASUALTIES.	
			APPENDIX II. – REINFORCEMENTS. 2/Lieut. S.J. PARR, M.C. joined from Base 27/2/17. 3 other ranks " " 23/2/17.	
			APPENDIX III. – HONOURS and REWARDS.	

Geo Callaghan
2/Lieut. & a/Adjt.,
The Royal Dragoons.

SECRET   THE ROYAL DRAGOONS.   WAR DIARY   March 1917.   Army Form C. 2118.
Volume XXX.

INTELLIGENCE SUMMARY

(Sheet I) (Erase heading not required.)

Place	Date	Hour	Summary of Events and Information	Remarks and references to Appendices
	2		Lieut-Col.F.W.WORMALD,D.S.O. and Capt. GRANT (R.A.M.C.) to Anti-Gas School	
	3		2/Lieut. J.F.HOUSTOUN-BOSWALL returned from Leave to U.K.	
	4		Lieut.H.E.F.deTRAFFORD, Lieut.R.B.HELME, and 2/Lt.J.S.DUNVILLE rejoined from Divnl. Training School.	
	5		Lieuts.deTRAFFORD, HELME and DUNVILLE proceeded to Pioneer Battalion.	
	7		2/Lieuts.P.R.D.COOKE and J.R.WINGFIELD-DIGBY rejoined from Pioneer Battn. 2/Lieuts.S.C.DUMBRECK, C.O.H.HILTON-GREEN, D.COOKE and J.R.WINGFIELD DIGBY proceeded to Divnl. Training School.	
	10		No.5768 Pte.BARTLETT,A. won Middle-weight Boxing Cavalry Corps Championship.	
	11		Lieut.H.M.P.HEWETT proceeded to Divn.l School as Instructor. 2/Lieut.H.SMITH and 12 other ranks proceeded to 3rd.Field Sqdn.R.E. for 1 weeks Pioneer Class.	
	13		2/Lieuts.D.P.LITHGOW and D.P.WILSON joined Regiment from Base.	
	14		Capt. E.W.T.MILES proceeded to Anti-Gas School.	
	15		4 Officers and 260 other ranks rejoined from Pioneer Battalion.	
	19		2/Lieut. R.F.HEYWORTH-SAVAGE rejoined Regiment from Cav.Corps.Signals.	
	20		2/Lieut. R.F.HEYWORTH-SAVAGE and 2 other ranks 3 days Course with 35th. Squadron R.F.C. L/C.WARREN,G. proceeded to Cadet School BLENDECQUES.	
	21		Lieut. W.P.BROWNE rejoined Regiment from 3rd.Cav.Divn.HQ.	
	22		Capt. F.W.WILSON-FITZGERALD,M.O. rejoined Regiment from 3rd.Cav.Divn.Training School and resumes duties of Adjutant.	
	24		Summer Time adopted.	
	25		A Working Party consisting of 1 officer(2/Lieut.D.H.WATSON) and 41 other ranks proceeded for attachment to 14th.Divn.VII Corps.near ARRAS.	
	26		A further working party consisting of 2/Lieuts.E.St.G.STEDALL and Hon.G.R.D. BROWNE and 35 other ranks proceeded to same place.	
	28		Scheme with Contact Aeroplane.	
	29		Regiment fitted with new Hotchkiss Equipment.	
	30		Inspection of Transport 4.pm.	

Capt. & Adjt.,
The Royal Dragoons.

SECRET — Duplicate

Army Form C. 2118.

Instructions regarding War Diaries and Intelligence Summaries are contained in F. S. Regs., Part II. and the Staff Manual respectively. Title Pages will be prepared in manuscript.

WAR DIARY or INTELLIGENCE SUMMARY

THE ROYAL DRAGOONS.   March 1917.   Volume XXX

(Erase heading not required.)

(Sheet II.)

APPENDIX I. - CASUALTIES DURING MONTH.

APPENDIX II. - HONOURS and REWARDS.

APPENDIX III. - REINFORCEMENTS RECEIVED.

2/Lieut. J.O.CAPE-ELLISON)   From Base 3/3/17.
2 other ranks
2/Lieut. D.P. LITHGOW   "   14/3/17.
   "   P.L. WILSON   "   14/3/17.
4 other ranks   "   18/3/17.
2/Lieut. W.O. STEWART   Joined Regt. 24/3/17.
5 other ranks   From Base 29/3/17.

J Wilson Stewart
Capt. & Adjt.,
The Royal Dragoons.

Place	Date	Hour	Summary of Events and Information	Remarks and references to Appendices

Army Form C. 2118.

DUPLICATE

THE ROYAL DRAGOONS.

WAR DIARY
or
INTELLIGENCE SUMMARY.

APRIL 1917   Volume XXXI

(Sheet I.)

(Erase heading not required.)

Instructions regarding War Diaries and Intelligence Summaries are contained in F. S. Regs., Part II. and the Staff Manual respectively. Title Pages will be prepared in manuscript.

Place	Date	Hour	Summary of Events and Information	Remarks and references to Appendices
PLUMOISON	1st		Brigade Service 11.30.am. Following presented with Military Medals by G.O.C. Division :- Corpl. TALBOT, L/Cpl. DUFF, Pte. KELMAN and Pte. Gallagher, for services rendered in early days of the war.	
"	3rd		Major H.A. TOMKINSON and Capt. Hon. O.A.J. ANNESLEY rejoined from Divisional School.	
"	3rd		Sergts. BLUNDELL, MONKHOUSE and ROGERS to Cadet School in ENGLAND for commission in Artillery.	
	5th		The Brigade concentrated in PLUMOISON area. This necessitated "B" and "C" Sqdns. moving to MAROONNELLE. 2/Lieut.W.O.STEWART to ARRAS as Quartermaster to Dismounted Battn. Sergt. RATCLIFFE as a/R.Q.M.S. 2/Lieut. J.C. CARR-ELLISON to Dismounted Party. 2/Lieut. P.L. WILSON supernumary to Base. 2/Lieut. D'A.F.H. HARRIES joined from Base at 12 noon and was evacuated same day being supernumary.	
FORTEL	7th		Left PLUMOISON - 13 miles to billets at FORTEL.	
FORTEL FOSSEUX	8th		Left FORTEL at 2.pm. - 20 miles to FOSSEUX, where the Brigade was concentrated in huts, horses in bivouac. Remainder of Division GOUY-en-ARTOIS.	
FOSSEUX DUISANS ARRAS DUISANS	9th		"Stood to" at 5.30am. 10am.moved to DUISANS in rear of 8th. Brigade. 2pm. moved through ARRAS to Eastern outskirts near the railway station. Houses in ARRAS all appeared to be deserted and all windows broken but the buildings themselves did not appear to be very badly damaged. Waited at Eastern outskirts of ARRAS till dark when we were ordered to off-saddle and bivouac in the town for the night. At 11.30pm. we were ordered to turn out and withdraw to neighbourhood of DUISANS where we spent the rest of the night in bivouac. Bitterly cold - snow in blizzards. Information received during the day was good and the infantry appeared to have got all their first and second objectives and in many cases the third.	

Hubert Fitzwil
Captain & Adjt.
The Royal Dragoons.

Army Form C. 2118.

DUPLICATE

THE ROYAL DRAGOONS.

WAR DIARY or INTELLIGENCE SUMMARY.

APRIL 1917. Volume XXI

(Sheet 2)

(Erase heading not required.)

Instructions regarding War Diaries and Intelligence Summaries are contained in F. S. Regs., Part II. and the Staff Manual respectively. Title Pages will be prepared in manuscript.

Place	Date	Hour	Summary of Events and Information	Remarks and references to Appendices
DUISONS ARRAS HILL 100.	10th	12 noon	We turned out at short notice and followed the 8th. Brigade through ARRAS via Cavalry Track to a position in readiness West of ORANGE HILL in H.53.d.(Scarpe Valley Sheet) The Cavalry Track was a passage constructed by the Dismounted Party of the Division from ARRAS through the German first and second line defences to hill 100 South of ORANGE HILL. The track was good enough though very heavy in places, and the Brigade passed through without any casualties though a few horses came down. Except in the immediate vicinity of the German line the surrounding country was practicable for cavalry in open order in spite of numerous shell holes. During these operations Major H.A. TOMKINSON had been acting liaison officer between the 3rd. Cav. Divn. and 37th. Division and was with 112th Bde. He was bringing an important message to the 8th. Cav. Bde. when he was wounded in the face and leg - not seriously -. 3 orderlies, DAVIDSON, SAUNDERS and ROBERTSON were also wounded whilst carrying messages for him. 2/Lieut. O.C.R.HILTON-GREEN and 2/Lieut. J.R.WINGFIELD.DIGBY were sent to establish liaison with 112th.Bde. and 5th. Cav.Bde. respectively. On reaching vicinity of ORANGE HILL the Brigade halted as it was understood that MONCHY-LE-PREUX and GUEMAPPES were both still held by the enemy and cavalry could not move forward. Consequently the Brigade bivouacked West of the FEUCHY Road. The cold was intense and there were continual snow blizzards. The only form of shelter available were shell holes which afforded a little cover.	
HILL 100.	11th	At 5.30.am. the infantry assaulted the line from the SCARPE to the COJEUL and by 8.am. MONCHY and BERGERE were in our hands. The cavalry were then ordered forward.- 8th.Brigade to seize BOIRY-NOTRE-DAME moving North of MONCHY. 6th.Cav.Bde. to seize VIS-EN-ARTOIS connecting on the left with the 8th. Cav. Bde. and on the right with the 5th.Cav.Bde. In consequence the 8th.Cav.Bde moved to MONCHY-LEZ-PREUX and 3rd.D.Gds. were directed upon the spur South of that village. In the event of the 3rd.D.Gds. reaching their first Main Bound namely the BOIS-de-SART, BOIS VERT, the Regiment was to seize the village VIS-en-ARTOIS just South of the COJEUL River.	

Arthur Titheral Captain & Adjt.
The Royal Dragoons.

DUPLICATE

Army Form C. 2118.

WAR DIARY
or
INTELLIGENCE SUMMARY

THE ROYAL DRAGOONS. APRIL 1917 Volume XXXI.

(Erase heading not required.) (Sheet III)

Place	Date	Hour	Summary of Events and Information	Remarks and references to Appendices
HILL 100	11*		8th.Brigade reached the village and there came under heavy artillery fire from the East and S.E. and lost very heavily both in horses and men. The Xth.Hussars and Essex Yeomanry each lost 9 and 11 Officers respectively. Lieut-Colonel P.E. HARDWICK,D.S.O.,Comdg.Xth.Hussars, was shot through the lower part of the leg. Each of these Regiments lost about 150 men. The "Blues" moving up in reserve did not reach the village. The Brigadier, General BULKELY-JOHNSON was killed. Later a squadron of the "Blues" under Lord PEMBROKE was sent up to reinforce. This squadron dismounted for action in squadron column S.W. of the village. The enemy had direct observation from the S.E. and a large number of the horses in this squadron were blown to pieces. It was a most horrible sight seeing these horses galloping back under a storm of crumps. Practically all the horses of the 8th.Cav.Bde. which survived had stampeded.	
			Meanwhile the 3rd.D.Gds. (6th.C.Bde.) were sent forward and reached line of the spur between MONCHY and BERGERE. They could get no further East of them. was strongly held and the enemy had a fortified line just East of them. This opposition prevented any further forward action on the part of the Brigade, and the Royals and N.Somerset Yeo. remained in a position of readiness just in rear of the crest of Hill 100 just South of ORANGE HILL. Regiments were disposed in line of troop columns at irregular intervals.	
			There was considerable hostile shelling but apparently not directed on us, and our losses were chiefly due to fire aimed at horses of 3rd.D.Gds. and 8th. C.Bde. Nearly all our losses occurred in "A" Sqdn. especially Lieut.HENDERSON'S troop which lost 21 horses.	
			Later the Brigade moved 800 yards further West near the FEUCHY Road. Here we were safe till about 6pm. when the enemy starting putting up a barrage directed probably upon infantry reinforcements who were coming up from ARRAS. result we had to move again.	
W. of ARRAS.			About 8pm. Bde. received orders to move back West of ARRAS after being relieved by infantry.	
			Total Casualties. - 68 horses killed wounded or missing.	
			Killed - 2 O.Ranks.	
			Wounded - Major H.A.TOMKINSON 26 Other Ranks.	
			2/Lieut. A.R.COOPER (attd.6th.M.G.Sqdn.) was wounded in the chest.	
			2/Lieut.D.P.LITHGOW and Lt.W.H.CUBITT acted as gallopers the former to General HARMAN and the latter to Divnl.HQrs.	

[signature] Captain & Adjt.,
The Royal Dragoons.

Army Form C. 2118.

DUPLICATE

THE ROYAL DRAGOONS.

WAR DIARY

or

INTELLIGENCE SUMMARY

APRIL 1917. Volume XXXI (Sheet IV)

(Erase heading not required.)

Instructions regarding War Diaries and Intelligence Summaries are contained in F.S. Regs., Part II. and the Staff Manual respectively. Title Pages will be prepared in manuscript.

Place	Date	Hour	Summary of Events and Information	Remarks and references to Appendices
ARRAS (Racecourse) FOSSEUX	12th		After spending a miserably cold night bivouacking in the snow on the so-called ARRAS racecourse, The Brigade moved at 9.30.am. and marched to FOSSEUX to our old camp which we had left on the 9th. Here we were joined by Capt. Hon.C.A.J. ANNESLEY and "B" Echelon which had spent the intervening time at BOUFFLERS. Many of the men were so cold after their night on ARRAS racecourse that they could hardly stand.	
FOSSEUX	13th		A considerable number of men sick with frostbitten feet or hands, as result of exposure during the past 3 days. The horses had stood the strain particularly well and there were no cases of exhaustion.	
FOSSEUX LE PONCHEL	16th		Brigade left FOSSEUX and marched to an area west of AUXI-LE-CHATEAU a distance of about 27 miles. The Regiment went into billets at LE PONCHEL. Lieut. W.P.BROWNE to Divnl. HQtrs. as G.S.O.III. Vice Capt. E.A.FIELDEN Brigade Major 5th. Cav.Bde.	
LE PONCHEL VRON	19th		The Brigade moved to new billets. Bde.HQtrs. to MAINTENAY, 3rd.D.Gds.SAULCHOY. Royals to VRON. N.S.Y. ARGOULES and NEMPONT. Our area was on the whole a good one. The chief difficulty being water. There was no running stream and we were confined to ponds. This was subsequently remedied by pumping water up to the Sugar Factory and using troughs.	
VRON	21st		Return of Dismounted Party. This party had been employed since March 25th. in neighbourhood of ARRAS in making the Cavalry Track and in Salvage Work.	
VRON	21st to 30th		Attention was devoted chiefly to the improvement in the condition of horses after the hard times they had been through. The corn ration was raised to 12lbs.Oats and 2lbs.Bran occasionally. The Hay ration to 12lbs. this was supplemented by as much grazing along the road sides as possible. Training was devoted chiefly to visual signalling, musketry, training of Hotchkiss rifle detachments. STRENGTH of Regiment on 1st.APRIL :- Men 648 Horses 593. " " " " 30th. " :- Men 656 Horses 597.	

Captain & Adjt.,
The Royal Dragoons.

Army Form C. 2118.

DUPLICATE

WAR DIARY
or
INTELLIGENCE SUMMARY

THE ROYAL DRAGOONS.   **APRIL 1917.**   **Volume XXXI** (Sheet V)

(Erase heading not required.)

Place	Date	Hour	Summary of Events and Information	Remarks and references to Appendices
	10.4.17		APPENDIX II CASUALTIES.	
	11th		Wounded (Officers) Major H.A. TOMKINSON 10/4/17. 2/Lt. A.F. COOPER (Attd. M.M. Sdn) 11/4/17.	
			Killed (O.R.) 11/4/17	
			9506 L/Cpl. Rankellor G.	
			2193 Pte. Jordan J.	
	10th		Wounded (O.R.) 10/4/17.	
			3561 Pte. Saunders H.	
			7704 " Davidson J.	
			10030 " Robertson J. (Died from Wounds 27/4/17.)	
	11th		Wounded (O.R.) 11/4/17.	
			5998 L/Cpl. Duff F.	3594 Pte. Bertram T. (Shell shock at duty)
			12805 Pte. Dickson G.	3757 L/C. Craven B. (Wded. 8/4/17 Dis. Party)
			6561 " Fergus A.	3969 Pte. McGuire W. (" 8/4/17 " ")
			9138 " Fraser F.	
			4903 S.S. Morgan A.	
			9277 Pte. Baird J.	
			4321 " Clutterbuck W.	
			9150 " Skinner R. (Died from Wds. 12/4/17)	
			986 " Ravell B.	
			4736 S.S.Farr. Allen F.	
			10638 Pte. Clarke R.	
			5765 " McIntyre E.	
			4425 " Sullivan W.	
			4103 TStr. Goodbody W.	
			8284 Cpl. McKenzie D. (Died from Wds. 11/4/17.)	
			631 Pte. Kelman R.	
			9251 " Duncan W.	
			50 " McKay K.	
			6642 " Harrower W.	
			2241 " Payne W. (Slightly at Duty)	
			8082 Sgt. Lavender W. " "	
			5500 Cpl. Talbot J. " "	

Captain & Adjt.
The Royal Dragoons.

DUPLICATE

Army Form C. 2118.

WAR DIARY APRIL 1917.
or
INTELLIGENCE SUMMARY Volume XXXI.
(Erase heading not required.) *(Sheet VI)*

THE ROYAL DRAGOONS.

Instructions regarding War Diaries and Intelligence Summaries are contained in F. S. Regs., Part II. and the Staff Manual respectively. Title Pages will be prepared in manuscript.

Place	Date	Hour	Summary of Events and Information	Remarks and references to Appendices
PLUMOISON	5th		APPENDIX III. Reinforcements from Base (Evacuated same day Supernumery to Base)	
VRON	21st		2/Lieut. D'A.F.H.HARRIES from Base 21/4/17.	
VRON	30th		8 other ranks from Base 21/4/17.	
			52 other ranks from Base 30/4/17.	
			APPENDIX I HONOURS AND REWARDS — NIL.	

Fitzhon Tiffany
Captain & Adjt.
The Royal Dragoons.

SECRET Duplicate

Army Form C. 2118.

1st R. Dragoons
VOL 32

WAR DIARY
or
INTELLIGENCE SUMMARY
(Erase heading not required.)

THE ROYAL DRAGOONS.   VOLUME XXXII   MAY 1917.

Instructions regarding War Diaries and Intelligence
Summaries are contained in F.S. Regs., Part II.
and the Staff Manual respectively. Title Pages
will be prepared in manuscript.

(Sheet 1.)

Place	Date	Hour	Summary of Events and Information	Remarks and references to Appendices
VRON	1st		52 Reinforcements joined on April 30th. These included some men who had recently been evacuated with Trench Feet, and others who had just arrived from England.	
"	6th		2/Lieuts. D'A.F.H.HARRIS and P.L.WILSON joined from Base with 20th other ranks. 8 horses were transferred to "O" Battery R.H.A. as this battery was unable to get suitable remounts from Base.	
"	8th		A Party of 30 men with 3 wagons were sent to do some work West of RUE on a field which had been damaged by the Royal Naval Division.	
"	11th		Capt. Hon.C.A.J.ANNESLEY was evacuated to the Duchess of Westminster's Hospital with bad teeth.	
DOMINOIS	12th		The Regiment marched out of billets in VRON to DOMINOIS and PETIT CHEMIN. Dismounted Party to BEAURAINVILLE and thence by train to PERONNE.	
FROHEN-LE-PETIT	13th		Marched to FROHEN-LE-PETIT.	
BEAUFAUCOURT	14th		Marched to BERTEAUCOURT.	
LA NEUVILLE	15th		Marched to LA NEUVILLE where we remained during 16th.	
BAYONVILLERS	17th		Marched to BAYONVILLERS and remained for 18th.	
N. of BUIRE	19th		Marched via BRIE to Camp just North of BUIRE on the River COLOGNE. A very desolate march through country which had been entirely devastated first of all by artillery and finally by fire made by the Germans on their retreat. The village of BRIE was a mass of ruins from which good bivouacks and shelters could be made.	
	20th		Dismounted Party rejoined. 1 Subaltern and 50 men for work on roads near CARTIGNY - after working on the roads for six hours without receiving orders this party was sent back to Camp. Remainder of Regiment grazing and work on Camp.	
	21st		Major T.S.IRWIN on a week's leave to PARIS.	
	22nd		1 Subaltern and 50 men working on roads - remainder grazing and work on Camp. Working Party continued - remainder grazing and working on mess huts. Captain F.W.WILSON-FITZGERALD,M.C. went to 8th. Cav.Bde as acting Staff Captain and 2/Lieut. G.T.O'CALLAGHAN took over duties of a/Adjutant. Divisional Canteen was opened supplying fresh eggs, butter, etc. "C" Sqdn. under Capt. HEWETT with 2/Lieuts.P.R.D. COOKE and E.St.G.STEDALL, and the 3rd.D.Gds. under Lt.Col.BURT proceeded at 6.pm. mounted to near EPEHY.	
	23rd		"C" Sqdn. and ẌẌ "A" Sqdn. relieved a Sqdn. ẊẌ 16th.Lancers in Copse 13.	

2449 Wt. W14957/M90 750,000 1/16 J.B.C. & A. Forms/C.2118/12.

Army Form C. 2118.

Duplicate

WAR DIARY or INTELLIGENCE SUMMARY

THE ROYAL DRAGOONS VOLUME XXXII

MAY 1917

(Erase heading not required.)

Instructions regarding War Diaries and Intelligence Summaries are contained in F.S. Regs., Part II. and the Staff Manual respectively. Title Pages will be prepared in manuscript.

Place	Date	Hour	Summary of Events and Information	Remarks and references to Appendices
			(Sheet 2.)	
	24"		"A" Sqdn. under Lieut. R.H.W.HENDERSON with 2/Lieuts.C.C.H.HILTON-GREEN and J.R.WINGFIELD-DIGBY, and "B" Sqdn. under Captain C.W.TURNER with 2/Lieuts. S.J.PARR, M.C. and D.P.LITHGOW (the whole under Captain E.W.T.MILES) proceeded at 6.pm. mounted to near EPEHY and relieved "C" Sqdn. and "A" Sqdn. in Copse 13, and remained in support whilst "C" and B "A" proceeded to the outpost line and took over the BIRD CAGE* and QUARRIES* from the "Greys". A hostile patrol was fired on from the BIRD CAGE and enemy M.Gs. were very active from OSSUS WOOD	
	25"		Trench mortars were fired on the QUARRY during the morning but were silenced by our guns. M.Gs. fired at "A" Post BIRD CAGE during the night. This post was crumped just after they had left it at dawn. The remainder of the Regiment were on fatigue carrying water and rations to the BIRD CAGE all night.	
	26"		Much activity in the air during the morning. Pte. Dysart (O) was slightly wounded in the arm be a splinter from an anti-aircraft gun. The QUARRIES and communication trench again bombarded by trench mortar (no damage). Capt. MILES visited the BIRD CAGE. A quiet night. The remainder of the Regiment carried up three days' emergency water and iron rations to the BIRD CAGE.	
	27"		At 6.a.m. 12 trench mortar shells were landed in the QUARRY. Ptes.KERR Head and Cooper(O) were wounded. Our guns silenced the mortars. During the night ½ Sqdns. N.SOMERSET YEO. relieved "C" and ½ "A" Sqdn. in the outpost line. ½ "B" and ½ "A" Sqdn. in Copse 13. The Regiment under Capt. MILES took over the GREEN Line (the main position) from the 3rd.Dragoon Gds. as follows:- "A" Sqdn. - G. Redoubt. "C" Sqdn. - H. Redoubt near PRIEL Farm. "B" Sqdn. - CATELET Copse Redoubt and CRUCIFORM Redoubt. Relief completed by 3.0. am.am. The above line was in the D.L. Sub-Sector commanded by Lieut.Col.BURT, D.S.O. The D. Sector was commanded by Brig-Gen.A.E.W.HARMAN, D.S.O. The Catelet Copse trenches were bad and not much work had been done on them.	
	28"		The usual shelling of LITTLE PRIEL Farm took place.(no damage). Much work was done during the night on fire-steps, communications, trench-drains and floor-boards put down. Sergt.BOWLES took out a patrol from G.Post.	

2449 Wt. W14957/M90 750,000 1/16 J.B.C. & A. Forms/C.2118/12.

Army Form C. 2118.

Duplicate

WAR DIARY

THE ROYAL DRAGOONS.

VOLUME XXXII

or

INTELLIGENCE SUMMARY MAY 1917.

(Erase heading not required.)

Instructions regarding War Diaries and Intelligence Summaries are contained in F. S. Regs., Part II. and the Staff Manual respectively. Title Pages will be prepared in manuscript.

Place	Date	Hour	Summary of Events and Information (Sheet 3.)	Remarks and references to Appendices
	29th		A few After shrapnel over G.Post in the morning. Much work again done on all trenches. 2/Lieut. WINGFIELD.DIGBY and party wired towards TOMBOY Farm. Sergt BOWLES again took the same patrol out from G.Post and located a small wired post about 300 yards in front of the Redoubt. No enemy were met.	
	30th		LITTLE PRIEL Farm again shelled in morning (20 shells of which 17 were duds) General HARMAN walked round the line early. Work continued on T heads and sandbag traverses in G. and CATELET Copse posts. The Regiment was relieved during the night by the N.Somerset. Yeo. Relief completed about 2.30.am. The Regiment then took over the BROWN Line (2nd.Line). The Regtl.HQtrs. and "A" and "C" Sqdns. in billets and shelters in EPEHY. "B" Sqdn. in dug-outs and shelters in the railway embankment. Nothing doing all day. During the night Capt. TURNER and 2/Lt. COOK and 100 men wired from G. towards QUARRIES. Another party of 80 men under 2/Lt.PARR and WINGFIELD_DIGBY wired at the BIRD CAGE.	
	31st		The enemy shelled EPEHY about 1.pm. The HQtrs. mess had to be evacuated and Capts. MILES, and TURNER , Lts. HENDERSON and HILTON-GREEN removed to a sunk road. Another shell landed in this road about ten yards away and wounded HILTON-GREEN in leg, side and head. He was immediately removed in motor-ambulance. The Regiment was relieved about 10.pm. by the "Blues" under Lord TWEEDMOUTH, and marched back on their horses, arriving in Camp about 3.15 am. June 2nd.	
	2nd May		During this period 12 Officers and 326 Other Ranks were up with the Trench Party, the details in Camp grazed and exercised, and worked on mess-huts, wash-houses etc.	

2/Lieut. & a/ Adjt.,
The Royal Dragoons.

Army Form C. 2118.
Duplicate

THE ROYAL DRAGOONS. WAR DIARY VOLUME XXXII.
or INTELLIGENCE SUMMARY MAY 1917.
(Erase heading not required.)

(Sheet 4.)   Summary of Events and Information

Appendix I. HONOURS&and& CASUALTIES.

```
3969 Pte. McGuire   W.  previously reported missing, now reported wounded 8/4/17.
10030  "  Robertson J.  (Wounded 10/4/17) died from wounds 27/4/17.
9130   "  Skinner   R.  (Wounded 11/4/17) Died from wounds 12/4/17.
5765   "  McIntyre  E.  (Reported missing 12/4/17) declared killed in action
                         11/4/17.
15166  "  Stribling J.  Wounded 24/5/17.
4151   "  Dysart    D.      "    27/5/17.
3555   "  Reed      C.      "    28/5/17.
2871   "  Cooper    J.W.    "    28/5/17.
```

Apx. II. HONOURS and REWARDS.

```
Major H.A. TOMKINSON           ) Mentioned in Despatches (Lon.Gaz.Suppt.
4576 S.S.M. RATCLIFFE R.A.J.   )                         d/- 5/5/17.)
     (O.R.S.)

Major H.A. TOMKINSON           Awarded D.S.O. (Birthday Honours 3/8/17.)
```

Apndx. III. REINFORCEMENTS.

```
2/Lieut. D'A.F.H.HARRIS  )  Joined from Base 6/5/17.
  "      P.L. WILSON     )

20 Other Ranks              Joined from Base 18/5/17 (To Dismounted Party)
10   "     "                    "     "    "  20/5/17.
 2   "     "                    "     "    "  27/5/17.
 8   "     "
```

2/Lieut. & a/Adjt.,
THE ROYAL DRAGOONS.

SECRET

Army Form C. 2118.

Duplicate

VOL 3

WAR DIARY
or
INTELLIGENCE SUMMARY

THE ROYAL DRAGOONS.
VOLUME XXIII. June 1917.

(Erase heading not required.)

Instructions regarding War Diaries and Intelligence
Summaries are contained in F. S. Regs., Part II.
and the Staff Manual respectively. Title Pages
will be prepared in manuscript.

Place	Date	Hour	Summary of Events and Information (Sheet I)	Remarks and references to Appendices
BUIRE	2		The Trench Party under Captain E.W.T.MILES consisting of 8 Officers and 263 O.R.returned to Camp at 3.0.am. on the 'Blues' horses, which Regiment had gone up to relieve ours. A working party under 2/Lieut. D.P.LITHGOW was left at EPEHY. The day was devoted to cleaning up, washing clothes etc.	
	3		Major CONDON Inspector of Catering, visited the Regiment and lectured to cooks and S.Q.M.Ss.on economy of rations and dripping saving. He seemed well satisfied with the arrangements made for the men's comfort in the messing line, but suggested several improvements chiefly with regard to covered in kitchen ranges. The Commanding Officer saw Squadron Leaders in the morning to discuss the Training to be carried out during the ensuing week.	
	4		Squadrons did Musketry, Remount training, and a little Troop Drill. Weather continues brilliantly fine and very hot.	
	5		Same training as yesterday. Hotter than ever. 2/Lieut. LITHGOW returned from working party and was relieved by Lieut. R.B.HELME.	
	6		Remount training and Musketry in morning. In afternoon the Regt. carried out a dismounted counter-attack; "C" Sqdn. represented the enemy - "A" and "B" Sqdns under Capt. MILES attacked; General HARMAN attended and criticised the operations and a good many useful points were brought out. The hottest day we've had yet but quite a gale of wind got up in the evening. Major H.A.TOMKINSON gazetted to the D.S.O. in the Birthday Honours List.	
	7		The Regiment stood to at 1 hour's notice from 4.0.am.and got the order to turn out at 5.15.am. - From the Brigade rendezvous we marched to near LONGAVENES where the Brigade carried out a dismounted attack which was watched and criticised by the Divisional Commander. Amongst the points which were noticed were the fact that the Brigade was too concentrated at the place of assembly, and that the preliminary dismounted advance the pace in front was too fast. - Regt. returned to Camp about midday.	
	8		Squadrons continued Musketry, Equitation and Bayonet Exercise. Three Officers were sent out to reconnoitre routes to the 'place of assembly' in each Divisional Sector.	
	9		Training continued the same as yesterday. Orders received for 1½ Squadrons to go up to the line on night of 10/11 and for rest of Regt.to go up on 11/12th. Dull day and much cooler	

Army Form C. 2118.

WAR DIARY or INTELLIGENCE SUMMARY

THE ROYAL DRAGOONS

VOLUME XXXIII.
June 1917

(Sheet II.)

(*Erase heading not required.*)

Instructions regarding War Diaries and Intelligence Summaries are contained in F.S. Regs., Part II. and the Staff Manual respectively. Title Pages will be prepared in manuscript.

Place	Date	Hour	Summary of Events and Information	Remarks and references to Appendices
Neighbourhood of EPEHY.	10.		"B" Squadron and 2 Troops "A" Sqdn. under Capt. C.W.TURNER left Camp at 7.0.pm. and rode to EPEHY, and from there to Intermediate Support Line,D.2.Sub-sector 500 yards N.E. of 14 WILLOWS(Sub-sector HQrs.) They took over from Liecester Yeomanry who returned to Camp on their horses.	
	11.		"C" Sqdn. and 2 Troops "A" under Major T.S.IRWIN, left Camp at 7.15.pm and rode to EPEHY to take over Intermediate Support Line from Capt.TURNER. The latter took over the Outpost Line from 6 Troops Leicester Yeomanry. Heavy thunderstorm during ride to EPEHY. 2 Zeppelins were reported over VILLERS GUISLAIN at 9.0pm. flying S.E. 2/Lieut. D.P.LITHGOW to 4th. Army School for a course in Sniping.	
	12.		The Colonel (Lieut-Colonel F.W.WORMALD D.S.O.) who was commanding D.2 Sub-sector went round Outpost Line with Major IRWIN. Squadrons in support worked on communications to Green Line. - Day quiet.	
	13.		From today onwards all the troops in Intermediate Support were detailed for work at night on Outpost Line, work to be carried out under Major IRWIN. - Quiet day.	
	14.		"C" Sqdn. and ½ "A" Sqdn relieved "B" Sqdn and ½ "A" Sqdn. in Outpost Line, work of relief was completed early but "B" Sqdn. remained up and worked on trenches till dawn.	
	15.		General SEYMOUR and the Colonel went round Outpost Line about 4.30.a.m. and owing to a thick fog, ordered night dispositions to be taken up again. L.Cpl.FROST(C.Sqdn.)went out from No.2 Post to reconnoitre supposed M.G.emplacement and brought back useful information. - Quiet day. About 1.30.am. an enemy patrol estimated 6 to 12 men crept up from OSSUS Wood and bombed our covering party in front of No.1.Post. 4 bombs were thrown and 2 men were wounded (Ptes. CAMPBELL and GROEGER both C. Sqdn.) The covering party opened fire and the enemy patrol retired. 2/Lieut. J.S.DUNVILLE went out with a patrol of 10 men in front of No.2 Post but saw nothing.	
	17		"C" Sqdn. and ½ "B" Sqdn., N.S.Yeo. relieved "C" Sqdn. and ½ "A" Sqdn. Royals in Outpost Line, and the remaining 6 Troops N.S.Y. relieved Royals in Intermediate Support. "A" Sqdn. took over Redoubt from "C" Sqdn.3rd.D.Gds. "B" Sqdn. took over M Redoubt from "A" Sqdn. 3rd. D.Gds. and "C" Sqdn. took over L Redoubt from "B" Sqdn. 3rd.D.Gds.. Relief was complete about 2.0.am. The enemy put a lot of shrapnel over between L and K Redoubts but fortunately many were blind.	
	18.		The Royals now worked entirely on Green Line, most of the work being widening and sloping the trenches and making a BERM all round.	

2449 Wt. W14957/M90 750,000 1/16 J.B.C. & A. Forms/C.2118/12.

Army Form C. 2118.

THE ROYAL DRAGOONS.

WAR DIARY or INTELLIGENCE SUMMARY

VOLUME XXXIII.
JUNE 1917.

(Erase heading not required.)

(Sheet III.)

Place	Date	Hour	Summary of Events and Information	Remarks and references to Appendices
	19. 20.		Work carried on on Green Line, rained hard all afternoon. - Quiet day. Trenches were very wet and muddy, and drainage was improved and new drains started. Officer reliefs took place as follows:- Capts. MILES and HEWETT relieved Capt. TURNER and Lt.deTRAFFORD. Lts.D.COOKE, STEDALL, WILSON, BROWNE, CARR, ELLISON relieved Lts. HENDERSON, DUMBRECK, HARRIS, WINGFIELD, DIGBY and WILSON. Major T.S. IRWIN went back to Sub-Sector HQrs. to await relief from Major H.A. TOMKINSON, D.S.O., (who had joined the Regiment from HAVRE) the remainder returned to Camp.	
	21.		Major TOMKINSON relieved Major IRWIN and took over 2nd. in Command under Colonel ING. L Post shelled about 5.30. by 5.9s. one traverse damaged and shelter blown in.	
	22.		Trench Mortars active on Outpost HQrs. Slight shelling round L Post, otherwise quiet day.	
	23.		General HARMAN and Colonel ING visited Green Line. N. SOMERSET YEO. relieved Regiment in Green Line. Relief complete by 3.0.a.m. 24th. and Squadrons march independantly to PEIZIERES. Lieut. CUBITT to 4th. Army School for a course in Stokes Mortars till July 2nd. (account attached)	
	24. 25.		The Regiment started out to raid 10.30.pm. Lieut.R.B.HELME's funeral was at VILLERS-FAUCON - parties from Trenches and Camp attended. Ptes. NISBET and LEITCH were also buried.	
	26.		2/Lieut. J.S. DUNVILLE died from wounds and was buried at VILLERS-FAUCON next to Lieut. HELME.	
	27.		Rained heavily all day. Horses went up in the evening from Camp under Major IRWIN to bring back Trench Party. Major IRWIN returned and took over "C" Sqdn.	
	28. 29. 30.		Rained heavily again, consequently horse lines were all changed in the afternoon. "B" Squadron inspected by the Colonel in Squadron Drill and small tactical exercises for subaltern officers and N.C.Os. The Colonel inspected "A" and "C" Sqdns. at the same schemes.	

Strength of Regiment 1/6/17
Men - 638. Horses - 585.

Strength of Regiment 30/6/17
Men - 606. Horses - 585.

WAR DIARY

THE ROYAL DRAGOONS

INTELLIGENCE SUMMARY
VOLUME XXXIII.
JUNE 1917.

(Sheet IV)

Place	Date	Hour	Summary of Events and Information	Remarks and references to Appendices
outpost D.2 Sub sector	14		APPENDIX I. - CASUALTIES.	
	14		9492 Pte. Harris E. Wounded.	
	15		9059 " Hunter G. "	
	15		10543 " Campbell J. "	
	15		5838 " Groeger F.A. "	
	25		6370 " Thompson J.M. Killed.	
			Lieut. R.B.Helme A. "	
			8865 Pte. Nisbet A. "	
			2/Lieut.J.S.Dunville wounded (died from wds.26/6/17.)	
			8809 Pte. Leitch J. " (died from wds.25/6/17.)	
			3075 Sgt. Mander F. wounded.	
			16412 Pte. Wilkinson A. "	
			3735 " Evans G. "	
			5768 " Bartlett A. "	
D.2 Sub sector	27		10003 " Lauder J. "	
			5370 " Goghlan J. "	
			6185 " Bennett J.T. "	
			2974 " McKiddie W. "	
			3270 " Logan J.D. " (slight,at duty)	
			911 " Grizzell R. missing.	
			7698 " Miles J. "	
			5753 " Morrison W. wounded.	
			6098 " McNeil W. "	
			APPENDIX II. HONOURS AND AWARDS.	
			Major H.A. Tomkinson To be Companion of the Distinguished Service Order.(Lon. Gaz: Sup: dated 4/6/17.)	
			2702 S.Q.M.S.Rogers G.E. ⎫	
			4179 Ck.Sgt. Bunker J. ⎪ Awarded Silver Medal for Long Service and	
			4320 Sergt. Seaton W.J. ⎬ Good Conduct, with Gratuity, A. Order 125 of	
			4269 Sgt.Tptr.Dyer W. ⎪ 1917.	
			4192 Tptr. Goodbody W. ⎭	

WAR DIARY
or
INTELLIGENCE SUMMARY

THE ROYAL DRAGOONS   VOLUME XXXIII.   JUNE 1917.

(Sheet V)   Summary of Events and Information

APPENDIX III.- REINFORCEMENTS.

1 Other Ranks	from British Cavalry Entrenching Battalion. 3/6/17.
4 " "	from Base 9/6/17.
3 " "	" 17/6/17.
2 " "	" Brit: Cav: Entrenching Battn. 18/6/17.
Major H.A. Tomkison, D.S.O.,	from HAVRE 19/6/17.
4 Other Ranks	from Brit: Cav: Entrenching Battn: 23/6/17.
1 " "	" " 30/6/17.

Captain and Adjt.,

THE ROYAL DRAGOONS.

REPORT ON RAID CARRIED OUT BY MEN OF ROYAL DRAGOONS
WITH SCOUTS OF 6th. CAV. BDE. AND DETAILS OF 3rd. D.GDS.
AND 3rd. FIELD SQUADRON R.E. ON THE MORNING OF 25/6/1917.

Ref. LE CATELET Map. 1/20,000.

OBJECT. 1. The object of the raid as laid down in Instruction dated 22/6/17 and marked X (attached).

DETAILS OF PARTIES. 2. Details of parties 'A' & 'B' under Lt. HENDERSON & HELME respectively.
Composition as in Appendices marked Y.1 and Y.2. are attached.
All ranks were of the Royal Dragoons, with the exception of :-
Lt. V.C.RICE, N.S.Y. i/c Scouts with B.Party.
LT. J.B.BICKERSTETH. 6th. M.G.S. i/c Covering party A. Party.
6 N.C.Os and men H.R.Detachments, 3rd. D.Gds.
6 Scouts 3rd. D.Gds.
6 Scouts N.S.Y.
Total of all ranks in the two parties was 121.

TIME TABLE ETC. 3. The programme was carried out punctually and in accordance with "Instructions for Raid" marked (X). and addenda fixing Zero hour (Z).

REPORT ON ACTION OF RAIDING PARTIES. 4. Owing the deaths of Lt. HELME & DUNVILLE, and the fact that Lt. RICE was wounded it has been difficult to obtain a corroborative evidence of all that occurred. I attach however repots of Lt. HENDERSON marked (A) of Lt. RICE marked (B) and a number of N.C.Os of the B.Party marked (C).

A.PARTY.
(a) From Lt. HENDERSON'S report it would appear that everything had gone alright up to 0 + 4½, but that delay occurred owing to an accident to the first torpedo and delay in firing the charge.

(b) That the assaulting party withdrew a short distance from the most advanced point which it had reached owing to the sappers running back to warn them that they were too close to the torpedo.

(c) That the raiding party did get through the wire but were unable to reach the enemy's trench owing to rifle fire and bombing.

(d) That the party had to withdraw without accomplishing its object, owing to the firing of the 'recall' rocket.

(e) That the enemy were aware of the attack and that the torpedo had to be placed in position under the fire of their rifles and bombers.

B.PARTY.
(a) From Lt. RICE's report (the only officer surviving of this party) it appears :-
(a) That everything went according to scheduled time

up

to 0 + 4½ and that there was no enemy opposition up to the moment he reached the 2nd. wire. Also that the first wire was cut by hand, and that there was an already formed gap through the second wire - and that he laid a tape up to and through the second wire.

(b) It seems probable that there was a shallow trench joining up the listening post just inside the enemy's first wire, and that the assaulting parties mistook this trench along which they heard fighting for their objective not noticing the tape which ran on to the 2nd. gap.

That this tape was laid is vouched for by two men of the Royals who are wounded and at 39 C.C.S. both of whom saw the tape and state that the assaulting parties did not follow it up.

(c) That the assaulting parties, having made their assault prematurely found themselves in a pocket of wire up against the trench which was their real objective.

(d) It appears certain that this party inflicted damage on the enemy.

ARTILLERY. 5. The artillery co-operation was perfect.
It is suggested however by Lt. HENDERSON that it was not sufficiently heavy to keep the enemy's heads down, as the party was exposed to heavy rifle fire at 0 + 4½.
On return of B.Party and when that party was reported 'all in', and having hard that some wounded of A.Party had still to be brought in I asked Major Young R.H.A. (my artillery Liaison Officer) to arrange for artillery to fire a few rounds at enemy's trenches to cover the stretcher bearers whilst coming in.

MACHINE GUNS. 6. Their co-operation was undoubtedly of greatest use.

R.E. 7. The R.E. personnel behaved throughout with the greatest coolness and determination. I have not yet received the report from C.R.E. as to the causes of delay in firing the torpedo of A.Party. The defect was repaired under fire and the original torpedo was used.
Only one of the torpedos was used.

LOSSES TO THE ENEMY. 8. It seems certain that the B.Party accounted for at least 3 of the enemy, and Cpl. TALBOT with the right party states that he saw 5 dead Germans.

OUR LOSSES. 9.

	K.	D of W.	W.	M.
'A'.Party. Officers.	-	1	-	-
O.Rs.	1	-	4	2
'B'.Party. Officers.	1	-	1	-
O.Rs.	2	1	4	-
	4	2	9	2

GENERAL REMARKS. 10. (a) The approach to starting points and onwards to points of attack over a distance of over 800ᵡ from our Outposts was brilliantly carried out the direction of 2/Lt. DUNVILLE and Lt. RICE. The approach in each case was conducted on a compass bearing and the exact points to be attacked were struck in the scheduled time.

(b)

(b) Failure of 'A' party was due to :-

    (1) Delay in firing torpedo.
    (2) The fact that the enemy were not surprised.

Failure of 'B' Party to reach its objective, viz :- the main enemy trench, was due to :-

    (1) The fact that behind the 1st. wire was a shallow trench, which is not evident from the photograph, on which all plans were laid.

    Everyone being under the impression that the listening posts were joined up by a track through the grass only.

    (2) Failure of assault leaders to follow the tape which would have taken them through the 2nd. gap in the wire.

REPORT ON RAID CARRIED OUT NIGHT 24th/25th.

BY A. PARTY.

At 12.50 the scouts under 2/Lt. DUNVILLE, and 3 sappers with Bangalor torpedo left the Northern end of No. 1. outpost. They marched 450 yards on a bearing of 104° (true) laying a tape to the starting point.

At 1 a.m. the assualting party, the covering party, 2 Hotchkiss rifles left the North end of No. 1. outpost, following the tape to the starting point. Here the men lay down, and bearings were checked.

At. 1.10 a.m. our barrage fire opened and the whole party moved forward to the assualt point. The barrage fire was most accurate, but did not seem quite heavy enough to keep the enemy down.

At 1.14½ the scouts under 2/Lt. DUNVILLE and the 3 sappers moved forward to the wire. The 2 assualting parties crept forward as far as possible. The support party was placed in position and 2/Lt. BICKERSTETH placed his Hotchkiss rifles on the right flank.

Having placed the support party under a Corporal I went up the tape and found the 2 assualting parties coming back; this was caused by them having got too close to the wire and being warned by the sappers to get clear of the torpedo. Heavy rifle fire was coming from the enemy.

The word was then passed back for the reserve torpedo. This I sent up. 2/Lt. DUNVILLE must have been wounded at about this time.

Meanwhile the wire remained uncut and the torpedo did not explode till about 1.23½. Again I ordered the assualting parties forward. Lt. BICKERSTETH was in action with his Hotchkiss guns on the right. The enemy kept up his rifle fire, and threw bombs.

Sergt. MANDER, in command of one of the assualting parties was wounded and I sent him back.

Cpl. TALBOT, who was in command of the covering party, got into what he considered his correct position.

This only left 4½ minutes before the signal to withdraw was due.

At the end of this 4½ minutes the rocket for withdrawal went up from Hd. Qrs., and I sounded the hunting horn as a signal for the assualting parties to withdraw.

They withdrew - Lt. BICKERSTETH and covering party came in last leaving no wounded men out. I also cut the tape. Cpl. TALBOT states he saw 5 dead Germans by his position.

It is probable that the wire cut was not the main wire, but a line of wire further West marked B - B in the sketch. It is also almost sertain that the enemy was not shooting and bombing from his main trench but from posts marked A.

The height of the thistles and the light on these tracks must have been responsible for giving the impression these tracks were sunk saps with sapheads.

The following points were the cause of the proposed programme not being carried out to the letter.

(1) The torpedo was much too late exploding.
(2) It was unexpected to find "apparent trenches or or saps running at right angles to our line of advance."
(3) The enemy was quite prepared for our attack and there was no surprise.
(4) The men only had 4½ minutes between the time when the torpedo exploded and the withdraw.

Sketch.

RAID CARRIED OUT ON THE NIGHT OF JUNE 24/25th. 1917.

BY THE ROYAL DRAGOONS.

The following statement by Lieut. RICE North Somerset Yeomanry, was taken down by Lieut. Col. WORMALD at No. 39 Clearing Station at BUIRE on 26th. June.

Lieut. RICE States :-

I was the scout officer attached with 6 scouts ato 'B' Raiding Party.

I passed through the Outposts at No. 2 Post at 12.50 am with 6 scouts and a party of sappers with torpedo.

We moved straight out to our starting point laying a tape as we went.

The whole party was assembled at the starting point at the scheduled time. At Zero hour the Artillery opened fire, and the raiding party closed up to the barrage, moving on a bearing of 90° (true). When I arrived at the enemy's wire I turned the 6 scouts on to cutting it. It was only a thin belt, and they had cut a way through in about 1 minute. As soon as the wire was cut I proceeded forward to the second belt of wire which I had intended to blow up. After going about 15 yards as far as I can judge I came upon the 2nd. line of wire. This appeared to be more recently erected wire, and had 3 rows of pickets. On reaching the wire, I found that there was already a track through the wire, so I sent back a message to Lieut. HELME to bring up his assualting party, along the tape which I had laid up to the second gap. I went on myself with my 6 scouts to a trench immediately in front of me. Two of the enemy showed themselves in this trench and fired at us killing Sergt. HICKS, 3rd. D.Gds., and wounding me in the left arm rendering it useless. I killed one with my revolver and the other ran away. I then tore the shoulder straps off the dead German.

Lieut. HELME with the assualting party had joined me by this time. The enemy in the trench on our right were now firing on us, and Lieut. HELME called on the men to attack with the bayonet. Lieut. HELME was shot immediately after he had given the order for the assualt. I told off a party to remove Lieut. HELMES' body.

The withdrawal rocket had been fired just before Lieut. HELME was killed. I gave the order to withdraw at Zero + 21 mins. The enemy did not molest us during the withdrawal, and there was no hostile barrage to go through on the way back. We brought the direction tape back with us as we withdrew.

~~I desire to recommend the undermentioned N.C.Os and men for recognition.~~

REPORT ON B. RAIDING PARTY "JOCK".

(map attached).

No. 4356 Sergt. Pope states :-

I was Sergt. i/c of the "B" assualting party.
We left our outpost line at 12.55 a.m. We reached the strating point at LONE TREE without mishap. At Zero minus 3 we went forward another 100 yds. and waited there until Zero. When the barrage started 100 yds. short of enemy wire, we crept up behind it and eventually reached what we thought was the enemy main wire.

The next thing we heard was Lt. RICE shouting "This way" and we walked through a small gap in the wire which was about 4 feet deep and immediately found ourselves in a shallow trench running parallel to the wire. There were two Germans in this trench whom Lt. RICE shot. One German wounded Lt. RICE in the arm.

We then proceeded up the trench to the right (i.e. to the South) for about 20 yds. Lt. RICE then ordered us out of the trench. We walked on for about 12 yds. along the top of the trench still in a Southerly direction, where we met wire running across our front and joining up with the advanced line of wire through which we came.

Lt. HELME and LT. RICE walked up and down the wire looking for a gap. Not finding any gap LT. HELME shouted "bring up the torpedo to cut the wire". All this time there was a German with an automatic rifle firing in small bursts from a shelter about 6 yds. away. Lt. HELME shot at him with his revolver and immediately Lt. HELME was shot dead through the head. Bombs were thrown at this automatic rifle and he ceased to fire. We put Lt. HELME on a stretcher and walked to the trench up which we had advanced. A green rocket for withdrawal then went up and I blew my whistle and went back through the same gap in the wire by which we had entered. During the whole period my assualting party were with me and were trying to find a way through the 2nd. line of wire and all withdrew with me.

When withdrawing through the gap in the wire I saw the torpedo lying by the wire and as far as I know it was left there.

Lt. RICE and I then walked back/for some distance together as fas as the Y roads behind No. 2 Post. I then took my party to FALLEN TREE DUMP and Lt. RICE went to the Dressing Station at New Outpost H.Q..

No. 6396 Cpl. JULL states :-

I was in charge of No. 2 assualting party of B. Raiding party.
We followed up the barrage and I heard Lt. RICE shout out "This way" and I went through a gap in a line of wire about 4 feet thick and immediately found myself in a trench. I passed Lt. RICE standing in the gap in the wire.

I then proceeded to the right (i.e. in a Southerly direction) along this trench for about 30 yds. where the trench came to an end. I then got out and saw two Germans running away to my left. I then walked on for about 12 yds. and came on another line of very thick coiled wire running straight across my front.

I.

I then turned left handed and walked for about 20 yds. where I came on a pit with no one in it. 20 yds. further on a German ran out of another pit. I then ran on and found another pit in which there was one German whom I bayonetted, as he was not dead, I and private Jones pulled him out and told him to walk and started back to the trench up which I had come. The German only walked 20 yds. when he fell dead. I then took identifications off him and whilst doing so heard the order given to come out. We then walked back to the gap in the wire through which we had entered. I was then told that there was some wounded in the trench. I walked back and found Pte. LEICH, and with the assistance of Pte. Jones and Cpl. Stevens and carried him outside the wire where the party was waiting, we then proceeded back.

No. 4309. Sgt. STURGES states :-

I was in charge of the covering party of B. Raiding Party.

I followed the assualting party through a gap in a line of wire. Immediately in front there was a shallow trench about 2'6" deep. I followed this trench along to the left for about 20 yds. where I came on a line of wire running across my front.

I then put out my covering party along this line of wire between the trench and the line of wire through which we had entered.

I saw no Germans.

I waited with my party until the green rocket went up and until the assualting party had withdrawn.

I then collected my posts and withdrew.

No. 165292. Sgt. HOWELL. N.S.Y. states :-

I am the Scout Sergt. who accoipanied Lt. RICE with B.Raiding party.

We followed up the barrage and came on a line of wire under which the R.Es. started to place the torpedo. Whilst doing this a bursting shell showed us that the main line of wire was 20 yds to 30 yds beyond the line of wire we had reached. Lt. RICE therefore told the R.Es. to keep the torpedo and told us to cut this first line with wirecutters, which we did. This line of wire was old and rusty about 3 feet high and more or less hidden by high thistles.

After cutting the gap I followed Lt. RICE to the main line of wire. Here Lt. RICE found a gap already made, through which he went. On returning he shouted "All clear, I have cut the wire".

We then went back to fetch the others and when half-way between the two lines of wire Lt. RICE spotted two Germans climbing out of the trench immediately inside the first line of wire. Lt. RICE shot one and clubbed the other with his revolver.

Lt. HELME then came up and Lt. RICE said to him its "all clear".

Rifle fire was all this time coming from our right.

The assualting party then came through the gap in the 1st. line, turned to the right up the trench to go for the of wire and instead of going across to the gap in the 2nd. line
Germans

Germans firing at them from that direction. Lts. HELME & RICE accompanied this party at the same time as Lt. RICE shot the German. I threw three bombs down a dug-out, at the other end of the left hand trench, where I heard groans. I also found 4 dead Germans killed by shell fire. I took identifications off them. Close to this trench was an automatic rifle firing from a bomb-proof shelter.

I heard Lt. RICE say he had broken his arm, so I climbed out of the trench and shortly after the green rocket went up and I withdrew with the others.

The above was taken down by me.

Sd. W.T.Miles, Captain,
Commanding "JOCK".

26/6/17.

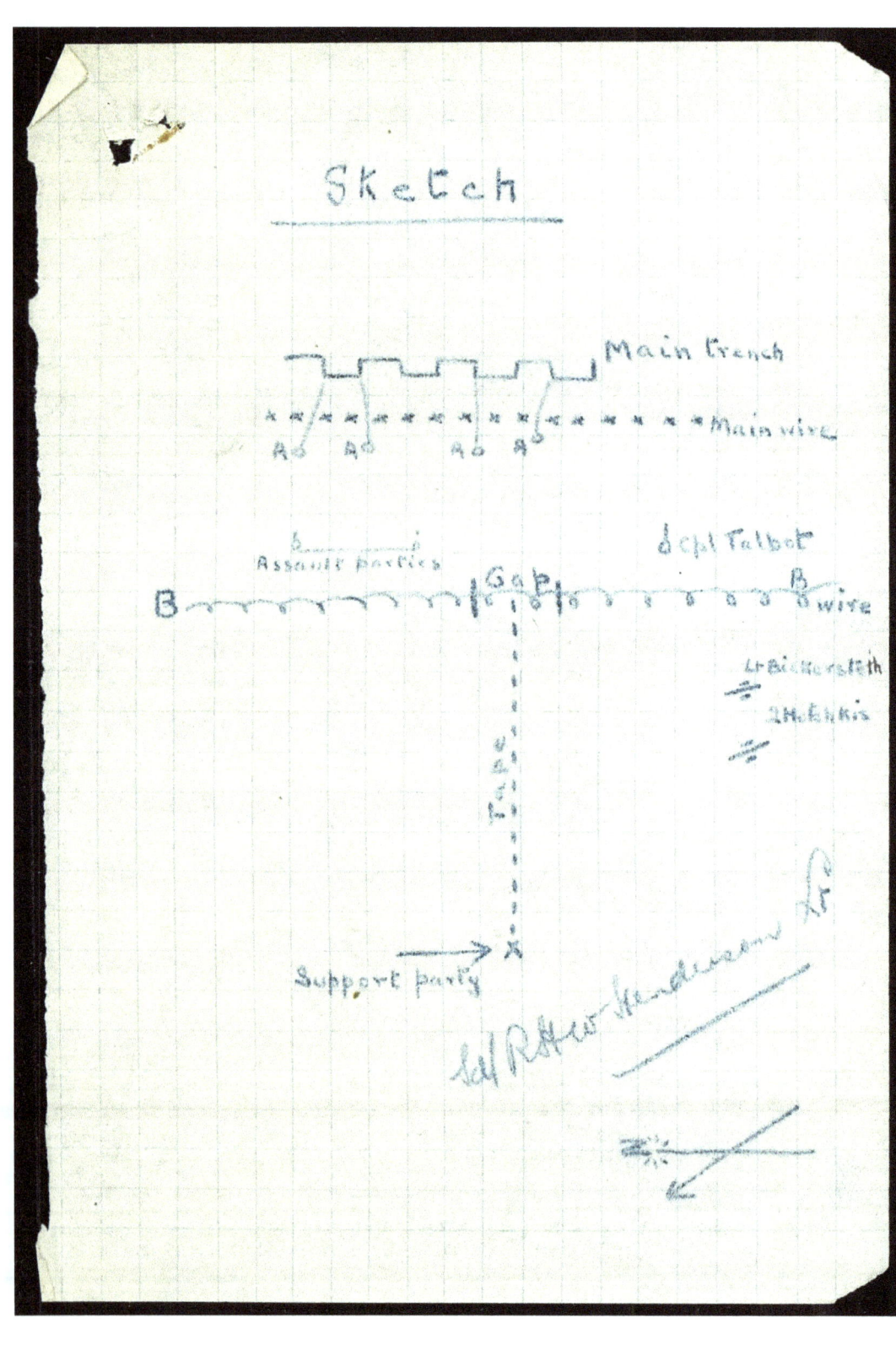

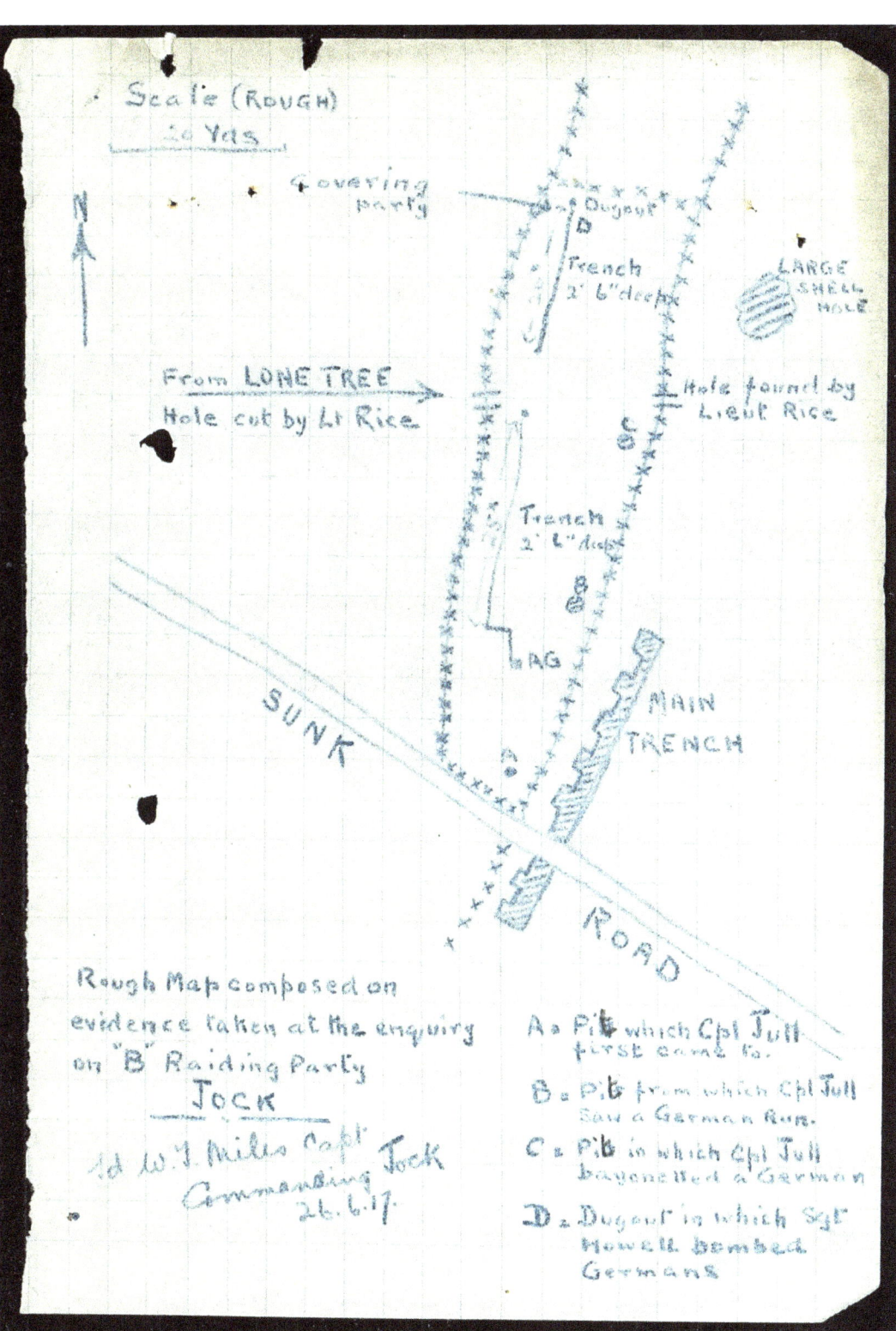

ORIGINAL

Vol 34

Army Form C. 2118.

Instructions regarding War Diaries and Intelligence Summaries are contained in F. S. Regs. Part II. and the Staff Manual respectively. Title pages will be prepared in manuscript.

THE 1OYAL DRAGOONS WAR DIARY or INTELLIGENCE SUMMARY. VOLUME XXXIV

JULY 1917.

(Erase heading not required.)

Place	Date	Hour	Summary of Events and Information	Remarks and references to Appendices
BURE.	1st		Major T.S. ARMY went to a Senior Officers' Course at Fourth Army School. Regiment was preparing to move to a new area.	
	2nd		Cleaned up Gen. Squadrons held marching Order Inspections.	
BURE - SUZANNE	3rd		Regiment marched at 8.30.am. to SUZANNE.	
SUZANNE - MERICOURT	4th		Regiment marched at 7.45.am to MERICOURT.	
MERICOURT-AMPLIER S.A.	5th		Regiment marched at 8.30.am to AMPLIER.	
AMPLIER - RIE BRUNETTE	6th		Regiment marched at 9.30.am. to REBREUVIETTE.	
REBREUVIETTE - LAPUGNOY	7th		Regiment marched at 10.30.am. to LAPUGNOY. This meant visiting the coal mine country which we had vacated in November 1915.	
LAPUGNOY	7-16		Remained at LAPUGNOY. Training chiefly consisted grazing remounts and Musketry on the Range belonging to the 6th Division Mining Companies.	
	10th		Dismounted Party rejoined by train from COUCHELLES Area. This party had been working in "D" Sector. Two Sergeants were wounded - Sergts. PHILCOX and CUBITH.	
HAVERSKERQUE.	16th		Marched from LAPUGNOY at 5.30.am. Arrived HAVERSKERQUE about 9 a.m. Distance about 12 miles. We have now got back to the Area of our first rest billets after the First Battle of YPRES. Brigade Headqrs. are actually at LES LAURIERS where General Davis C.V.M. established his HQrs in 1914. There is little to show that the war has been going on for nearly three years. If anything the people are better off than they were then. The FORET de NIEPPE has been taken over by the Government and is out of bounds to all troops.	
			Regimental Headqtrs. in HAVERSKERQUE. The three Squadrons in billets towards LA MOTTE BAUDET.	
	19th		Inspection of A.I. Section by the Brigadier.	
	21st		Inspection of regiment in Marching Order by the Brigadier G.O.C.	
	22nd		Great aerial activity on the part of the enemy who was continually coming over our lines area. 2/Lieut. D.T. WILLOW proceeded for range duties at ROMBLY.	
	23rd		Lieut. R.E.F. deTRAFFORD and 7 N.C.Os. commence jr. the Course of Pioneering.	
	24th		Major A.A.MARKINSON,D.S.J. proceeded to GAILLES, as commandant of Hotchkiss Rifle School. 2 Hotchkiss Rifle Detachments per Squadron together with one Officer and one N.C.O. per Squad. on proceeded for first Course.	
	26th		Whole Regiment marched to First Army Musketry School near ROMBLY and spent the day Shooting on the Range.	

HAVERSKERQUE

ORIGINAL

Army Form C. 2118.

THE ROYAL DRAGOONS WAR DIARY JULY 1917.
INTELLIGENCE SUMMARY. VOLUME XXXIV
(Erase heading not required.)

Place	Date	Hour	Summary of Events and Information	Remarks and references to Appendices
HAVERSKERQUE	27th		3 Officers from Kings Dragoon Guards joined the Regiment from the Base - T/2nd.Lieuts. E.H. RICHARDSON, A. DREW, and J. DREW.	
	29th		Party of Hotchkiss Gunners left for 2nd. Line Course at CAMIERS. 2/Lieut. E.St.G.SIDALL, Sergt. ELLIOTT, Sergt.MACE and Cpl. CLARKE proceeded to St.POL for a Course of Bayonet fighting and Physical Training.	
	28th		1st. Party of Hotchkiss Gunners returned on 29th. from CAMIERS less Lt. CUBITT and Sergt. HEWETT who were retained as Instructors. The scores obtained by the Regiment during this course were a hundred marks higher than those obtained by any other unit in the Division.	
	30th			
	31st		Fifth and Second Army attacked N. and E. of YPRES at 3.50. am. The attack appears to have gone well in the North but not so well in the wooded ground near HOOGE. Sergt. CRESWELL, Sergt. NORMAN and L.Cpl. REID went to Cavalry Corps Gas School on a two days' course. A recent order published states that no further reinforcements for Cavalry will be supplied until all dismounted men with Regiments are absorbed. At present we have about 70.	

STRENGTH OF REGIMENT

JULY 1st. 1917.   Men.....607.   Horses.....579.

JULY 31st. 1917. Men.....607.   Horses.....584.

Hobson Fitzfield
Capt. & Adjt.,
The Royal Dragoons.

ORIGINAL

Army Form C. 2118.

THE ROYAL DRAGOONS. WAR DIARY JULY 1917.

INTELLIGENCE-SUMMARY. VOLUME XXXIV

or

(Erase heading not required.)

Place	Date	Hour	Summary of Events and Information	Remarks and references to Appendices
			(APPENDIX I.)	
			APPENDIX I. - CASUALTIES.	
D.Secb.	5th		1624 Sergt. Philcox R. Wounded 5/7/17.	
	"		4759 L/" Cubitt A.E. " 5/7/17.	
			APPENDIX II. - HONOURS AND AWARDS.	
			2nd. Lieut. J.S.Dunville Awarded 'Victoria Cross' (Lon.Gaz:Supp: d/- 2/8/17)	
			6396 Cpl. Jull E. Awarded 'Military Medal' 2/7/17.	
			APPENDIX III. - REINFORCEMENTS.	
	2nd		7 Other Ranks joined from British Cavalry Entrenching Battn 2/7/17.	
	13th		1 " " " " " " Base 13/7/17.	
	14th		8 " " " " " " " 19/7/17.	
	24th		Temp.2/Lieut. B.H.Richardson) Reposted from 1st. Kings Dragoon Guards	
	"		" " A.Drew.) 12/7/17.	
	"		" " J.Drew.) Joined Regiment 24/7/17.	
	17th		" " J.Massy-Lynch Reposted from 3rd. Dragoon Guards 12/7/17.	
			Joined Regiment 17/7/17.	

Ikbilson Tifkuall

Capt. & Adjt.,

The Royal Dragoons.

Army Form C. 2118.

THE ROYAL DRAGOONS

WAR DIARY
or
INTELLIGENCE=SUMMARY.

(Erase heading not required.)

AUGUST 1917.   VOLUME XXXV

(Sheet I.)

Place	Date	Hour	Summary of Events and Information	Remarks and references to Appendices
HAVERSKERQUE.	1-5		Continual rain. Operation round YPRES were consequently much handicapped. No Training was possible. S.Q.M.S. B.WISCHHUSEN to be act.S.S.M. in "C" Sqdn. vice NEWTON.	
	3rd		Second party returned from Hotchkiss Course at CAMIERS. Major H.A.TOMKINSON, D.S.O. and Lt.Hon.W.H.CUBITT returned with this party.	
	6th		Dismounted Party - Lieut. D.H.WATSON, 2/Lt. W.O.STEWART and 52 Other Ranks proceeded to work under Fifth Army in the vicinity of BRANDHOEK.	
	7th		Divisional Rifle Meeting at LINGHEM. Sniping and Observation Competition was won by Cpls. AMOR and ELDRIDGE.	
	10th		Lieut. P.R.D.COOKE and Sergt.TALBOT proceeded to LINGHEM for a week's course in Sniping. At 2.30.am. a hostile air raid took place in our vicinity lasting about 30 minutes. A number of bombs were dropped near ISBERGES and some horses of the 2nd Life Guards were killed. No bombs were dropped near HAVERSKERQUE but the inhabitants mostly took cover in the cellars.	
	11th		Aeroplane Scheme near RELY. Weather is improving slightly but rain is still frequent and the country is absolutely waterlogged. This is largely due to the fact that all the field drains have become blocked. Lieut. P.R.D.COOKE and Sergt. TALBOT returned from Sniping Course at LINGHEM in which course they came out top of the Division.	
	12th		2/Lieut. D.P.LITHGOW and Cpl. ELDRIDGE returned from Sniping School at LINGHEM, where they had been acting as Instructors. Sergt.BUTLER proceeded on Course of Sniping at First Army School. 1 Sergt. and 10 men proceeded to ECKINGHEM to fetch remounts.	
	14th 16th 18th 19th		Remounts arrived. - 10 were allotted to the Regiment. 2/Lieut. W.J.MASSY-LYNCH joined the Regiment and was posted to "C" Sqdn. 2/Lieut. E.St.G.STEDALL, Sgts. MACE and ELLIOTT, and Cpl. CLARKE returned from Course at Bayonet & Physical Training School, St.POL. Sgt. PULLEN and Sgt. HOINVILLE to Musketry Course at First Army School for 12 days. Major W.T.HODGSON appointed G.S.O.I. 5th. Cav.Divn. and to be temp. Lieut-Colonel, August 2nd. 1917.	
	24th 25th		Brigade Horse Show. Divisional Horse Show.	

Army Form C. 2118.

WAR DIARY
or
INTELLIGENCE SUMMARY

THE ROYAL DRAGOONS.

AUGUST 1917.

VOLUME XXXV

(Sheet II).

Place	Date	Hour	Summary of Events and Information	Remarks and references to Appendices
HAVERSKERQUE	27*		L.Cpl. GUY ('A'Sqdn.) to AIRE on Corps Gas Course. 2/Lieut. D.P.LITHGOW to be Lieutenant 5/8/17. 2/Lieut. J.C.CARR_ELLISON rejoined from actin gas A.D.C. at Brigade Headquarters.	
	26*		Relief of Dismounted Party. Lieut. D.H.WATSON, 2/Lieut. W.O.STEWART and 51 Other Ranks were relieved by Lieut. P.R.D.COOKE and 51 Other Ranks.	
	29*		L.C. GUY returned from course at Corps Gas School.	
	28*		The Divisional Gas Officer gave a lecture to the Regiment concerning the new German Gas.	

STRENGTH OF REGIMENT

August 1st. ...... Men 606 .... Horses 584.
August 31st. ...... Men 612 .... Horses 580

C O Callaghan
Lieut., & a/Adjt.,
The Royal Dragoons.

Army Form C. 2118.

Duplicate

Vol 35

THE ROYAL DRAGOONS. WAR DIARY AUGUST 1917.
INTELLIGENCE SUMMARY. VOLUME XXXV

(Erase heading not required.)

(Sheet III.) Summary of Events and Information

Appendix I. - CASUALTIES.

```
15124 Pte. Anderson   J.   wounded 22/8/17.
 7769 Sgt. Mitchell   W.   killed in action 31/8/17.
 8254 Pte. Struthers  J.   wounded 31/8/17. (Slight, at duty)
 1286  "   Hayden     W.   wounded 31/8/17. (Slight, at duty).
```

Appendix II - HONOURS & REWARDS.

6396 Cpl. Jull   E.   Awarded Military Medal 2/7/17.

Appendix III - REINFORCEMENTS.

```
T/2.Lt. W.J.Massy-Lynch  reposted from 3rd. Dragoon Gds. 18/8/17.
1 Other Ranks            Received from Base 7/8/17.
7   "    "               Retransferred from 7th. D.Gds. 7/8/17.
```

Lieut. & a/Adjt.,
The Royal Dragoons.

DUPLICATE

SHEET 1

THE ROYAL DRAGOONS

September 1917. WAR DIARY VOLUME XXXVI
or
INTELLIGENCE SUMMARY

Army Form C. 2118.

Instructions regarding War Diaries and Intelligence Summaries are contained in F. S. Regs., Part II. and the Staff Manual respectively. Title pages will be prepared in manuscript.

(Erase heading not required.)

Place	Date	Hour	Summary of Events and Information	Remarks and references to Appendices
HAVERSKERQUE	Sept. 1		Cavalry Corps Horse Show.	
	3.		Regimental Scheme. Cast Horse Parade by D.R., Cav. Corps.	
	4-8.		Individual training and carried out on stubbles and practice for Regimental Sports	
	9.		Regimental Sports - The Corps Commander presented the prizes.	
	11.		Brigade Scheme in the area BLARINGHEM - SERCUS.	
	13.		Regimental Scheme. "B" and "C" Sqdns. made a dismounted attack on LABELLE HOTESSE defended by "A" Sqdn.	
	15.		Captain J.C. SCLATER BOOTH seconded for duty with Cavalry Corps Signals.	
	17.		Regimental Scheme. Advance Guard and Intercommunication, WALLON CAPPEL - HAZEBROUCK.	
	19.		Regimental Scheme. Dismounted attack by "A" and "C" Sqdns. on LES AMUSOIRES (SE. of St. VENANT) held by "B" Sqdn. 10 other ranks to Base for transfer to Infantry.	
	21.		Brigade Scheme. Same as scheme on 17th., but advancing over area allotted to N.S.Y.	
	24.		Inspection of Regiment in tactical exercise by Major-General VAUGHAN. 2/Lieuts. DREW A., DREW J., RICHARDSON B.H. reposted to 1st. K.D.Gds. 2/Lieut. MASSEY-LYNCH to 3rd. D.Gds.	
	30.		Lieut. P.R. DAVIES-COOKE and dismounted party rejoined Regiment from I ANZAC CORPS.	
			The whole of this month was devoted to Individual training in Riding, Swordsmanship, Despatch Riders etc. with an average of 2 Regimental Schemes a week. Full use being made of the short time the country is possible for mounted work.	

8th. October 1917.

E.C. Callaghan
for Lieut-Colonel,
Commanding The Royal Dragoons.

DUPLICATE

Army Form C. 2118.

Sh. II.

THE ROYAL DRAGOONS. WAR DIARY VOL. XXXVI. September 1917.
INTELLIGENCE SUMMARY.
(Erase heading not required.)

Instructions regarding War Diaries and Intelligence Summaries are contained in F. S. Regs., Part II. and the Staff Manual respectively. Title pages will be prepared in manuscript.

Place	Date	Hour	Summary of Events and Information	Remarks and references to Appendices
			Strength of Regiment :—	
			Offrs. O.R. Horses.	
			September 1st. 33 567 580	
			September 30th. 31 555 571	
			C. O. Allfrey	
			Lieut-Colonel,	
			Commanding The Royal Dragoons.	

DUPLICATE

Army Form C. 2118.

Sheet III

THE ROYAL DRAGOONS. WAR DIARY VOLUME XXXVI. September 1917.
or
INTELLIGENCE SUMMARY.

(Erase heading not required.)

APPENDIX I

HONOURS AND AWARDS.

N I L.

APPENDIX II

CASUALTIES DURING MONTH.

7789 Sergt. MITCHELL W. Killed 31/8/17. (At duty)
9254 Pte. STRUTHERS J. Wounded " "
1286 " HAYDEN W. " 26/9/17 "
9120 " MOTION R. " " "

APPENDIX III.

REINFORCEMENTS RECEIVED DURING MONTH.

Date.	Officers.	O.R.	Horses.
7/9/17	—	1	From Base.
22/9/17	—	3	"
29/9/17	—	1	"

8th. October 1917.

C O'Callaghan
Lieut. & a/Adjt.,
The Royal Dragoons.

DUPLICATE

Army Form C. 2118.
October 1917

THE ROYAL DRAGOONS.
WAR DIARY VOLUME XXVII.
or
INTELLIGENCE SUMMARY.— 4th. November 1917.

Sheet I.

(Erase heading not required.)

Place	Date	Hour	Summary of Events and Information	Remarks and references to Appendices
HAVERSKERQUE.	1.		L/Cpl.McLEAN to Hotchkiss Course at LE TOUQUET. Lieut.S.C.DUMBRECK to Stokes' Mortar Course at XI Corps Sch. MERVILLE. Lieut.J.R.WINGFIELD.DIGBY to Bombing Course at XI Corps Sch., MERVILLE.	
	2.		Lieut.R.F.HEYWORTH-SAVAGE conducted a party of 30 men to the Base - 12 to be posted to Infantry and 18 to be retained as reinforcements.	
	3.		Regimental Scheme. Dismounted attack on LES AMUSOIRES from the S.E.	
	4.		R.Q.M.S. YOUNG to ROUEN pending discharge on completion of 22 years.	
	5.		Brigade Scheme. The Regiment acting as enemy against N.S.Y. and 3rd.D.Gds, defending the cabal.	
	6.		Capt.F.W.WILSON-FITZGERALD, M.C. to Cav.Corps for advanced course.	
	7.		Regiment warned tombe ready to move at short notice on 9th.	
	8.		C.O. inspects Squadrons in Swordsmanship.	
	9.		Move cancelled. Capt.F.W.WILSON-FITZGERALD, M.C. appointed Staff Captain 8th Cav. /Bde.	
	10.		Lieut.C.T.O'CALLAGHAN appointed Adjutant with effect from 12th.September.	
	12.		Lieut.WILLIAMS WYNN rejoined Regiment from Base.	
	15.		2/Lieut.W.O.STEWART proceeded on 5 days course of Stokes Mortars at XI Corps Sch. /MERVILLE.	
	16.		Lieut.R.H.W.HENDERSON to Hotchkiss School, LE TOUQUET.	
	17.		Lieut.C.T.O'CALLAGHAN granted acting rank of Captain whilst holding appointment of Adjutant. Lieut. W.R.LINES to be Hon. Captain 25th.August 1917.	
EPS.	19.		The Regiment marched to EPS, S.W. of FERNES.	
BOUBERS.	22.		The Regiment marched to BOUBERS-SUR-CANCHE.	
BERNEUIL.	23.		The Regiment marched to BERNEUIL.	
LONG.	24.		The Regiment marched to permanent area at LONG.	
	25.		Lieut.A.R.COOPER, Lieut.A.S.CASEY, 2/Lieut.A.O.COOK and 2/Lieut.F.W.RHODES joined Regiment from Base.	
	26.		"B" Sqdn. Moved out of LONG and went to billets in VAUCHELLES-les-DOMART and MOUFLERS.	
	27.		The Royals dismtd. detach. consisting of Capt.H.E.F. de TRAFFORD 1/c 6th.Cav.Bde. Coy. Lieut.H.SMITH, Lieut.D'A.F.HARRIS & 99 O.R. proceeded by lorry to DOINGT for work on Divisional Camp and Stables in that area.	
	27-30.		Work was entirely devoted to consolidation of area.	

C.T. O'Callaghan
Capt.

DUPLICATE

Army Form C. 2118.

THE ROYAL DRAGOONS.
WAR DIARY VOLUME XXVII.

Sheet II. **INTELLIGENCE SUMMARY.** 4th. November 1917.

(Erase heading not required.)

Summary of Events and Information

	Off.	O.R.
Strength of Regiment Oct. 1st.	29	571.
" " " Oct. 31st.	33	529.

APPENDIX I.

N I L.

APPENDIX II.

N I L.

APPENDIX III.

Lieut. W. WILLIAMS WYNN joined from Base 12/10/17.
Lieut. A. R. COOPER ⎫
Lieut. A. S. CASEY   ⎬ joined from Base 25/10/17.
2/Lieut. A. O. COOK ⎪
2/Lieut. F. W. RHODES⎭
1 other rank from Hospital 5/10/17.
1 " " " " 23/10/17.
1 " " " Military Prison, ROUEN 23/10/17.

4/11/17.

CW Whatha
Capt. & Adjt.,
The Royal Dragoons.

DUPLICATE

Sheet I.

Army Form C. 2118.

THE ROYAL DRAGOONS.

WAR DIARY
or
INTELLIGENCE SUMMARY   VOLUME XXXVIII.
(Erase heading not required.)   December 7th. 1917.

Place	Date	Hour	Summary of Events and Information	Remarks and references to Appendices
	Nov.			
LONG.	3.		Lieut. R.H.W. HENDERSON proceeded to DAOURS as Adjutant of 3rd. Cav. Divnl. School.	
"	4.		Major H.A. TOMKINSON, D.S.O. proceeded to DAOURS as Commandant of 3rd. Cav. Div. Sch.	
"	6.		Lieut. H. HARRISON joined Regiment from 34th. Division. 2/Lieut. P.L. WILSON proceeded to P. & B.T. School, St. POL.	
"	7.		Team of 8 Officers and 8 N.C.Os. shot against PONT REMY Musketry School.	
"	8.		Regimental Staff Ride.	
"	9.		Inspection of horses by G.O.C. 3rd. Cavalry Division.	
"	12.		Major H.A. TOMKINSON, D.S.O. and Lieut. R.H.W. HENDERSON proceeded to PERONNE to take over charge of Dismounted Battalion.	
"	14.		Lieut. H. SMITH and 44 other ranks rejoined from BUIRE.	
"	15.		Major H.A. TOMKINSON, D.S.O., Capt. Hon. F. de TRAFFORD, Lieut. R.H.W. HENDERSON, Lieut. D'A.F.H. HARRIS and 54 other ranks rejoined from BUIRE.	
"	17.		The Regiment marched to CONTAY.	
CONTAY	18.		Night march to SUZANNE; arrived there at 10.30pm. 2/Lieut. F.W. RHODES proceeded to Hotchkiss School, LE TOUQUET.	
SUZANNE	19.		2/Lieut. R.C.G. JOY joined Regiment and was posted to "C" Sqdn. Ordered to 'stand to' at short notice and had to saddle-up to turn out to water.	
"	20.		Still 'standing-to'. Lieut. C.B. SCOTT, attd. Cav. Corps died of wounds and was buried at FINS. / Continued on another sheet.	

DUPLICATE

Army Form C. 2118.

Sheet II.

WAR DIARY
or
INTELLIGENCE SUMMARY.
(Erase heading not required.)

Instructions regarding War Diaries and Intelligence Summaries are contained in F. S. Regs., Part II. and the Staff Manual respectively. Title pages will be prepared in manuscript.

Place	Date	Hour	Summary of Events and Information	Remarks and references to Appendices
SUZANNE.	Nov. 23		Went back to billets at WARGNIES (HQrs). NAOURS ("A" & "C"). HAVERNAS ("B"). Left SUZANNE 7.45am., arrived in billets 5.30pm.	
WARGNIES	24		About mid-day ordered to 'stand-to' at short notice ready to move back to BRAY area	
"	25		Ordered to 'stand-down' again about 5.0pm.	
"	26		Lieut.E.St.G.STEDALL admitted to Hospital.	
"	27		Information received that the Dismounted Bde. would occupy the line in a few days. Lieut.R.H.W.HENDERSON went to Divisional School as Adjutant, taking advance party with him.	
"	28		Major H.A.TOMKINSON, D.S.O. went to Divisional School.	
"	29		Information received that the Dismounted Party would proceed on 1st. December. Lieut.R.F.HEYWORTH-SAVAGE went on a Power Buzzer Course to Cav.Corps Signal Sch. at YZEUX. Capt.A.NEILSON, R.A.M.C. left Regiment and Capt. A.J.LYONS, R.A.M.C. joined.	
"	30.		Lieut.Col.F.W.WORMALD, D.S.O., Capt. H.M.P.HEWETT, Capt. E.W.T.MILES and Capt. A.J. LYONS, R.A.M.C. left by car as 6.0am. as advance party to the trenches in the HARGICOURT Sector. Major T.S.IRWIN took over Command of the Regiment. 11.30am. - Orders received to 'stand-to' at 1 hour's notice to move in Cap Organ- isation also to have Dismounted Party ready to move if required. 11.30pm. - The Colonel and Capt. H.M.P.HEWETT returned in Motor Lorry unexpectedly also Lieut. R.F. HEYWORTH-SAVAGE from the Signalling School.	

STRENGTH.
1st. November — 33 officers — 529 other ranks.
30th. November — 35 " — 530 "

[signature] Lieut. & a/Adjt.
The Royal Dragoons.

7/12/17.

DUPLICATE

Army Form C. 2118.

Sheet III.

WAR DIARY
or
INTELLIGENCE SUMMARY
(Erase heading not required.)

Instructions regarding War Diaries and Intelligence Summaries are contained in F. S. Regs., Part II. and the Staff Manual respectively. Title pages will be prepared in manuscript.

Place	Date	Hour	Summary of Events and Information	Remarks and references to Appendices
			APPENDIX I.- Casualties.	
			Lieut.C.B.SCOTT, Attd.Cav.Corps Died of Wounds 20/11/17.	
			APPENDIX II.- Honours & Rewards.	
			N I L.	
			APPENDIX III.- Reinforcements received.	
			2/Lieut. H.HARRISON joined from Northumberland Hussars 6/11/17.	
			Capt. A.NEILSON, R.A.M.C. attached to Regt. 14/11/17.	
			2/Lieut. R.C.G.JOY joined from Base 19/11/17.	
			Capt. A.J.LYONS, R.A.M.C. attached to Regt. 29/11/17.	
			5 other ranks from Base 3/11/17.	
			2 " " " 12/11/17.	
			1 " " " 3rd. Cav.Div.HQrs. 12/11/17.	
			1 " " " 21st.Divnl.HQrs. 30/11/17.	
7/12/17.			H. Honeybun Sewell Lieut. & a./Adjt., The Royal Dragoons.	

Duplicate

Royal Dragoons Vol 39

Army Form C. 2118.

WAR DIARY
or
INTELLIGENCE SUMMARY.

(Erase heading not required.)

VOLUME XXXIX.

Instructions regarding War Diaries and Intelligence Summaries are contained in F.S. Regs., Part II. and the Staff Manual respectively. Title Pages will be prepared in manuscript.

Place	Date 1917 Dec	Hour	Summary of Events and Information	Remarks and references to Appendices
In the Field	1		At 12.15 a.m. orders were received for the Dismounted Party to move off at 5.30 a.m. ride to TALMAS and embus for the trenches in the neighbourhood of EPEHY where the Germans had made an attack. Col. Wormald was in command of 6th. Cav. Bde. Battalion.	
	2		The Regiment less trench party moved billets from WARLUS area to ALLONVILLE area. H.Q. and "B" Sqdn in ALLONVILLE, "A" Sqdn. in HAINNEVILLE, and "A" Sqdn. in CARDONNETTE. Lieut. W.R.Birch joined from Base and posted to "B" Sqdn.	
	3		5 reinforcements joined from Base with 9 chargers and 7 remounts. 150 horses required to parade for selection of horses for EGYPT.	
	4		81 horses selected by selection committee for EGYPT. (27 per Sqdn.)	
	5		2 reinforcements (shoeing Smiths) joined from Base.	
	6		2/Lieut. F.W. Rhodes rejoined from Hotchkiss School.	
	7		Lieuts. W.W. Wynn, A.R. Cooper and D.P. Lithgow went to 1st. Course at Dismtd. School	
	10		81 horses selected for EGYPT entrained at LONGUEAU at 7.30 p.m. under Lieut. P.R. Davies Cooke. The party was to conduct them to MARSEILLES, and return. Major T.S. Irwin had a staff ride of 6 Officers at 9.0 a.m.	
	11		Col. Wormald, Maj. Hodgson, M.C., Bt.Major Cosens and Capt. Miles mentioned in despatches. G.O.C., inspected Regtl. billets.	
	12		Lieut. Ho. W.H. Cubitt proceeded to Cav. Corps Equitation School.	
	14		Lieut. S.C. Dumbreck admitted to Hospital from trenches.	
	15		Capt. C.T. O'Callaghan proceeded to Dismtd. Bde. to relieve Capt. H.M.F. Hewett.	C.O. Delafosse
	16		Major H.A. Tomkinson, D.S.O., granted acting rank of Lieut.-Col. whilst Cmdt. Regt., and Capt. R.H. Henderson granted acting rank of Capt. whilst	

Army Form C. 2118.

WAR DIARY
or
INTELLIGENCE=SUMMARY.
(Erase heading not required.)

Place	Date	Hour	Summary of Events and Information	Remarks and references to Appendices
Lucheux	1917 Dec 16		Adjutant of Divisional School. 2/Lieut. H.Harrison proceeded to Dismtd. Bde. to relieve Lieut. S.C.Dumbreck evacuated sick. Snowed heavily all day.	
	18		Many roads impassable owing to snow drifts. Ration wagons had to move across country.	
	19		Lieut. P.R.D.Cooke rejoined from MARSEILLES. Sgt. Shackell proceeded to 3rd Echelon to relieve Q.M.S.Ratcliffe sick to England. 2/Lieuts. D. A.F.H.Harris, L.St. J.Stedall, and C.G.H.Hilton Greene to be Lieuts.	
	20		2/Lieut. W.O.Stewart proceeded to 24th. Divnl. Tramways.	
	21		The Regiment moved to new area.- HQ at VILLERS SOUS AILLY, "A" Sqdn. at BRUCAMPS "B" Sqdn. at VAUCHELLES and MOUFLERS, and "C" Sqdn. at ERGNIES. Difficult march due to snow drifts and shortage of men.	
	22		Lieut. P.R.D.Cooke, Capt. Turner, and Lieuts. Digby and Smith proceeded to join Dismtd. Bde.	
	23		Col. Wormald, having handed over command to Col. Ing, N.S.Y., rejoined Regt.also Capts. Miles, O'Callaghan and Lyons, and Lieut. Watson. Lieuts. Harris and Browne proceeded to jointhe Dismtd. Bde.,	
	25		Major. T.S.Irwin ceased to command Regiment.	
	26		Lieut. Wynn, Cooper and son Lithgow rejoined from Divnl. School.	
	27		Lieuts. Casy and Parr, M.C., proceeded to jointhe Dismtd. Bde.,	
			Lieut. Stedall rejoined from Hospital.	
	29		Lieut. J.G.G.Hilson proceeded to join the Dismtd. Bde., to relieve Lt.Harrison.	C D Callaghan Capt & Adjt
	31		Lieut. S.C.Dumbreck struck off, having been evacuated to England. Lieut.	The Reg^t. a g----

Duplicate

Army Form C. 2118.

WAR DIARY
or
INTELLIGENCE SUMMARY.

(Erase heading not required.)

Instructions regarding War Diaries and Intelligence Summaries are contained in F. S. Regs., Part II. and the Staff Manual respectively. Title pages will be prepared in manuscript.

Place	Date	Hour	Summary of Events and Information	Remarks and references to Appendices
Lucheux	1917 Decr		R.F. Heyworth Savage to Power Buzzer Course at YZEUX. Lieuts. Boswall and Lithgow to Dismtd. Bde.	
			NOTE:— The Diary of the Royals Company in the trenches has not been entered but will be made up on relief of Dismtd. Bde. The weather has been very severe since the first week of the month and caused difficulties in rations and reliefs. All time has been devoted to improvement and consolidation of the new area.	
			Officers. Other ranks. Strength of Regiment 1st. Decr. 1917. 35 530 " " " 31st. Decr. 1917. 35 538	

C.D. Clayton
Captain
The Royal Dragoons

Army Form C. 2118.

WAR DIARY
or
INTELLIGENCE SUMMARY.
(Erase heading not required.)

Place	Date	Hour	Summary of Events and Information	Remarks and references to Appendices
			APPENDIX I.	
			NIL.	
			APPENDIX II.	
			Lieut-Col. F.W. Wormald, D.S.O., Major W.T. Hodgson, M.C., } Mentioned in despatches. Bt. Major G.P.L. Cosens, Capt. E.W.T. Miles,	
			APPENDIX III.	
			Lieut. W.R. Birch joined from Base, 2/12/17. 5 other ranks joined from Base, 3/12/17. 2 " " " " " 5/12/17. 11 " " " " " 24/12/17. 2 " " " " " 30/12/17.	

C. F. O'Callaghan
Capt. and Adjt.,
The Royal Dragoons.

DUPLICATE'

Instructions regarding War Diaries and Intelligence Summaries are contained in F. S. Regs., Part II. and the Staff Manual respectively. Title pages will be prepared in manuscript.

1 Royal Dragoons Vol 40

WAR DIARY
or
INTELLIGENCE SUMMARY

(Erase heading not required.)

Place	Date	Hour	Summary of Events and Information	Remarks and references to Appendices
In the Field.	1918. Jany. 1		Lieut. Harrison rejoined from Dis. Bde.,	
	2		Lieut. W.R.Birch to 24th. Divnl. Tramways. Capt. Johnston A.V.C. to 8th. Bde R.H.A.	
	5		40 riding horses joined from Base. 20 other ranks proceeded to Tank Corps. Extract from New Year Honours' Gazette:- Capt. R.Houstoun to be Bt. Major. Bt. Major (temp. Lt-Col.) G.P.L.Cosens to be companion of D.S.O., 2/Lieut. W.O.Stewart seconded for service with Tank Corps.	
	7		Major Irwin, Capt. Lines and Lts. Savage and Joy to Dis. Bde., Lieuts. Parr, Stedall, and Wilson to Divisional School.	
	8		Lt-Col. Wormald to Paris for 7 days leave.	
	9		Lt. A.O.Cook to Dis. Bde., Extract from New Year Honours' List:- Awarded Meritorious Service Medal:- R.S.M. J.Oxford.	
	10		Capt. Turner, Lts. P.R.D.Cooke, Digby and Smith rejoined from Dis. Bde. S.S.M. Jeffrey granted a commission in the Regiment dated 5/1/18. After nearly a month's continuous and hard frost, thaw set in accompanied by heavy rainfall. Capt. Miles proceeded on leave to the United Kingdom.	
	11		Lt. Carr Ellison from Dis. Bde. to undergo a 6 weeks signalling course at YZEUX Sgts. Elliott and Michael wounded. Sgt. Talbot accidentally wounded.	
	12		Capt. Swire to Regimental duty from 35th. Sqdn. R.F.C. Capt. Swire to Cav. Corps as 'G' learner.	
	14		Lieut. Harris from Dis. Bde., Lt. Casey to Hotchkiss School, Le Touquet.	
	15		Sgts. Elliott, Michael, and Talbot reported wounded.	

Capt. and Adjt.,
The Royal Dragoons.

WAR DIARY
or
INTELLIGENCE SUMMARY

(Erase heading not required.)

Army Form C. 2118.

Place	Date 1918.	Hour	Summary of Events and Information	Remarks and references to Appendices
In the Field.	Jany. 16		Return of 5 Officers and 120 O.R. from Dis. Bde. to form 3rd. Cav. Div. Pioneer Regt., remainder of Regiment left up to form 3rd. Cav. Div. Pioneer Regt., under the Command of Major Irwin.	
	16/23		was devoted to cleaning, and re-equipping Trench party, fitting of saddlery and marching order parades, preparatory to the month's training.	
	23		Lt. Boswall rejoined from Dis. Divs., Capt. Johnston rejoined from 4th. Bde. R.H.A. Lieut. Cubitt rejoined from Equitation School. Lt-Col. Wormald gave a lecture on the use of the Tactical sheet to Officers of the Brigade.	
	24		68 O.R. proceeded by lorry from L'ETOILE to VIGNACOURT to relieve a similar number from the Pioneer Regiment. Lt. Cooper remains up as Adjt.,	
	25		Major Irwin and 67 O.R. rejoined from Pioneer Regt. 3 O.R. joined from Base.	
	26		Interpreter Pinto proceeded to join 4th. Cav. Div.	
	27		Lt. Casey rejoined from Hotchkiss School. Capt. Turner to Gas School.	
	28		The Regiment marched from VILLERS SOUS AILLY to AILLY SUR SOMME area.	
	29		The Regiment marched from AILLY SURS OMME to HARBONNIERES.	
	30		The Regiment marched from HARBONNIERES to final area vacated by 8th. Hussars 5th. Div. at TERTRY (Couvigny Farm). Lt. P.R.D.Cooke to Equitation School. Lt. Harris to Hotchkiss School.	
	31		7 O.R. joined from Base.	
			NOTE:- The weather during the month was fine and cold, except for one week from 16th. to 23rd.	

C D Colley
Capt. and Adjt.,
The Royal Dragoons.

DUPLICATE.

Army Form C. 2118.

WAR DIARY
or
INTELLIGENCE SUMMARY.

(Erase heading not required.)

Summary of Events and Information

STRENGTH OF REGIMENT.

	Officers.	O.R.
1st. January 1918	35.	536.
31st. January 1918	36.	506.

E W Callaghan
Capt. and Adjt.,
The Royal Dragoons.

DUPLICATE.

WAR DIARY
or
INTELLIGENCE SUMMARY

Army Form C. 2118.

(Erase heading not required.)

Place	Date	Hour	Summary of Events and Information	Remarks and references to Appendices
			APPENDIX 'I'. — CASUALTIES.	
			D/1860 Sgt. Elliott, T. Wounded.	
			D/3225 Sgt. Michael, D.E. Wounded.	
			D/20710 Sgt. Talbot, J.J. Wounded, accidentally.	
			**************************	
			APPENDIX 'II'. — HONOURS AND REWARDS.	
			Extract from New Year Honours' Lists:-	
			Capt. R.Houstoun to be Bt. Major.	
			Bt. Major (temp. Lt-Col.) G.P.L.Cosens, to be companion of D.S.O.,	
			R.S.M. J.Oxford, awarded the Meritorious Service Medal.	
			**************************	
			APPENDIX 'III'. — REINFORCEMENTS RECEIVED.	
			Capt. C.G.W.Swire from 35th. Sqdn. R.F.C. 12/1/18.	
			3 other ranks from Base. 25/1/18.	
			7 " " " " 31/1/18.	
			**************************	

C. Callaghan
Capt. and Adjt.,
The Royal Dragoons.

Army Form C. 2118.

SHEET I.

VOLUME IXL.

WAR DIARY
or
INTELLIGENCE SUMMARY.
(Erase heading not required.)

Instructions regarding War Diaries and Intelligence Summaries are contained in F.S. Regs., Part II. and the Staff Manual respectively. Title pages will be prepared in manuscript.

Place	Date	Hour	Summary of Events and Information	Remarks and references to Appendices
In the Field.	Feb 1918 1		Capt. G.W.Turner rejoined from Gas School. 1 Officer and 35 O.R. went up to work on GREEN LINE (W.6.8.2.6. Sheet 62.Q., S.E.) near CAULAINCOURT.	
	2		Extract from Lond. Gazette d/- 28th. Jany. 1918 - 2/Lieut. A.S.Casey to be Lieut. 1st. July 1917.	
	3		Lieut. E.St.G.Stedall rejoined from Divisional School. Lieuts. Parr and MMM Wilson admitted to Hospital. Capt. E.W.T.Miles, Sgt. Seaton and Pte. Neal, R. awarded the Croix de Guerre (Belgian).	
	7		Lieuts. Watson, Birch and Joy proceeded to Divisional School.	
	8		2/Lieut. A.O.Cook and 70 O.R. rejoined from Pioneer Regt at VENDELLES. They were relieved by the 7th. Brigade.	
	9		Lieut. A.R.Cooper rejoined from Pioneer Regt. The Regiment now finding 2 officers and 100 O.R. for work on GREEN LINE and 1 officer and 55 O.R. on BROWN LINE near JEANCOURT. Capt. C.G.W.Swire awarded the Croix de GUERRE (Belgian).	
	10		Extract from Lond. Gazette, d/- 8/2/18 - Sec.Lieuts. to be Lieuts:- W. Edwerds 17/9/17. Hon.G.R.D.Browne 7/10/17. S.J.Lawrence, 3/12/17. J.R.Wingfield Digby 4/12/17.	
	11		11 O.R. rejoined from Base. Lieut. Parr rejoined from Hospl.	
	13		Lieut. J.C.Carr Ellison rejoined from Cav. Corps Sigg. School.	
	15		Capt. H.M.P.Hewett proceeded to England to join R.F.C.,	
	16		Lieut. D'A.F.H.Harris rejoined from Hotchkiss School, LE TOUQUET.	
	18		Enemy aircraft bombed Divisional Billets killing 12 horses of 7th. Bde.	

Geo Calley
Capt. and Adjt.
The Royal Dragoons.

Army Form C. 2118.

SHEET II.

VOLUME IXL (Continued)
WAR DIARY
or
INTELLIGENCE-SUMMARY.
(Erase heading not required.)

Place	Date 1918 Feb.	Hour	Summary of Events and Information	Remarks and references to Appendices
In the Field.	21		Lieut. J.B.Bickersteth rejoined Regiment from 6th. M.G.Sqdn. and took up duties as Brigade Intelligence Officer.	
	22		5 O.R. joined from Base. A further working party detailed to work under R.E. officer on ROISEL - TEMPLEUX Road. 'B' Working party withdrawn from digging at JEANCOURT.	
	24		2/Lieut. S.L.Jeffrey proceeded with 11 O.R. and 24 riding horses to instruct in equitation at V Corps School.	
	27		45 Riding Horses joined Regiment from Northumberland Hussars (Corps Cav. Rgt) 2/Lieut. J.C.Carr Ellison to be Lieut.	
	28		Lecture at Divisional Hqrs. on 'Interpretation of Aeroplane Photographs' by Capt. Heppold, Fifth Army. All working parties withdrawn.	
			**********************	
			NOTE:- Weather has been mild and fair all this month. The Regiment was finding working parties daily. All those remaining in camp worked on improving and bombproofing huts and stables.	
			**********************	
				Officers.	O.R.
			Strength on 1st. February 1918	36	515.
			" 28th. "	36	521.
			**********************	

C.O'Callaghan
Capt. and Adjt.,
The Royal Dragoons.

Army Form C. 2118.

VOLUME IX. (Continued)
WAR DIARY
or
INTELLIGENCE-SUMMARY.
(Erase heading not required.)

Summary of Events and Information

APPENDIX I. - CASUALTIES.

NIL.

APPENDIX II - HONOURS AND REWARDS.

Capt. E.W.T.Miles   awarded Croix de Guerre (Belgian) 3/2/18.
D/20646 Sgt. W.J.Seaton,   "   "   "   "   3/2/18.
D/12856 Pte. Neal, R.J.   "   "   "   "   3/2/18.
Capt. C.G.W. Swire.   "   "   "   "   9/2/18.

APPENDIX III - REINFORCEMENTS.

Lieut. J.B.Bickersteth joined Regiment from 6th. M.G.Sqdn. 21/2/18.
1 O.R. rejoined from Base,   11/2/18.
5 O.R. joined from Base,   21/2/18.

****

C V Callaghan
Capt. and Adjt.,
The Royal Dragoons.

Army Form C. 2118.

WAR DIARY
or
INTELLIGENCE SUMMARY.

(Erase heading not required.)

1st R. Dragoons

Place	Date	Hour	Summary of Events and Information	Remarks and references to Appendices
In the field	1 Mar.		Marching Order inspection of Regiment by Commanding Officer. Training Programme compiled for the fortnight the Division is in reserve.	
	2		Weather turned very cold; N.E. wind with a light fall of snow.	
	3		Brigade came into corps reserve. Regiment became duty Regiment for 48 hours, i.e., standing to at half hour's notice. Lieuts. Birch, Watson, and Joy returned from Divisional School.	
	4		Training commenced - Troop and Squadron drill in marching order close to camp. The Regiment took part in a Brigade counter attack scheme, receiving orders to counter attack TERTRY (62.C.1/40,000) from the East.	
	6		Capt. W.P.Browne rejoined from Regimental duty from 3rd. Cav.Div.Hqrs, and took over command of "C" Squadron.	
	8		33 riding horses taken over from 7th. Bde. Lieut. P.R.D.Cooke rejoined from Equitation School.	
	11		Divisional School closed.	
	12		Major Tomkinson and Lieut. Henderson rejoined from Divisional School,	
	14		Lieut. C.C.H.Hilton Greene joined from Base.	
	15		Major Tomkinson assumed command of X Royal Hussars and Major Irwin became 2nd. in command of Regiment.	
	18		Pioneer party of 3 Officers and 147 O.R. commenced work on rear zone defences E. of BOUVINCOURT.	
	19		Lieut. R.E.T.H.Savage to Cav.Corps Signals. Lieut. Henderson went to Brigade as acting Staff Captain.	

Capt. and Adjt.
The Royal Dragoons.

Army Form C. 2118.

WAR DIARY
or
INTELLIGENCE SUMMARY.
(Erase heading not required.)

Place	Date	Hour	Summary of Events and Information	Remarks and references to Appendices
In the field	1918 Mar 21		Enemy bombardment opened up at about 4.40 a.m. Reveille ordered at once and Regiment stood to. TERTRY shelled by light gun and aerodromes at MONS EN CHAUSSEE Brigade left DEVISE at 4.45 p.m. arriving at BEAUMONT EN BEINE about 10.0 p.m. where it went into bivouac. Shortly afterwards, orders were received to form Dismounted Brigade under Col. Burt with Capt. Miles as his 2nd. in Command. The Regimental detachment was commanded by Capt. W.P.Browne, with Lieuts. Birch, Stedal Hilton-Greene, Smith and Casey and 217 O.R.	
	22		Soon after midnight, Dismounted Brigade rode to UNGY-LE-GAY where they embussed for the front, horses returning to BEAUMONT. The Brigade Staff having left also to form staff of Dismounted Division, Major Irwin was left in charge of Brigade details with Capt. O'Callaghan as Staff Officer. Orders received to march Bde. details to PONTOISE which was reached about 2.0 p.m. where we went into billets, horses in open.	
	23		About 10.0 a.m. message came through from Division by telephone to say Germans had broken through at HAM and were on HAM - ESMERY HALLON Road, accordingly all available men were to be mounted leaving one man to five horses in the lines; this was subsequently altered to 50 men per unit forming a 6th. Bde. Squadron under Major W.Williams, X Hussars, with Capt. Turner as 2nd. in command. The Officers with Regimental party were Lieuts. Cubitt, Cooper and Harris. They marched at 11.20 a.m. to join Col. Patterson, Fort Garry Horse, at BRETIGNY and subsequently joined Gen. Harman's mounted detachment. About 3.0 p.m. Bde. details marched to CARLEPONT and went into bivouac.	
	24		Remained at CARLEPONT.	
	25		Men of all three Regiments returned in early morning with wounded horses from the mounted party and said the 6th. Cav.Bde.Sqdn. had had a mounted charge the previous afternoon (24th.) near FLAVY-LE-MELDEUX and killed about 60 and captured about 100 Germans. Lieuts. Cubitt and Cooper had been wounded and Harris had got concussion owing to his horse being shot, and the Brigade Sqdn. had had other casualties but not heavy. This news was afterwards confirmed. Later on, heard Cubitt had died of wounds but this was not confirmed till much later. Left /horses	

Capt. and Adjt.,
The Royal Dragoons.

WAR DIARY
or
INTELLIGENCE SUMMARY.

(Erase heading not required.)

Army Form C. 2118.

Place	Date 1918 Nov.	Hour	Summary of Events and Information	Remarks and references to Appendices
Littlefield	25		horses at CARLEPONT for Dismounted party with one man to ten, remainder of Bde. details marched to OLLENCOURT arriving about 1.0 p.m. Ordered to stand to with all available mounted men at 8.0 p.m. in order to go up and cover crossings over the OISE at PONTOISE and BRETIGNY; our Infantry were withdrawing from line BABOEUF - SALENCY north of the river; this order subsequently cancelled and stand to ordered instead for 5.45 a.m. following morning.	
	26		Mounted party of 50 men per Regiment left at 5.45 a.m. under Major Irwin to join Gen. Portal's detachment at LES CLOYES to hold river crossings at SEMPIGNY and PONTOISE. On arrival there, however, these crossings were found to be held by French Infantry, so Portal's detachment remained at LES CLOYES in support. Remaining Bde. details removed to CHOISY-AU-BAC, 3 miles N.E. of COMPIEGNE. Col. Wormald rejoined from leave.	
	27		Dismounted party rejoined having had 13 O.R. killed and 39 wounded in four days rear guard fighting from NOUREUIL to QUIERZY on the OISE. Gen. Portal's detachment also rejoined their respective Regiments at CHOISY.	
	28		Regiment stood to ready to move mounted at 5.45 a.m. Hostile aeroplanes bombed wood in which bivouac was about 5.15 a.m. and wounded 3 O.R. of "C" Sqdn.	
	29		Marched to AIRION via COMPIEGNE and CLERMONT, reaching there about 3.30 p.m. Gen. Harman's detachment rejoined having had three officers and 6 O.R. wounded and 6 missing, all in the charge. Very heavy rein all morning, weather having broken previous night.	
	30		Marched at 6.0 a.m. 30 miles due north, and Bivouaced in wood a mile S.E. of SAINS-EN-AMIENOIS together with 7th. Bde. Very wet all day. Horses and men in open but Officers of both Brigades all got shelter in a large farm.	
	31		Remained in bivouac all day; stood to at 5.45 a.m. but off saddled after water, though ready to move at short notice. More rain and men got very wet.	

C. O. Colyer
Capt. and Adjt.,
The Royal Dragoons.

Duplicate

Army Form C. 2118.

WAR DIARY
or
INTELLIGENCE=SUMMARY

(Erase heading not required.)

Instructions regarding War Diaries and Intelligence Summaries are contained in F. S. Regs., Part II. and the Staff Manual respectively. Title pages will be prepared in manuscript.

Place	Date	Hour	Summary of Events and Information	Remarks and references to Appendices
	1st. March 1918		STRENGTH OF REGIMENT.	
			Officers. O.R.	
	3.st. " "		36 521	
			34 403	
			APPENDIX I. CASUALTIES.	
			Lieut. Hon.W.H.Cubitt, wounded, 24/3/18. (died of wounds)	
			" A.K.Cooper, " 24/3/18.	
			" D.A.F.H.Harris, " (concussion) 24/3/18;	
			" E.St.G.Stedall, " (at duty) 26/3/18.	
			Capt. A.W.Forrest, R.A.M.C., attached,(wounded at duty) 26/3/18*	
			Other ranks:- Killed. Wounded. Missing. Date.	
			1 - - 21/3/18.	
			7 11 - 23/3/18.	
			2 21 6 24/3/18.	
			4 11 - 25/3/18.	
			- 3 - 28/3/18.	
			Total 14 47 6	
			APPENDIX II. HONOURS AND REWARDS.	
			N I L.	
			APPENDIX III. REINFORCEMENTS.	
			Lieut. C.C.H.Hilton Greene joined from Base, 14/3/18.	
			E O Callaghan	
			Capt. and Adjt.,	
			The Royal Dragoons.	

6th Cav.Bde.
3rd Cav.Div.

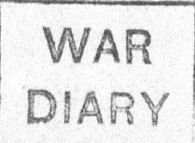

THE ROYAL DRAGOONS.

A P R I L

1 9 1 8

Attached:

Appendices I, II
& III.

Army Form C. 2118.

WAR DIARY
or
INTELLIGENCE SUMMARY

VOLUME XLIV.

(Erase heading not required.)

Place	Date	Hour	Summary of Events and Information	Remarks and references to Appendices
In the Field.	April 1st.		"Stood-to" at 5.45am. and marched through BOVES to BOIS de GENTELLES where we remained all day standing-to in support to 2nd.Cav.Div. who were employed Dismtd. about HANGARD. The 7th.Bde. moved up further during the afternoon but were not employed though the 7th.D.Gds. lost a lot of horses. At about 6.30pm. our Bde. moved to a small Fir Wood about 1 mile S. of BLANGY-TRONVILLE and went into bivouac. The 7th.Bde. joined us there during night. Lieut.HEYWORTH-SAVAGE to 6th.Signal Troop, seconded for service with Signals. Lieut.J.C.CARR-ELLISON became Regtl.Signalling Officer.	
	2nd.		Remained in bivouac all day. Whole Regiment turned out at 8.0pm. to go up and dig support trenches N.E. of VILLERS-BRETONNEUX. Led horses we e left at X roads 1 mile S. of FOUILLOY and diggers had to march up 2 miles through mud to their work. Heavy rain most of night.	
	3rd.		Diggers returned to led horses at 3.0am. and whole Regiment moved into bivouac in Northern portion of the BOIS L'ABBE, just N. of AMIENS-PERONNE Railway where we remained all day. Lieut.HENDERSON returned from 5th.Bde.HQrs. Some digging party formed as for previous night so men had a second night out of bed. Very wet night again.	
	4th.		Digging party only returned just before 5.0am. Germans started shelling our bivouac at 5.30am. and it was necessary to evacuate it but not before Captain JOHNSTON, A.V.C. (attached) had been wounded and 1 O.R. killed and 3 wounded besides about 20 horses being killed. About 9.0am. the Regiment was ordered to move up mounted to Valley just N. of VILLERS-BRETONNEUX, (the 3rd.D.Gds. and 10th. Hussars having already gone up) and eventually was employed to fill a gap in the line just E. of that place between the 9th. Australian Inf.Bde. and the 14th.Div. Led horses after moving about all day to avoid shell fire, were eventually sent back to bivouac S. of BLANGY-TRONVILLE. Further casualties during day's operations 3 killed, 5 wounded, 1 missing.	
	5th.		The Dismounted Party holding front line were relieved about 2.0am. by 2 Sqdns. of the 17th.Lancers and 1 of Inniskilling Dragoons and returned to Dismtd.Bde.HQ. (about 1 mile N.E. of VILLERS-BRETONNEUX Church) where they dug in in support before daylight. Capt.BROWNE with 4 Subalterns remained in charge of Dismtd.Party /and all others	

C W Clafson
Captain & Adjt
1st Royal Dragoons

Army Form C. 2118.

WAR DIARY
or
INTELLIGENCE=SUMMARY.
(Erase heading not required.)

Instructions regarding War Diaries and Intelligence Summaries are contained in F. S. Regs., Part II. and the Staff Manual respectively. Title pages will be prepared in manuscript.

Place	Date 1918	Hour	Summary of Events and Information	Remarks and references to Appendices
In the Field.	April			
			and all other Officers returned to led horses. This support line was heavily shelled between 10 & 11 am. but they had no casualties and no Infantry attack developed. The 6th.Cav.Bde. was relieved about midnight by 5th.Anzac Division and led horses were sent up to bring back Dismtd.Party. Further casualties reported from previous day – 4 wounded, 3 missing.	
	6th.		Dismounted Party reached bivouac about 4.30am. completing the 4th. night running most of the Regiment had had no rest whatever. Fine warm day at last. Brigade paraded at 9.0am. and marched to CAMON just East of AMIENS where we went into billets to refit. 64 O.R. post to Regiment from N.S.Y. as reinforcements under Lieut.R.E.F.COURAGE (attached to Regt.). Capt.J.WILLMOTT, R.A.M.C. ceased to be attached on return of Capt.LYONS, R.A.M.C. from leave. 13 O.R. joined from Base. Heard in evening from No.5 C.C.S. that Capt.H.McCOLL, JOHNSTON, A.V.C. (attached to the Royals since they came out in October 1914) had died of wounds on the 4th. inst. to everyone's great regret. Pte.LEANING wounded same day had died also. Wet night and orchard where horses were picketed became very muddy.	
	7th.		Remained at CAMON. Bright Spring day and got things well dried. 23 O.R. joined from Base. 2/Lieut.J.WALKER joined on promotion to commissioned rank from 6th.M.G.Sqdn. Lieuts.D'A.F.H.HARRIS and H.D.HOLLAND joined from Base.	
	8th.		Still at CAMON. The whole Regiment had hot baths in AMIENS in course of morning. 4 N.C.Os., N.S.Y. posted to Regiment.	
	9th.		G.O.C. had "Marching Order Inspection" of each unit in the Brigade during which the Corps Commander came round. A good many of the deficiencies have been made up but by no means complete especially in Hotchkiss Strips, and clothing. 17 O.R. from N.S.Yeo. (previously drafted to 10th.Hussars) posted to Regiment.	
	10th.		Stood-to during day, first at 1½ hours notice then at 2½.	
	11th.		The Bde. marched at 7.0am. to AUXI-le-CHATEAU, the Regiment going into billets at HARAVESNES, about 5 miles N. of that place. A very long march – about 25 miles The whole of the rest of Cav.Corps was moving North the same day and road very much congested. The idea seemed to be that Cav.Corps would remain about AUXI-le-CHATEAU	

/12.........

Army Form C. 2118.

WAR DIARY
or
INTELLIGENCE=SUMMARY.
(Erase heading not required.)

Instructions regarding War Diaries and Intelligence Summaries are contained in F. S. Regs., Part II. and the Staff Manual respectively. Title pages will be prepared in manuscript.

Place	Date	Hour	Summary of Events and Information	Remarks and references to Appendices
In the Field.	1918 April 12th.		About midday received orders to move at once and packed up in a great hurry. Brigade concentrated at CONCHY-Sur-CANCHE and marched to HUMIERES where we halted some hours in a wood. Eventually received to move into billets at HESTRUS which was not reached till long after dark. On the way whilst watering near WAVRANS some aeroplanes came over and dropped two bombs within 100 yards of the Regiment but no damage.	
	13th.		Brigade marched early through TANGRY and SACHIN to AUMERVAIL where we watered, eventually moving into billets - Bde.HQrs. and Royals at PERFAY, 10th. and 6th. M.G. at AUMERVAL and 3rd.D.Gds. at BAILEUL-les-PERNES. Remained standing-to at 1½ hours notice. Here we came under orders of G.O.C. 1st.Army.	
	14th.		" Standing-to at 1½ hours notice.	
	15th.		Standing-to at 3½ hours notice.	
	16th.		ditto. ditto.	
	17th.		ditto. ditto. Lieut.S.J.PARR,M.C. released from Military Service for three months to attend to his farms.	
	18th.		Still standing-to at 3½ hours notice.	
	19th.		Standing-to at 1½ hours notice from 7.0am. being duty Brigade. If required the Brigade is to move up in support of 61st.Division (XI Corps) holding line E. of St.VENANT and take over support trenches on either side of CANAL de la LYS between LA HAYE and LA MALADERIE. Capt.H.A.Thorne, A.V.C. attached to Regiment. Lieut.Courage and 69.O.R. with 70 Remounts rejoined from Dismounted Party. Nos.12827 L/Cpl.T.Guy, 9564 L/Cpl.W.Ritchie and 4254 Pte.Fentley S. awarded MILITARY MEDAL.	
	20th.		Remained at 1½ hours notice. Capt.C.G.W.Swire rejoined from Cav.Corps HQrs. and posted to "A" Sqdn. Nos.4338 Sgt.C.A.Bowles and 20691 Sgt.J.Rickeard awarded MILITARY MEDAL.	C.Callaghan /21............... Lieut & Adjt. The Royal Dragoons

Army Form C. 2118.

WAR DIARY
or
INTELLIGENCE SUMMARY.
(Erase heading not required.)

Instructions regarding War Diaries and Intelligence Summaries are contained in F.S. Regs., Part II. and the Staff Manual respectively. Title pages will be prepared in manuscript.

Place	Date	Hour	Summary of Events and Information	Remarks and references to Appendices
In the Field.	April 21st.		Still at 1½ hours notice. Lieut.R.B.Bowerman, N.S.Y. attached to the Regt. as Signalling Officer. Lieut.Carr-Ellison to Cav.Corps Signalling School.	
	22nd.		Came off 1½ hours notice at 7.0.m.; after that at 3½. Canadian Bde. took over Duty Bde. Defence Scheme for all Officers, Troop Sergts. and Hotchkiss Nos.2 in afternoon N. of AUMERVAL.	
	23rd.		Practised coming on to Dismtd.Est-blishment fr&x in the lines at 8.0am. Nos.D/4219 Cpl.(a/L/Sgt.)H.Neale and D/5961 Pte.McKenzie A. awarded MILITARY MEDAL	
	24th.		Turned out of FERFAY by HqQtrs., XIII Co ps and moved billets to VEDONCHELLE where we arrived about 5.0pm. Capts.F.W.T.MILES and W.P.BROWNE and Lieuts.D/A.F. H.HARRIS and E.St.G.STINDALL award.d MILITARY CROSS. No.D/8311 Pte.W.J.Smart awarded D.C.M.	
	25th.		Stood-to at ¾ hour notice from 6.0 — 8.0am.; after that on 3½ hours. Commenced training. 1 Squadron has Drill Ground at BAILLEUL-les-PERNES every morning. Hotchkiss Classes, Musketry and Training Remounts on roads.	
	26th.		G.H.Q. Lieut.W.W.WYNN proceeded to XVIIICorps Hotchkiss School. The 'Archies' Concert Party of XIIICorps HQrs. came over and gave us an excellent show.	
	27th.		Same notice. The plan of employing the Brigade was altered; instead of hold- ing support line E. of ST.VENANT, it is now to hold all Canal Crossings from the Drawbridge S. of ROBECQ to that on the ST.VENANT - BUSNES Road, and find nucleus garrison for the BUSNES - STEENBECQUE Line from just S. of BUSNES to the latter Drawbridge mentioned above.	
	28th.		Came off being Duty Bde. Major (T/Lt.Col.)H.A.TOMKINSON, D.S.O. awarded Bar to D.S.O. Capt.C.W.TURNER award.d MILITARY CROSS and No.D/13871 Pte.Cockburn, T.O. awarded D.C.M.	

/29......

The Royal Dragoons

WAR DIARY
or
INTELLIGENCE SUMMARY

(Erase heading not required.)

Army Form C. 2118.

Place	Date	Hour	Summary of Events and Information	Remarks and references to Appendices
In the Field	April 29th.		Capt.C.G.W.SWIRE proceeded to G.S., 3rd.Cav.Div. Capt.T.W.T.MILES proceeded on 8 days leave to PARIS-PLAGE. Capt.H.F.de TRAFFORD assumed Command of "A"Sq.	
	30th.		Lieut.E.St.G.Stedall admitted to HOSPITAL. 2 O.R. joined from Base. Lieut. HOLLAND with 7 O.R. joined from Dismtd.Details. 12 Riding horses joined.	
			Offrs. O.R.	
			Strength on 1st.April 1918. 34 467.	
			" 30th.April 1918. 36 521.	
			C V Callaghan	
			Capt. & Adjt.,	
			The Royal Dragoons.	

APPENDICES

I, II and III.

WAR DIARY
or
INTELLIGENCE SUMMARY
(Erase heading not required.)

Summary of Events and Information

APPENDIX I. - CASUALTIES.

Capt.H.McCOLL JOHNSTON, A.V.C. attd. wounded 4/4/18.

Killed		Wounded		Missing		Date.
4		15		1		4/4/18.
/20						

APPENDIX II - HONOURS AND REWARDS.

Major (T/Lt.Col.)H.A.TOMKINSON, D.S.O. awarded Bar to D.S.O. 22/4/18.
Capt. E.W.T.MILES   }
  "   W.P.BROWNE   } Awarded MILITARY CROSS 24/4/18.
Lieut. D.A.F.H.HARRIS   }
Lieut. E.ST.C.SMYDAIL   }
Capt. C.W.TURNER awarded MILITARY CROSS 25/4/18.
No. D/8511 Pte.W.J.SMART awarded D.C.M. 24/4/18.
No. D/13971 Pte.T.O.COCKBURN awarded D.C.M. 23/4/18.
No. D/12827 L/Cpl.T.GUY   }
No. " 9564   " W.RITCHIE } Awarded MILITARY MEDAL 19/4/18.
No. " 4234 Pte. E.FAULTLEY }
No. " 4228 Sgt.C.A.BOWLES }
No. " 20691   " J.RICKEARD } Awarded MILITARY MEDAL 20/4/18.
No. " 4819 Cpl.(/L/Sgt.)H.NEALE }
No. " 5961 Pte.A.MCKENZIE } Awarded MILITARY MEDAL 23/4/18.

C D Callahan
Capt. & Adjt.,
The Royal Dragoons.

INTELLIGENCE SUMMARY

(Erase heading not required.)

Place	Date	Hour	Summary of Events and Information	Remarks and references to Appendices
			APPENDIX III.- REINFORCEMENTS.	
			2/Lieut.J.WALKER joined from 6th.M.G.Sqdn. 7/4/18.	
			Lieut.D¹ˢ.F.F.HARRIS } from Base 7/4/18.	
			" H.D.HOLLAND }	
			Lieut. E.F.COURAGE from North Somerset Yeo. (attd.) 6/4/18.	
			" R.P.BOWERMAN, " " " 21/4/18.	
			Capt.H.A.THORPE, A.V.C. attached from 12/4/18.	
			64 O.R. from N.S.Yeo. 6/4/18.	
			15 " " " " 6/4/18.	
			23 " " Base 7/4/18.	
			4 " " N.S.Yeo. 8/4/18.	
			17 " " 10th.Hussars 9/4/18.	
			2 " " Base 30/4/18.	

C S Callaghan
Capt. & Adjt.,
The Royal Dragoons.

DUPLICATE.

Army Form C. 2118.

WAR DIARY
or
INTELLIGENCE SUMMARY.

THE ROYAL DRAGOONS.   VOLUME XLV.

(Erase heading not required.)

Vol 44

Place	Date	Hour	Summary of Events and Information	Remarks and references to Appendices
In the field	May 1918 1.		Standing-to 6.0 to 8.0am at ½ hour notice.	
	2.		ditto. First warm spring day.	
	3.		ditto. Corps Commander visited the Drill Field.	
	4.		Marched with rest of Brigade to area N.E. of AUXI-LE-CHATEAU and went into billets at CONCHY-SUR-CANCHE. Sergt. BARNARD and Cpl. WINSLADE proceeded to 2nd.Battn. Worcester Regt. on promotion to Commissioned Rank.	
	5.		Moved billets in afternoon to NOEUX. Very heavy rain during day.	
	6.		Marched to CONTAY (8 miles W. of ALBERT) arriving there 4.30pm. and went into bivouac. The rest of 3rd. Divn. was concentrated there. Very wet night. Lieuts.G.BROWNE and RHODES to Cav.Corps Equitation School.	
	7.		At 2 hours notice from 6.0am. Capt. & QMr. W.LINES proceeded to U.K. Capt.C.G.W. SWIRE to be G.S.O.3, 3rd. Cav.Div. Digging party found for work at HENENCOURT. Major R.HOUSTOUN.(attd.G.S.58th.Divn.) came over to see us.	
	8.		Stood-to at 5.0am. Off-saddled 5.30am. after which on 2 hours notice. 2 chargers joined from Base. Working party at night.	
	9.		Standing-to at 5.0am. every morning until further notice. Lieut. ACKROYD joined from Details at ABBEVILLE.	
	10.		Capt.H.A.THORNE, A.V.C. taken on strength of Bde.Hqrs. but remains attached to Regt. Lieut.W.WYNN rejoined from Hotchkiss School.	
	11.		Working party for day work at HENENCOURT at 9.30am. The Division is at present in Army Reserve to 4th.Army and might be used in the event of enemy breaking through front line system on 3rd.Corps front or in its capacity as Mobile Reserve anywhere required.	
	12.		Night working party at HENENCOURT. Wet cold day; lines got very muddy.	
	13.			

DUPLICATE.

Army Form C. 2118.

WAR DIARY
or
INTELLIGENCE SUMMARY

THE ROYAL DRAGOONS   VOLUME XLV. (Sheet II.)

(Erase heading not required.)

Instructions regarding War Diaries and Intelligence Summaries are contained in F. S. Regs., Part II. and the Staff Manual respectively. Title pages will be prepared in manuscript.

Place	Date	Hour	Summary of Events and Information	Remarks and references to Appendices
In the Field	MAY 1918 14.		Did not stand-to. At 2 hours notice from 6.0am. 2/Lieut.R.V.Weatherstone joined Details at ABBEVILLE.	
	15.		Stood-to at 5.0am. again. 2/Lieut.STEWART re-joined from Tank Corps and apptd. Acting Quartermaster.	
	16.		2/Lieut.J.WALKER proceeded to M.G. Training Centre in U.K. and struck off. 2/Lieut. H.Harrison admitted to Hospital.	
	17.		Marched to BELLOY-SUR-SOMME and went into bivouac with rest of Brigade in wood N.E. of village. Very hot day.	
	18.		G.O.C. inspected all Officers' chargers in morning.	
	19.		Corps Commander presented ribbons of decorations awarded after recent operations at a Brigade Church Parade. Lieut.TEDALL invalided to England from old gunshot wound in leg and struck off strength.	
	20.		Troop and Sqdn. Training in morning. Major IRWIN commenced afternoon Class of recently joined Officers in Map reading, elementary tactics, etc. Pte.CRAIG ("C" Sqdn.) drowned whilst bathing in SOMME VALLEY.	
	21.		Training as yesterday. Pte.CRAIG'S body recovered by dragging. 2 O.R. and 13 riding horses joined from Base and 5 O.R. from ABBEVILLE off command.	
	22.		Dismounted Attac. Scheme by Regiment at 8.30am. Just E. of Camp. Lieut.H.Boswell to Cav.Corps HQrs. for Intelligence Course. Very hot day and some thunder.	
	23.		Working party found to pitch tents at VIENACOURT. 2/Lieut.S.H.BROMLEY(Northants.Yeo.) and 2 O.R. joined from Base. 2/Lieut.R.V.Weatherstone joined from details and struck off command. S.S.M.Stalker and Sergt.Rickeard proceeded to U.K. for admission to Cadet Unit. Major T.S.Irwin } Mentioned in Capt.C.W.Turner, M.C. } Despatches Lieut(a/Capt.)F.B.Ratcliffe(attd.M.G.C.)} Lon.Gaz. Sergt. Whaite F. } 20/5/18.	

C. Callaber
Capt. & Adjt.,
The Royal Dragoons.

DUPLICATE.

Army Form C. 2118.

THE ROYAL DRAGOONS WAR DIARY VOLUME XLV. (Sheet III).

or

INTELLIGENCE SUMMARY.

(Erase heading not required.)

Instructions regarding War Diaries and Intelligence Summaries are contained in F. S. Regs., Part II. and the Staff Manual respectively. Title pages will be prepared in manuscript.

Place	Date	Hour	Summary of Events and Information	Remarks and references to Appendices
In the Field	MAY 1918 24.		Training as usual.	
	25.		Regtl.Parade at 6.30am. for All Officers, Sergts. and Section Leaders for instruction in carrying out a Dismtd.Attack. 2/Lieut.LESLIE HENSON (late of the Gaiety Theatre) gave an entertainment to the Brigade with his troupe, the "Gaieties".	
	26.		Capt. de Traffors and L/Cpl.Glen to G.H.Q.Hotchkiss School, LE TOUQUET for Course. 2/Lieut.H.Harrison rejoined from Hospital. 1 Riding horse from XIII Corps HdQtrs.	
	27.		Regtl.Drill and Scheme in morning W. of PICQUIGNY rather interfered with by finding Drill Ground occupied by French Infantry. Practised taking up a position to fill gap in line. In afternoon an aeroplane of No.6 Sqdn. gave a demonstration of flying at 3000, 2000 and 1000 feet to give an idea of what it looked like at the different altotudes. 2/Lieut.R.E.Bowerman and Lieut.R.E.F.Courage posted to Royal Dragoons from North Somerset Yeomanry.	
	28.		Regtl.Drill on 3rd.L.Gds. Field near VIGNACOURT WOOD. Each Sqdn. did a short reconnaissance and Dismtd.Attack Scheme in turn. Lieut.R.H.W.Henderson to Cav. Corps Gas School.	
	30.		Staff Ride of Officers and Troop Sergeants in morning. Did a rear Guard Scheme withdrawing from high ground-N.E. of LA CHAUSSEE on BELLOY WOOD.	
	31.		Paraded at 7.0am. and marched to BEHENCOURT going into bivouac in wood West of village. Took over from Inniskillings.	

			Strength of Regt. on 1st.May 1918 Offrs. O.R.
			                                               35 524
			               ditto. 31st.May 1918. 34 487.	

                                        Capt. & Adjt.,
                                  The Royal Dragoons.

DUPLICATE

Army Form C. 2118.

WAR DIARY
THE ROYAL DRAGOONS.   VOLUME XLV. (Sheet IV.)
INTELLIGENCE SUMMARY
(Erase heading not required.)

Instructions regarding War Diaries and Intelligence Summaries are contained in F. S. Regs., Part II. and the Staff Manual respectively. Title pages will be prepared in manuscript.

Place	Date	Hour	Summary of Events and Information	Remarks and references to Appendices
			APPENDIX I. - CASUALTIES.	
			N I L.	
			APPENDIX II. - HONOURS AND REWARDS.	
			Major (T/Lt.Col.)W.T.Hodgson, M.C. ⎫	
			Major T.C.Irwin. ⎬ Mentioned in Despatches	
			Capt.C.W.Turner, M.C. ⎬ (Lon.Gaz. 20/5/18).	
			Lieut.(a/Capt.)F.B.Ratcliffe (attd.M.G.C.) ⎬	
			20692 Sgt.Whaite F. ⎭	
			APPENDIX III. - REINFORCEMENTS.	
			1 Other rank from Base 1/5/18.	
			1 " " " " 5/5/18.	
			2/Lieut.R.V.Weatherstone from Base 12/5/18.	
			2/Lieut.W.O.Stewart joined from Tank Corps 15/5/18.	
			1 Other rank from Base 14/5/18.	
			1 " " " " 18/5/18.	
			2/Lieut.S.H.Bromley ⎱ joined from Base 23/5/18.	
			2 Other ranks ⎰	
			C O Callahan	
			Capt. & Adjt.,	
			The Royal Dragoons.	

Army Form C. 2118.

THE ROYAL DRAGOONS. WAR DIARY VOLUME XLVI.

INTELLIGENCE SUMMARY.

(Erase heading not required.)

Instructions regarding War Diaries and Intelligence Summaries are contained in F.S. Regs., Part II. and the Staff Manual respectively. Title pages will be prepared in manuscript.

Place	Date	Hour	Summary of Events and Information	Remarks and references to Appendices
	1.		A lot of activity during the night on the part of hostile aircraft and many bombs dropped in neighbourhood but none near our bivouac.	
	2.		Regiment found working party of 150 Officers and men under Capt. HUNTER paraded at 7.0pm. and marched to HENENCOURT returning about 9.15am.	
	3.		Major IRWIN'S Class for young Officers re-assembled in afternoon.	
	4.		G.O.C. 6th.Cav.Bde. Inspected Regiment in Marching Order and expressed his appreciation of excellent turn-out.	
	5.		Working party of 150 Officers and O.R. left Camp at 7.0pm. under Capt.MILES returning about 3.0am.	
	6.		Lieut.A.R.COOPER and Lieut.L.J.HUNTER Joined Details ABBEVILLE. Lieut.R.H.W. HENDERSON to Hospital with P.U.O. Major (T/Lt.Col.) W.T.HODGSON, M.C. to be Brevet Lieut-Colonel (Lon.Gaz.Supp. d/- 3/8/18).	
	7.		An attack being expected on the III Corps front we were ready to turn out in 40 minutes after 4.0am.	
	8.		The 8th.Australian Field Coy., R.E. in next bivouac to us held Sports and a Concert to which they invited us. Working party found as before under Capt. BROWNE.	
	9.		2/Lieut.K.E.N.WILLIAMS Joined Details at ABBEVILLE. Dull day and a little rain.	
	10.		Lieut.L.J.HUNTER Joined from Details, ABBEVILLE.	
	11.		Eliminating competition, to decide best Troop in Regiment for A.R.A. Inter-Troop Competition Medal, held. Result 1st. 4th.Troop "C" Sqdn. (Lieut.DAVIES COOKE) 2nd. 4th.Troop "B" " (Lieut.COOK). 3rd. 1st.Troop "A" " (Lieut.HILTON GREEN).	
	12.		The "C" Sqdn. Troop won on its rifle shooting, its Hotchkiss only scoring 17 points	

DUPLICATE

Army Form C. 2118.

(Sheet II.)
WAR DIARY
or
INTELLIGENCE SUMMARY.

THE ROYAL DRAGOONS. (Volume XLVI.)

(Erase heading not required.)

Instructions regarding War Diaries and Intelligence Summaries are contained in F. S. Regs., Part II. and the Staff Manual respectively. Title pages will be prepared in manuscript.

Place	Date 1918	Hour	Summary of Events and Information	Remarks and references to Appendices
In the Field	June 12.		The "B" Sqdn. Troop only scored 1 hit with Hotchkiss and "A" Sqdn. 42. "B" Sqdn. was slightly better than "C" in the bayonet work scoring more hits. Same party as before under Lieut. BIRCH.	
	13.		Lieut. D'A.F.H.Harris, M.C. proceed d on leave to U.K.	
	14.		The Brigade returned to its old bivouac at BELLOY-SUR-SOMME each Regiment going into the same lines as before. Paraded at 9.30am. and arrived in Camp about 3.0pm.	
	15.		a/S.S.M. Workman to be S.S.M. vice Stalker to England.	
	17.		22 Reinforcements joined Regiment from ABBEVILLE. Lieut.Hon.G.R.D.Browne and 2/Lieut.F.W.Rhodes rejoined from Cav.Corps Equitation School. Lieut.W.M.Wynn went on leave. 20657 Q.M.S.(O.R.S.) Ratcliffe R. ⎫ Awarded Silver Medal with 20661 F.Q.M.S. Allen F. ⎬ gratuity for L.S. & G.C. 20650 Sergt. Earl H. ⎭ 1/4/18. 4368 " Morgen S. without gratuity for L.S. 205648.S.M.Timson E. awarded S.M. and G.C. 1/4/18.	
	18.		Regtl.Scheme S. of SOMME - Regtl.Drill and Artillery attack by each Sqdn. in turn. Major P.HOUSTOUN visited Regiment on his way to Cav.Corps School after being attached to HQrs., 3rd.Corps.	
	19.		2/Lieut.R.V.Weatherstone to Hotchkiss School, LE TOUQUET.	
	20.		C.O. inspected horses proposed for casting.	
	21.		Regtl. Rear Guard Scheme S. of SOMME. Both the Divnl. and Brigade Commanders came out. Capt.W.P.Browne, M.C. admitted to Hospital owing to injured shoulder incurred by a fall in jumping competition at Canadian Bde. Sports on 19th.	

Lieut., for Capt.& Adjt.
The Royal Dragoons.

DUPLICATE

Army Form C. 2118.

THE ROYAL DRAGOONS. (Sheet III.) WAR DIARY VOLUME XLVI.
or
INTELLIGENCE SUMMARY.

Place	Date	Hour	Summary of Events and Information	Remarks and references to Appendices
In the field	June 1918 22		D.D.R., Cav.Corps held Casting Parade. - Lieut.Hon.H.W.Mansfield (late of Regiment) accompanied him. 2/Lieut.K.N.Williams joined from ABBEVILLE. 2/Lieut.A.R.Cook proceeded to Cav.Corps Equitation School.	
	23		The 4th.Troop of "C" Sqdn. (Lieut.Davies Cooke) won Bde.Inter-Troop A.R.A. Competition with 299 points(Hotchkiss 57), 3rd.D.Gds. 2nd. with 269 points and 10th.Hussar 3rd. with 286 points. The best Troop in 7th.Bde. which was firing at same time made 271 points. Lieut.Wingfield Digby to Cav.Corps Equitation School. Capt. & Adjt.O'Callaghan to Hospital with P.U.O.	
	24		Brig.de Signalling Scheme in morning. All Officers and O.R. passed through Gas Chamber at YZEUX to test S.B.Rs. An Epidemic of P.U.O. (pyrexis unknown origin) or influenza commenced in Regiment. 26 O.R. admitted to 6th.C.F.A. after 10 yesterday.	
	25		Bde. moved from BELLOY to the LANDON Valley, the Regt. going into bivouac at SOUES. Bde.HQrs. and 3"d.D.Gds. at LE MESGE and 10th.Hussars at RIENCOURT 13 O.R. admitted to 6th.C.F.A. Capt.O'Callaghan returned from Hospital.	
	26		5 Riding horses joined from Base. 15 O.R. admitted to 5th.C.F.A.	
	27		Sergts.Mynard and Scott to Cav.Corps School. Capt.Thorne, A.V.C. and Lieut. Lithgow and 28 O.R. admitted to 6th.C.F.A.	
	28		A.D.V.S.(Col.Clarke) inspected horses of Regiment. Lieuts.Casey & Harrison and 28 O.R. to 6th.C.F.A. 19 O.R. returned from 6th.C.F.A.	
	29		Lieut.Askroyd & Smith to Cav.Corps School at DIEPPE for 6 weeks Course. Sergt.Weeks A.V.C. attached to Regt. for 1 month with view to obtaining Cav. Commission. 26 O.R. admitted to 6th.C.F.A., 26 returned. Lieut.Bowerman on leave to England.	
	30		Lieut.Holland and 17 O.R. to 6th.C.F.A. Capt.Thorne, A.V.C. returned. Strength on 1st.June Offrs. O.R. 34 488 " 30th.June 36 513	

Army Form C. 2118.

THE ROYAL DRAGOONS. WAR DIARY VOLUME XLVI.
(Sheet IV)
or
INTELLIGENCE SUMMARY.

(Erase heading not required.)

APPENDIX I. – CASUALTIES.

  N I L.

APPENDIX II. – HONOURS AND REWARDS.

Major(T/Lt.Col.) W.T.HODGSON M.C. to be Brevet Lieut-Colonel 3/6/18.
xxxx.

APPENDIX III. – REINFORCEMENTS.

2/Lieut.L.J.Hunter) From Base 1/6/18.
26 O.R.
Lieut.A.R.Cooper From Base 2/6/18.
2/Lieut.K.B.N.Williams) From Base 8/6/18.
5 O.R.
1 O.R. from Base 25/6/18.
3 O.R. from Base 14/6/18.
1 O.R. from Hospital 8/6/18.
1   "   "   12/6/18.
1   "   "   17/6/18.
1   "   "   22/6/18.
1   "   "   30/6/18.

                                          Lieut., for Capt. & Adjt.,
                                           The Royal Dragoons.

DUPLICATE

Army Form C. 2118.

THE ROYAL DRAGOONS. WAR DIARY. VOLUME XLVII.
or
"INTELLIGENCE=SUMMARY."
(Erase heading not required.)

Instructions regarding War Diaries and Intelligence Summaries are contained in F.S. Regs., Part II. and the Staff Manual respectively. Title pages will be prepared in manuscript.

Place	Date.	Hour	Summary of Events and Information	Remarks and references to Appendices
In the Field	July 1		22 O.R. admitted 6th.C.F.A. with Influenza.	
	2		15 O.R. ditto. ditto. Lieuts.Casey & Harrison returned from hospital.	
	3		Lt.Birch proceeded to Cav.Corps Gas Sch. 6 O.R. to 6th.C.F.A. 2/Lt.BROMLEY to Hosp. Lt.Courage and L/Cpl.Forsyth to Hotchkiss Sch.	
	4		6 O.R. to 6th.C.F.A.	
	5		Staff Ride for Sqdn. Leaders and 2nd-in-commands near CAVILLON. Scheme,Advance Guard and taking of a position.	
	6		Lieuts.Lithgow & Henderson rejoined from Hosp.	
	8		Cav.Corps Rest Camp Opened for O.R. R.Q.M.S. ALLIOTT awarded M.S.M. (Lon.Gaz.17/6/18). R.Q.M.S.ALLEN promoted W.O.Class II.	
	11		Lts.Harris and Casey and 4 N.C.Os. commenced 3 days Course of Instruction in German M.Gs. at HQ. 6th.M.G.Sqdn.	
	12		Staff Ride near CAVILLON; continued same scheme as last week defending village.	
	13		Regtl. Dismounted Sports held in afternoon in Field at W. exit of SOUES. Band of 140th. Inf.Bde. played.	
	15		Lts.Hilton Green & Weatherstone and 4 N.C.Os. commenced 2nd.Course in German M.Gs. Inter-Troop Skill-at-Arms Competition commenced. In morning every troop did the A.R.A. Rifle & Bayonet Competition and in afternoon 2 troops of each Sqdn. competed in Indication of targets.	
	16		Very heavy thunderstorm in night. 2 troops of each Sqdn. competed in Swords-manship in morning and Indication of targets in afternoon.	
	17		2/Lt.Bromley from Hospital.	

C.O. Callahan
Capt. & Adjt.,
The Royal Dragoons.

DUPLICATE

Army Form C. 2118.

(Sheet II).

THE ROYAL DRAGOONS' WAR DIARY VOLUME XLVII.
or
INTELLIGENCE=SUMMARY

(Erase heading not required.)

Instructions regarding War Diaries and Intelligence Summaries are contained in F. S. Regs., Part II. and the Staff Manual respectively. Title pages will be prepared in manuscript.

Place	Date 1918 JULY	Hour	Summary of Events and Information	Remarks and references to Appendices
In the Field.	18		Rapid loading Competition in afternoon. 2/Lt.Jeffrey to 5th.Army Musk.Sch.	
	20		Lt.Courage rejoined from Hotchkiss School. Very wet afternoon. Bde.Sports were postponed.	
	21		Inter-Bde. A.R.A.Competition took place at BOUCHON. The Score was as follow 1. Royals 294 pts. 2. L.S.H. 243 " 3 Inniskillings. 234 "	
			Lts.P.Wilson and Forsyth Forrest joined from Base.	
	22		Lt.Birch from C.Corps Gas School. Regtl.Scheme S. of SOMME.	
	23		Lt.Lithgow to Hotchkiss School.	
	24		Judging of best Troop of horses took place in the morning - 1. Lt.Smith (B1) 2 2/" Joy (C1)	
	25		Lt.Casey & 2/Lt.Rhodes to England on leave.	
	26		Bde.Sports held in afternoon. 50 O.R. taken on the strength of the Regt. and remained at C.Corps Reinforcement Camp.	
	27		Horse Show postponed owing to heavy rain.	
	29		Lt.Carr Ellison rejoined from C.C.Signal School.	
	30		Bde.Horse Show took place in afternoon. 40 O.R. joined Regt.from C.C.Rft.C.	
			Strength of Regt. on 1/7/18 Offrs. 36 O.R. 513 " 31/7/18 38 543.	

Capt. & Adjt.,
The Royal Dragoons.

DUPLICATE

THE ROYAL DRAGONS. (Sheet III). WAR DIARY VOLUME XLVII.
INTELLIGENCE SUMMARY.

Army Form C. 2118.

APPENDIX I - CASUALTIES.

N I L.

APPENDIX II - HONOURS AND REWARDS.

R.Q.M.S. Alflott W. awarded Meritorious Service Medal 17/6/18.

APPENDIX III - REINFORCEMENTS.

Lieut. P.L. Wilson } Joined from Base 21/7/18.
"   P.M. Forsyth Forrest }
1 O.R. joined from Hpl. 10/7/18.
1 O.R. joined C.C.Rft.Camp 14/7/18.
1 O.R. from Hpl. 16/7/18.
1 O.R.   "   20/7/18.
50 O.R. joined C.C.Rft.Camp from Base 26/7/18.

C O'Callahan
Capt & Adjt.,
The Royal Dragoons.

Army Form C. 2118.

THE ROYAL DRAGOONS WAR DIARY VOLUME XLVIII.

INTELLIGENCE SUMMARY.

(Erase heading not required.)

August 1918.

Place	Date August 1918	Hour	Summary of Events and Information	Remarks and references to Appendices
In the Field.	1.		H.R.(Bde.) Test took place, result being as follows:- 1. X.R.H. 610 pts. 2. Royals 561 " 3. 3rd.D.Gds. 532 " Bde. Boxing competition took place : Cpl.McCann won the Welter Weights. Lt. Lt.Bowerman to 3rd.Signal Sqdn. for instruction.	
	4.		Fourth Anniversary of the War. Special Parade Service.	
	5.		Regtl.Scheme arranged to take place S. of SOMME cancelled. Regt. closed up with X.R.H. at RIENCOURT.	
	6.	10.30p.	Bde. marched into forward Concentration Area S.W. of AMIENS, the Regt. at RENANCOURT.	
	7.	9.0pm.	The Bde. (less A.2 Echelon) marched to Assembly Area N.31 (sheet 62D), arriving about 2.0am. on 8th.inst.	
	8.	4.20am. 5.40" 7.15" 9.30" 10.50" 1.0pm.	Zero hour. Bde. followed 7th.Cav.Bde. up Cavalry Track, Regt. leading. Regt. arrived W. of CACHY. Bde. moved to pt. E. of MORGEMENT WOOD, crossing front system about 9.50am. Bde. moved and crossed R. LUCE at DEMUIN and halted in D.16a. Regt. with 1 sect. 6th.M.G.Sqdn. was ordered to support 7th.C.Bde. The Regt. had "C" Sqdn. as Advanced Sqdn. and pushed on to high ground S. of CAIX in E.15 but were unable to advance further owing to high ground E. of LE QUESNEL being strongly held by M.G. The Regt. then held a series of posts with "B" & "C" Sqdns. from B.15.b.9.0 to E.21.b.9.2. "A" Sqdn. and M.Gs. were holding Southern section of Wood in E.15.	
		6.40pm.	Capt.TURNER reported enemy dribbling in small parties from Direction of VRELY into small Copse about 800 yards in front of his position. 'C' and 'K' Batteries then opened fire on this target.	
		8.25pm.	The Regt. was ordered to be prepared to reinforce with 2 dismounted Sqdns. in case of attack, which would have been difficult as majority of troops were on extended front in this line.	

Army Form C. 2118.

THE ROYAL DRAGOONS. (Sheet II.) WAR DIARY VOLUME XLVIII.
or
INTELLIGENCE SUMMARY.

(Erase heading not required).

Instructions regarding War Diaries and Intelligence Summaries are contained in F. S. Regs., Part II. and the Staff Manual respectively. Title pages will be prepared in manuscript.

Place	Date	Hour	Summary of Events and Information	Remarks and references to Appendices
In the Field.	August 1918 8	9.0pm.	"A" Sqdn. in Wood fairly heavily shelled. The situation on night of 8th. was as follows :- The Regt. was holding in conjunction with Canadian Infantry, Southern edge of Wood, posts and part of an old line running from E.16.b.7.7. to E.21.a. and b.	
	9.	8.15am.	The Regt. was relieved by Canadian Infantry; Bde. returning to area CAYEUX - CAIX, (less "C" Sqdn) which was left at request of O.C. 85th.Battn. in Support. until he was satisfied with progress of our new attack.	
		1.30pm.	"C" Sqdn. rejoined Brigade.	
		8.30pm.	Bde. ordered to off-saddle and ready to move at 5.0am.	
	10.	5.0am.	"A" Sqdn. marched to 2nd.Cav.Div.HQ. in E.30a. and took over patrols from 3rd.Cav.Bde. Remainder of Bde. concentrated in E.23. "A" Sqdn. were ordered to keep in close touch with Infantry and report how attack was progressing. The Sqdn. moved to neighbourhood of BOUVROY CEMETERY and pushed out 2 Officer's patrols under Lts.DIGBY and WILSON to keep touch with attack. The remainder of Regt. closed up E. of BEAUFORT in support of "A" Sqdn.	
		1.10pm.	Message from O.C. "A" Sqdn. that PARVILLERS was still held by enemy and that we were unable to advance.	
		1.50pm.	C.O. reported to Bde. that it was out of the question to act mounted owing to the impassable state of the country due to lines of old wire and entrenchments.	
		3.0pm.	Message from Lt.DIGBY who is in front line that left flank of 32nd. Divis on was out of touch with Canadians and attack on PARVILLERS was held up by M.G. and snipers.	
		4.10pm.	A Whippet Tank Attack which was due to take place was cancelled owing to nature of ground, attacking Tanks had already started, and Lt.BIRCH was sent forward to stop them which he successfully did.	
		5.43pm.	Regt. was concentrated E. of BEAUFORT. Capt. MITTWS having had orders to rejoin.	
		5.50pm.	Regt. was ordered to move in support to X.R.H. who had already gone up S. of main ROYE road to support Canadian Cavalry attack on Hill 100. Attack failed, and Bde. ordered to concentrate W. of FOLIES, the Regt. off-saddling and remaining there for the night.	
	11.	5.15pm.	Bde. moved W. along S. of AMIENS - ROYE road to area FOUENCAMPS, the Regt. bivouacing on line of River midway between DOMMARTIN - COTTENCHY.	

[signature] Lieut. & a/Adjt.,
The Royal Dragoons.

Army Form C. 2118.

THE ROYAL DRAGOONS' WAR DIARY (Sheet III.) VOLUME XLVIII.

INTELLIGENCE-SUMMARY.
(Erase heading not required.)

Place	Date August 1918	Hour	Summary of Events and Information	Remarks and references to Appendices
In the Field.	13.		The O.-in-C. visited the Division and rode round the Regtl. Lines.	
	14.		Lts. SMITH and ACKROYD from Cav.Corp School. 2/Lt. WILLIAMS to Cav.Corps Sch.	
	15.	8.30pm.	Bde. moved to their old area, Regt. billeting at SOUES. Lt.WYNN to Cav.Corps School. Lts. BIRCH and HARRIS to Cav.Corps Equitation School.	
	16.		Capt. O'CALLAGHAN to Canadian Cavalry Bde. Lt.P.R.DAVIES COOKE assumed duties of acting Adjutant. 3 chargers joined from Base. Billeting parties sent to ST. LEGER DOMART but move cancelled.	
	18.		8 O.R. and 2 Riding horses joined from Base.	
	19.		The Band of the 2nd. Life Guards, under Major H.C. HALL, M.V.O. who was Bandmaster of the Regt. 25 years ago, visited the Regt. and played during the afternoon and evening.	
	20.		No.12834 Cpl.T.C.HEWSON awarded the MILITARY MEDAL.	
	21.		2/Lt.JOY and 10 O.R. proceeded on leave. 2 O.R. from Base. 2 chargers from Base. Regt. marched from SOUES to MONTRELET (about 7 miles S.W. of DOULLENS as the Divn. was closing up into a preliminary concentration area in case it should be required to take part in the 3rd.Army operations.	
	22.		Capt. H.A. THORNE, A.V.C. admitted to Hospital.	
	24.		Lt.Col.F.W. WORMALD. D.S.O. went on leave to England and Major T.S. IRWIN assumed command of the Regiment.	
	25.		Marched at night to GUESCHART near AUXI-LE-CHATEAU arriving at about 3.0am.	
	26.		Marched at very short notice to SIBIVILLE (just E. of FREVENT) arriving about 9.30pm.	
	27.		On short notice to move but did not do so.	

The Royal Lieut. & a/Adjt.
Dragoons. Commanding The Royal Dragoons

(Sheet IV.)

THE ROYAL DRAGOONS' WAR DIARY or "INTELLIGENCE-SUMMARY."

VOLUME XLVIII. Army Form C. 2118.

(Erase heading not required.)

Place	Date Hour 1918 August	Summary of Events and Information	Remarks and references to Appendices
In the Field.	28.	Brigadier explained scheme to C.Os. and Sqdn. Leaders in case we should take part in operations under 1st.Army tomorrow. Lt.HILTON GREEN to Hospital. Lt.J.R.WINGFIELD DIGBY awarded M.C. (22/8/18).	
	29.	Operations of 1st.Army against DROCOURT – QUEANT line postponed.	
	30.	Brigadier explained a new scheme which was subsequently cancelled. The 10th. Hussars left to act as Corps Cavalry to Canadian Corps.	
	31.	Owing to departure of 10th.Hussars Billeting areas were rearranged; 3rd.D.Cds. moving in to FREVENT and Royals having the whole of SIBIVILLE and SERICOURT.	
		Strength of Regt. on August 1st. Offrs. O.R. 38 543.	
		ditto. " 31st. 38 528.	

M.Henderson
Lieut. & a/Adjt.,
The Royal Dragoons.
for O.C. Royal Dragoons.

(Sheet V.)

THE ROYAL DRAGOONS. WAR DIARY VOLUME XLVIII.

INTELLIGENCE-SUMMARY.

Army Form C. 2118.

(Erase heading not required.)

Place	Date	Hour	Summary of Events and Information	Remarks and references to Appendices
In the Field.	August 1918.			

APPENDIX I. - CASUALTIES.

5 O.R. wounded 8/8/18.
2 " " 9/8/18.
2 " " 10/8/18. *(1 wounded (at Duty).
1 " " 11/8/18.

APPENDIX II - HONOURS AND REWARDS.

No. D/12834 Cpl. HEWSON T.C. awarded MILITARY MEDAL 20/8/18.
Lt. J.R. WINGFIELD DIGBY awarded MILITARY CROSS 22/8/18.

APPENDIX III. - REINFORCEMENTS.

1 O.R. joined from 7th.Cav.Bde.HQrs. 1/8/18.
1 " " Base 16/8/18.
1 " " Hospital 18/8/18.
8 " " Base 18/8/18.
2 " " " 20/8/18.
3 " " " 13/8/18.

[signature]
Lieut. & a/Adjt.,
The Royal Dragoons.
for O.C. Royal Dragoons.

DUPLICATE

Army Form C. 2118.

THE ROYAL DRAGOONS WAR DIARY
VOLUME XLIX
INTELLIGENCE SUMMARY.
(Erase heading not required).

Instructions regarding War Diaries and Intelligence Summaries are contained in F.S. Regs., Part II. and the Staff Manual respectively. Title pages will be prepared in manuscript.

Place	Date September 1918	Hour	Summary of Events and Information	Remarks and references to Appendices
In the Field	2		Standing-to at short notice. 5 men and 44 riding horses joined Regt.	
	3		Notice increased to 2½ hours.	
	4		G.O.C. Division inspected the horses of the Regiment.	
	6		Marched from SERICOURT to St.GEORGES, S.E. of HESDIN. 5 O.R. joined Regt.	
	8		Lieuts. DUMBRECK and SUFDALL and 4 O.R. joined Regt. from Base.	
	9		Lt. PITT-RIVERS joined Regt. from 20th.Division. 5 O.R. and 2 chargers joined from Base.	
	16		Regt. moved to St.AUSTREBERTHE, to take part in Cavalry Corps manoeuvres on following day.	
	17		Cavalry Corps manoeuvres. Horses did about 45 miles in the day. Regt. bivouaced night just West of DOULLENS. Lt.ACKROYD went to Cav.Corps Signal School.	
	18		Regiment returned to St.GEORGES billets. Capt.NICHOLAS, A.V.C. joined Regt. as Veterinary Officer.	
	19		Regiment moved into billets at PREVENT. R.S.M.PHILLIPS joined Regt. to be Quartermaster.	
	20		Capt.CRAIG, A.V.C. left Regiment to rejoin Canadian Cav.Bde.	
	23		G.O.C. Division presented A.R.A. Medals to 4th.Troop of "C" Sqdn.	
	24		Bde. Communication Scheme. Lt. JEFFREY rejoined Regt. from Hospital.	
	25		Regt. marched by night to COIGNEUX. Lts.HOLLAND and DUMBRECK left Regt. for Cav.Corps Equitation School.	

Mr Henderson Lieut. & a/Adjt.,
The Royal Dragoons.

DUPLICATE

Army Form C. 2118.

(Sheet II).

THE ROYAL DRAGOONS. WAR DIARY VOLUME XLIX.

or

INTELLIGENCE SUMMARY.

(Erase heading not required.)

Instructions regarding War Diaries and Intelligence Summaries are contained in F. S. Regs., Part II. and the Staff Manual respectively. Title pages will be prepared in manuscript.

Place	Date 1918 September	Hour	Summary of Events and Information	Remarks and references to Appendices
In the Field	26		Regt. marched by night to BECORDEL-BECOURT.	
	27		Regiment moved by night to Camp N.E. of HEM.	
	29		Moved into bivouac by night near BINECOURT.	
	30		Standing-to at 2½ hours notice.	
			Officers. O.R.	
			Strength on 1st.September 1918 39 526.	
			ditto 30th " " 42 532.	
			[signature] Lieut. & a/Adjt..	
			The Royal Dragoons.	

DUPLICATE

Army Form C. 2118.

THE ROYAL DRAGOONS. (Sheet III). WAR DIARY VOLUME XLIX.
or
INTELLIGENCE-SUMMARY.

(Erase heading not required.)

Instructions regarding War Diaries and Intelligence Summaries are contained in F. S. Regs., Part II. and the Staff Manual respectively. Title pages will be prepared in manuscript.

Place	Date	Hour	Summary of Events and Information	Remarks and references to Appendices

APPENDIX - I. - CASUALTIES.

1 O.R. xxxxxxxxxxxxxxxxxxx Wounded 5/10/18.

APPENDIX II. - HONOURS AND REWARDS.

N I L.

APPENDIX III. - REINFORCEMENTS.

Lt.G.H.T.Pitt Rivers joined from 20th.Divn. 9/9/18.
Lt.S.C.Dumbreck   ) Joined from C.C.Rft.Camp
Lt.B.St.G.Stedall   )   8/9/18.
4 O.R. from C.C.Rft.Camp 2/9/18.
6 O.R. from Hospital 5/9/18.
2 O.R. from 1st.Life Guards 19/9/18.
1 O.R. from Hospital 14/9/18.
2 O.R. from C.C.Rft.Camp 21/9/18.
3 O.R. from 3rd.D.Gds. 22/9/18.
4 O.R. from Inniskillings 23/9/18.
3 O.R. from 3rd.D.Gds. 29/9/18.

[signature] Lieut. & a/Adjt.,
The Royal Dragoons.

Army Form C. 2118.

THE ROYAL DRAGOONS. WAR DIARY or INTELLIGENCE SUMMARY. VOLUME L.

(Erase heading not required.)

Place	Date October 1918	Hour	Summary of Events and Information	Remarks and references to Appendices
In the Field.	2.		Division moved up to BELLENGLISE to take part in operations with LE CATEAU as objective. Orders cancelled and Regiment returned to BINCOURT.	
	3rd.		Division again moved to Assembly Area at BELLENGLISE. At 3.30pm 5th.Cav.Bde. ordered to seize high ground S.E. of MONTBREHAIN. This was done by 3rd.Dragoon Guards. Owing to hostile counterattack, Bde. withdrew to bivouac near PONTRUEN, except 1 Sqdn. 3rd.D.Gds. who remained in observation near JONCOURT.	
	4.		"C" Sqdn. under Capt. BROWNE relieved Squadron of 3rd.D.Gds. near JONCOURT.	
	5.		Capt. BROWNE's Squadron relieved by a Sqdn., 17th.Lancers. Regt. moved into huts at THEECON.	
	8.		Brigade moved 4.0am. to MAGNY LA FOSSE for operations against LE CATEAU. At 11.0am. moved S. of BEAUREVOIR. At 5.30pm. as situation did not develop Bde. moved to MAGNY-LA-FOSSE for night.	
	9.		Moved 4.30am. E. of BEAUREVOIR. At 9.0am. Infantry reported enemy in retreat. Canadian Bde. moved forward N. of LE CATEAU Road, 5th.Bde. South with 7th.Bde. in reserve. Our advance temporarily held up E. of HONNECHY. At 2.0pm. Bde. ordered to seize high ground E. of HONNECHY with LE CATEAU as final objective. Regiment moved N. of HONNECHY, "C" Sqdn. still in advance and seized high ground S.W. of REUMONT without casualties. Advance here held up. Relieved by Cyclist Battalion 9.0pm. and spent night in Farm on Western outskirts of MAUROIS. Casualties 4 killed, 20 wounded. 34 horses.	
	10		Bde. moved S.E. of BROISVILLE. Infantry held up on line of SELLE all day. Eventually moved back into bivouac E. of MONTIGNY for night.	
	11.		Moved to billets in ELINCOURT.	
	12		Moved to bivouac at BANTEUX.	
	14		Moved into bivouac and huts at ETRICOURT.	

Lieut. & a/Adjt.,
The Royal Dragoons.

Army Form C. 2118.

(Sheet II).

THE ROYAL DRAGOONS. WAR DIARY or INTELLIGENCE-SUMMARY.
VOLUME I.

(Erase heading not required.)

Place	Date	Hour	Summary of Events and Information	Remarks and references to Appendices
In the Field	October 15, 16, 17, 18, 19		Capt.C.T.O'Callaghan and Lt.P.L.Wilson rejoined. Re-equipping, training, reinforcements, remounts, etc. Weather wet and changeable.	
			Brigade Advance Guard Scheme over the area BUS - HAPLINCOURT - VILLERS-au-FLOS.	
	22		Brigade Scheme. Lt.BICKERSTETH struck off strength of Regiment as Intelligence Officer to 6th.Cav.Bde. 23 O.R. from C.C.R't.Camp attached to 3rd.D.Gds. for temporary duty.	
	26		6 Riding horses joined from Base.	
	27		7 O.R. joined from C.C.R.C.	
	28		Bde. Scheme over ground NURLU - SAULCOURT. Very wet day.	
	29		The C.O. inspected "B" and "C" Sqdns. in Drill Order. Each Sqdn. of three 13 file Troops. C.O. inspected Transport in Marching order.	
	31.		17 O.R. rejoined from 3rd.D.Gds.	

	Offrs.	O.R.
Strength on 1st.October	42	541
" " 31st. "	41	509

Lieut. & a/Adjt.,
The Royal Dragoons.

DUPLICATE

Army Form C. 2118.

(Sheet III).

THE ROYAL DRAGOONS. WAR DIARY VOLUME L.
INTELLIGENCE SUMMARY.
(Erase heading not required.)

Summary of Events and Information

APPENDIX I. – CASUALTIES.

```
 1 O.R.  Wounded          4/10/18.
 4  "    Killed in Action 9/10/18.
 1  "    Died of Wounds   9/10/18.
19  "    Wounded          9/10/18.
 1 O.R.  Died of Wounds  10/10/18.
 2  "         do.        11/10/18.
```

APPENDIX II. – HONOURS AND REWARDS.

```
20649 Cpl. North  J. ⎫
13020  "   Lawry  A. ⎬ Awarded MILITARY MEDAL 18/10/18.
 9080 Pte. Timson A. ⎭

 3535 Cpl. Foote /W. Awarded "LA MEDAILLE D'HONNEUR AVEC GLAIVES EN ARGENT
                                                              26/10/18.
```

APPENDIX III. – REINFORCEMENTS.

```
Lt. P.L. Wilson     ⎫  Joined from C.C.R.C. 15/10/18.
 3 O.R.             ⎭
 8 O.R. from C.C.R.C.                       17/10/18.
 2  "    "     "                            15/10/18.
 7  "    "     "                            27/10/18.
18  "    "     "                            31/10/18.
```

Lieut. & a/Adjt.,
The Royal Dragoons

DUPLICATE

Army Form C. 2118.

THE ROYAL DRAGOONS. **WAR DIARY** VOLUME LI.
or
INTELLIGENCE SUMMARY.
(Erase heading not required.)

Instructions regarding War Diaries and Intelligence Summaries are contained in F. S. Regs., Part II. and the Staff Manual respectively. Title pages will be prepared in manuscript.

Place	Date	Hour	Summary of Events and Information	Remarks and references to Appendices
In the Field.	November. 1918			
	1.		G.O.C., 6th. Cav.Bde. inspected "C" Sqdn. in turn out - (1 Troop in Marching Order. (1 Troop in Drill Order. (1 " " Watering " (1 " " Stripped Saddles.	
	2.		Bde. Scheme. Another wet day. Capt. O'Callaghan to Division.	
	3.		Received orders that Division might move following evening.	
	4.		C.O. inspected HQrs., "A" & "B" Sqdns. in marching order.	
	5.		Very wet day.	
	6.		Left ETRICOURT for MARQUION - Miserable march of 18 miles - Very wet.	
	7.		Left MARQUION for ESQUERCHIN near DOUAI. A march of 25 miles.	
	8.		Left ESQUERCHIN for FRETTIN - a long march of 23 miles along pavé roads.	
	9.		Remained at FRETTIN.	
	10.		Left FRETTIN for GAURAIN-RAMECROIX - Got in very late, owing to crossing a pontoon bridge at TOURNAI. Distance covered - 27 miles.	
	11.		Armistice declared. Regiment had moved up to MOULBAIX, while "A" Sqdn. had gone to AUTREPPE. Stayed on our outpost position till about 14.30 when ordered to march back to GAURAIN-RAMECROIX. Got in late on a miserable wet evening.	
	12.		Left GAURAIN-RAMECROIX for POTENCHE about 6 miles away. Got in about 14.00, "B" Sqdn. in BRAFFE, and "C" Sqdn. in BAUGNIES.	
	13. 14.		Stayed at POTENCHE, and prepared for march East by cleaning generally.	
	15. 16.		Left POTENCHE at 07.45 for MARCQ about 23 miles away. Got in about 14.30.	

The Royal Dragoons.

Lieut. & a/Adjt.,

DUPLICATE

Army Form C. 2118.

THE ROYAL DRAGOONS. (Sheet II.) WAR DIARY VOLUME LI.
or
INTELLIGENCE-SUMMARY.
(Erase heading not required.)

Instructions regarding War Diaries and Intelligence Summaries are contained in F. S. Regs., Part II. and the Staff Manual respectively. Title pages will be prepared in manuscript.

Place	Date	Hour	Summary of Events and Information	Remarks and references to Appendices
In the Field	November 1918			
	18.		Left MARCQ at 08.00 for HONDZOCHT - 15 miles march. Arrived in 11.30. "A" & "C" Sqdns. in TUBIZE, and "B" Sqdn. and HQrs. in HONDZOCHT.	
	19. 20.		Stayed at HONDZOCHT.	
	21.		Left HONDZOCHT for COURT-ST.ETIENNE. Numerous German Guns in Railway here which were handed over to the British. Major Irwin returned with Regtl. Standard from England. Left a Guard of 1 Sgt. and 9 O.R. to look after the guns, etc.	
	22.		Left COURT-ST.ETIENNE at 08.00 for AISCHE-EN-REFAIL, about 9 miles N.W. of NAMUR - "A" Sqdn. in NEHAIGNE.	
	23.		Stayed at AISCHE. Baron VON GODSTNOVEN owned the Chateau where HQrs. were billeted.	
	24.		Moved from AISCHE to VEDRIN just N.W. of NAMUR. "A" Sqdn. is detached in NAMUR looking after various dumps, etc. "C" Sqdn. in DAUSSOULX - "B" Sqdn. and HQrs. in VEDRIN, the latter in Chateau belonging to Baron de MONTPELIER.	
	25.		Working party required E. of NAMUR on Railway. The Guard rejoined from COURT-ST.ETIENNE.	
	26.		Nothing to report.	
	27.		Rations and forage came up very late today, about 11.00, consequently men's breakfasts and dinners were combined into one meal.	
	28.		Nothing to report.	
	29.		Pitt-Rivers and Holland to U.K.	
	30.		Rations and forage were delivered very late today again, it being about 13.00 hrs. before they reached the Regiment.	

Lieut. & a/Adjt.,
The Royal Dragoons.

DUPLICATE

Army Form C. 2118.

(Sheet III.)

THE ROYAL DRAGOONS' **WAR DIARY** VOLUME LI.
or
INTELLIGENCE-SUMMARY.

(Erase heading not required.)

Instructions regarding War Diaries and Intelligence Summaries are contained in F. S. Regs., Part II. and the Staff Manual respectively. Title pages will be prepared in manuscript.

Place	Date	Hour	Summary of Events and Information	Remarks and references to Appendices

			Strength of Regiment on 1/11/18. — Offrs. O.R.
			 " " " 30/11/18. — 41 509
			                                             43 523.
			
			                                                    Lieut. & a/Adjt.,
			                                     The Royal Dragoons.	

DUPLICATE

Army Form C. 2118.

THE ROYAL DRAGOONS. VOLUME LI. (Sheet IV).

WAR DIARY
or
INTELLIGENCE SUMMARY.
(Erase heading not required.)

Place	Date	Hour	Summary of Events and Information	Remarks and references to Appendices
			APPENDIX - I. - CASUALTIES.	
			N I L.	
			APPENDIX - II. - HONOURS AND REWARDS.	
			N I L.	
			APPENDIX - III. - REINFORCEMENTS.	
			Lt.H.D.Holland and ⎫ From C.C.R.C. 14/11/18.	
			2/Lt.S.H.Bromley ⎬	
			" K.E.N.Williams ⎭	
			37 O.R.	
			1 O.F. from C.C.R.C. 19/11/18.	
			1 " C.C.HQrs. 26/11/18.	

Lieut. & a/Adjt.,
The Royal Dragoons.

DUPLICATE

Army Form C. 2118.

THE ROYAL DRAGOONS. **WAR DIARY** VOLUME LII.
or
INTELLIGENCE SUMMARY.
(Erase heading not required.)

Place	Date	Hour	Summary of Events and Information	Remarks and references to Appendices
In the FIELD	December 7		Regtl. Ceremonial Parade.	
	10		Regiment marched independantly to new area at HUCCORGNE.	
	13		Regiment marched to new area at JEHAY-BODEGNEE as permanent winter billets	
	16		C.O. went on leave to U.K. for 1 month."	
	21		Major Irwin to Hospital with fraytured wrist. Major Houstoun commands the Regiment.	
	22		14 O.R. left the Regiment for demobilization.	
	23		Lieut.Davies Cooke to U.K. on leave and Lieut.Henderson performed duties of Acting Adjutant.	
	24		7 O.R. to U.K. for demobilization.	
	25		Interpreter St..ers left Regiment for demobilization. 6 O.R. to U.K. for demobilization.	
	27		Major Tomkinson, D.S.O., Capt.Fitzgerald,M.C., Lieut.Smith and S.S.M. Wischhusen mentioned in Despatches. (Lon. Gaz. dd – 27/12/18)	
	28		12 horses to 13th.M.V.S. and struck off strength.	
	29		1 Cpl. and 12 men left to go on a Divisional Guard.	
	30		16 horses lent to 5th.Bde., R.A.F. and struck off strength.	

Strength of Regiment on 1/12/18.
" " " " 31/12/18

	Offrs.	O.R.
1/12/18	43	522
31/12/18	41	503

W.Henderson Lieut. & a/Adjt.,
The Royal Dragoons.

DUPLICATE

Army Form C. 2118.

THE ROYAL DRAGOONS' WAR DIARY VOLUME LII.

Sheet LI.

INTELLIGENCE SUMMARY.

(Erase heading not required.)

Instructions regarding War Diaries and Intelligence Summaries are contained in F.S. Regs., Part II. and the Staff Manual respectively. Title pages will be prepared in manuscript.

Place	Date	Hour	Summary of Events and Information	Remarks and references to Appendices
			CASUALTIES - APPENDIX I.	
			1 O.R. Missing 11/11/18.	
			APPENDIX II. - HONOURS AND REWARDS.	
			Major H.A.TOMKINSON? D.S.O. } Mentioned in Despatches	
			Capt. F.W. WILSON FITZGERALD, M.C. } 23/12/18.	
			Lieut. H. SMITH }	
			20656 S.S.M. WISCHEUSEN B.	
			APPENDIX III. - REINFORCEMENTS.	
			18 O.R. Joined from Base 9/12/18.	
			6 O.R. " " " 11/12/18.	
			2 O.R. Joined from Hospital 24/12/18.	
			1 " " " Base 23/12/18.	
			1 " " " Hospital 26/12/18.	
			Lieut. & ?/Adjt.,	
			The Royal Dragoons.	

DUPLICATE

Army Form C. 2118.

1 Royal Dragoons Vol 3

WAR DIARY
or
INTELLIGENCE SUMMARY.

(Erase heading not required.)

Instructions regarding War Diaries and Intelligence Summaries are contained in F. S. Regs. Part II. and the Staff Manual respectively. Title pages will be prepared in manuscript.

Place	Date	Hour	Summary of Events and Information	Remarks and references to Appendices
	January 1919.			
	1st.		1 N.C.O. and 12 men rejoined from Divisional guard. Capt.C.T.O'Callaghan M.C. rejoined Regt. from sick leave. Capt.F.W.Wilson Fitzgerald M.C. } Awarded D.S.O. } Lon.Gaz. Capt.C.T.O'Callaghan. } " M.C. } 1/1/19. Lieut.J.Bickersteth M.C. } " Bar to M.C. "	
	4th.		12 O.Ranks proceeded to the U.K. for Demobilization. (4 Watford Details. 8 Coalminers.) Lieut.E.St.G.Stedall M.C. rejoined from Cav. Corps Equit. School.	
	7th.		Lieut.W.Ackroyd and Lieut.R.B.Bowerman rejoined from Cav. Corps Sigg. School.	
	8th.		Lieut.C.G.H.Hilton Green rejoined from Cav. Corps Equit. School.	
	9th.		Lieut.A.S.Casey and Sergt. proceeded to 3rd. Army Rifle training School for course.	
	10th.		2/Lieut.K.E.N.Williams proceeded to the U.K. for Demobn.	
	12th.		Lieut.J.G.Carr Ellison to 6th.Cav.Bde. for Duty.	
	15th.		Lieut.R.F.Heyworth Savage rejoined Regt. from 6th.Cav.Bde. Interpreter F.Carter attached to Regt. for Duty.	
	20th.		Capt.A.V.Nicholas R.A.V.C. proceeded to 2nd.Cav.Div. for Duty.	
	24th.		Capt.H.A.Thorne R.A.V.C. rejoined Regt. Horse Classification commenced. H.Qrs. and "A" Sqdn. and "B" Sqdn. horses classified.	
	25th.		"C" Squadron horses classified.	
	29th.		Lieut.R.B.Bowerman proceeded to NAMUR for duty with the Directorate of Hirings and Requisitions.	
			Demobilisation continued during the month leaving a ration strength of 25 officers and 250 O.Ranks. Hard frost and snow towards the latter part of month.	

DUPLICATE.

Army Form C. 2118.

WAR DIARY
or
INTELLIGENCE SUMMARY.
(Erase heading not required.)

Instructions regarding War Diaries and Intelligence Summaries are contained in F.S. Regs., Part II. and the Staff Manual respectively. Title pages will be prepared in manuscript.

Place	Date	Hour	Summary of Events and Information	Remarks and references to Appendices
	January 1919.		APPENDIX 1.	
			NIL.	
			APPENDIX 2.	
			Capt.F.W.Wilson Fitzgerald M.C. awarded D.S.O. (Lon.Gaz.1/1/19.	
			Major H.A.Tomkinson D.S.O.) Mentioned in Despatches.	
			Capt.F.W.Wilson Fitzgerald M.C.) (Lon.Gaz.23/10/18.)	
			Lieut.H.Smith.	
			20656 S.S.M.Wischhusen B.	
			Capt.G.T.O'Callaghan awarded M.C. Lon.Gaz. 1/1/19.	
			Lieut.J.B.Bickersteth M.C. awarded Bar to M.C. Lon.Gaz.1/1/19.	
			APPENDIX 3.	
			NIL.	
			Strength on 1st.January. 35 Officers. 332 O.Ranks.	
			Strength on 31st.January. 23 Officers. 250 O.Ranks.	

DUPLICATE.

1st Royal Dragoons

Army Form C. 2118.

WAR DIARY
or
INTELLIGENCE SUMMARY.

(Erase heading not required.)

Instructions regarding War Diaries and Intelligence Summaries are contained in F. S. Regs., Part II. and the Staff Manual respectively. Title pages will be prepared in manuscript.

Place	Date	Hour	Summary of Events and Information	Remarks and references to Appendices
JEHAY-BODEGNEE.	March 1919 February 1919			
	1st.		3rd.Cavalry Division Concert Party performed at STOCKAY.	
	4th.		Lieut.A.S.Casey and Sergt.Shackell rejoined from 3rd.Army Rifle Training School. Lieut.P.I.Wilson and Interpreter F.Carter proceeded to PARIS on leave.	
	5th.		Mr.Phillips lectured at STOCKAY.(Subject. Small Holdings) 2/Lieut.R.Allan proceeded as Conducting officer to U.K. with Dispersal Draft.	
	6th.		2/Lieut.R.V.Weatherstone proceeded as Conducting Officer to U.K. with Dispersal Draft.	
	7th.		Lieut.C.C.H.Hilton-Green proceeded as Conducting Officer to U.K. with Dispersal Draft.	
	8th.		Lieut.D.H.Watson proceeded to SERAING for duty with Cav. Corps "Z" Horse Depot. 3rd.Cavalry Division Concert Party performed at STOCKAY. Lieut.J.F.Houstoun-Boswall proceeded on one months leave England.	
	9th.		Lieut.W.H.W.Henderson proceeded as Conducting Officer to U.K. with Dispersal Draft. 2/Lieut.A.R.Cook to be Lieut.(L.G. d/-6/1/19)	
	10th.		Lieut.W.Ackroyd posted to 6th. Reserve Cavalry Regiment.	
	11th.		Re-classification by Remount Board of all Packs and Riders	
	12th.		S.Q.M.S.Dyer to be Chevalier de l'Ordre de Leopold II. (Extract fro Belgian decorations d/- 7/12/18.)	
	14th.		Major T.S.Irwin rejoined the Regiment from sick leave.	
	17th.		Lieut.W.P.Lithgow proceeded as Sales Officer to "Z" Horse Depot.SERAING.	
	20th.		2/Lieuts.D.A.Longbottom and W.H.W.Gossage joined Regiment.	
	23rd.		2/Lieut.E.F.Mosley rejoined from leave.	
	24th.		2/Lieut.S.L.Jeffrey rejoined from leave.	
	25th.		Interpreter F.Carter struck of strength. Lieut.A.R.Cook relieved Lieut.D.P.Lithgow at "Z" Horse Depot.SERAING.	

C.Callaghan
Capt. & Adjt.
The Royal Dragoons.

DUPLICATE.

Army Form C. 2118.

WAR DIARY
or
INTELLIGENCE SUMMARY.
(Erase heading not required.)

Instructions regarding War Diaries and Intelligence Summaries are contained in F. S. Regs., Part II. and the Staff Manual respectively. Title pages will be prepared in manuscript.

Place	Date	Hour	Summary of Events and Information	Remarks and references to Appendices
			February 1919 (cont'd)	
	27th.		Capt. J. Lyons R.A.M.C. proceeded to 53rd. C.C.S. for ceases to be attached. Lieut. D.P. Lithgow and 2/Lieut. H. Harrison proceed on leave to U.K. 2/Lieut. R. Allan rejoined from leave.	
	28th. Notes.		Demobilization of personnel was suspended during the month. All the "Z" horse were disposed of, some at LIEGE, and some at HUY. Weather very variable. 3rd. Cavalry Division* assembled several times during the month in the Regimental Area.	

* beagles.

C.D. Callaghan
Capt. & Adjt.,
The Royal Dragoons.

Army Form C. 2118.

WAR DIARY
or
INTELLIGENCE SUMMARY.

(Erase heading not required.)

Place	Date	Hour	Summary of Events and Information	Remarks and references to Appendices
			February 1919. (contd)	
			APPENDIX I.	
			NIL.	
			APPENDIX II	
			S.Q.M.S. Dyer to be Chevalier de l'ordre de Leopold II.	
			APPENDIX III	
			NIL.	
			Strength on 1st.February. 38 Officers 331 Other Ranks.	
			Strength on 28th.February. 40 " 4251. " "	
			GO Callahan
Capt. & Adjt.
Royal Dragoons.	

DUPLICATE

DUPLICATE.

Army Form C. 2118.

WAR DIARY
or
INTELLIGENCE SUMMARY.
(Erase heading not required.)

Instructions regarding War Diaries and Intelligence Summaries are contained in F. S. Regs., Part II. and the Staff Manual respectively. Title pages will be prepared in manuscript.

Place	Date	Hour	Summary of Events and Information	Remarks and references to Appendices
JEHAY-BODEGNEE.	MARCH 1st. 1919. 3rd.		75 Riders taken over from 3rd. Dragoon Guards. Capt. E.W.T. Miles M.C. } Posted to 6th. Reserve Lieut. H. Smith. } Cavalry Regiment. Lieut. W.R. Birch. Lieut. R.E.F. Courage struck off pending demobilization. Lieut. E.St.G. Stedall M.C. proceeded to Cavalry Corps 'Z' Horse Depot for Duty.	
	5th.		Lieut. W. Williams Wynn proceeded to the U.K. i/c Dispersal Draft. Royals played Xth. Hussars in Divisional Football Competition and won by 2 goals to 1. 3rd. Dragoon Guards left the 6th. Brigade and proceeded to Cadre Area.	
	6th.		Capt. H.E.F. de Trafford struck off pending a Medical Board Lieut. A.R. Cook from Cavalry Corps 'Z' Horse depot, relieved by Lieut. A.S. Casey.	
	7th.		29 Draught horses taken over from 3rd. Dragoon Guards. Capt. Alsop M.C. 3rd. Dragoon Guards, joined temporarily for duty.	
	9th.		Lieut. S.G. Dumbreck to hospital with Bronchitis. Divisional Football Cup. 17th. Lancers beat the Regiment by 5 goals to 3.	
	10th. 11th. 12th.		17th. Lancers Race Meeting at JENNERET. 2/Lieut. R.V. Weatherstone posted to 6th. Reserve Cavalry Regiment. Lieutenants A.S. Casey and E.St.G. Stedall M.C. rejoined from Cavalry Corps 'Z' Horse Depot. Lieut. G.H.F. Pitt-Rivers to be Captain 24/6/17. (London Gazette d/- 12/3/19.)	
	13th.		Lieut. W.O. Stewart proceeded to No.2 Infantry Records Office WARLEY for duty, and struck off. Lieut. A.R. Cook proceeded to Cavalry Corps Animal Collect or for duty.	

C. Callaghan

CAPTAIN & ADJT.
THE ROYAL DRAGOONS.

DUPLICATE.

Army Form C. 2118.

WAR DIARY
or
INTELLIGENCE SUMMARY.
(Erase heading not required.)

Instructions regarding War Diaries and Intelligence Summaries are contained in F.S. Regs., Part II. and the Staff Manual respectively. Title pages will be prepared in manuscript.

Place	Date	Hour	Summary of Events and Information	Remarks and references to Appendices
HAY-BODOGNEE.	MARCH. 14th.		Capt.J.Lyons R.A.M.C. rejoined from 53 C.C.S. 96 other ranks 1st.Cavalry Division lent to Regiment for proposed move to new area.	
	15th.		2 Lieut.S.L.Jeffrey proceeded to Cavalry Corps Animal Collecting Camp ENGIS, as Adjutant. Lieut.W.S.Phillips to leave in U.K.	
	16th.		Capt.Alsop M.C. 3rd.Dragoon Guards, ceases to be attached on posting to Cavalry Corps '3' Horse Depot for Duty.	
	18th.		Major R.Houstoun to leave in U.K. Lieut.R.F.Heyworth Savage to leave in South of France. The Regiment having been ordered to join the Army of Occupation moved to SPRIMONT, leaving 3 officers and 110 other ranks at JEHAY-BODEGNEE, for demobilization.	
SPRIMONT.	19th.		The Regiment moved to THEUX.	
THEUX.	20th.		The Regiment moved to RAEREN AND NISPERT CROSSING THE FRONTIER.	
RAEREN.	21st.		RAEREN and NISPERT, crossing the Frontier at GOE. The Regiment moved to WARDEN, HONGEN, MARIADORF, and HEHLRATH.	
WARDEN. OBEREMBT.	22nd. 23rd.		The Regiment moved to OBEREMBT. The Regiment marched in to the Artillery Barracks, COLOGNE, and took over 241 horses belonging to the 18th.Hussars.	
COLOGNE.	24th.		The whole day was spent in settling in; grooming state worked out about 1 man to 8 horses.	
"	25th.		Col. R. Osborne XXth.Hussars, gave a very interesting lecture on the fighting in PALESTINE, particularly dealing with the final Cavalry Advance.	
	26th.		30 other ranks from the "QUEENS BAYS" were posted to the Regiment.	
	27th.		Orders were recieved that the 12th.Lancers were to relieve us in barracks, and we were to march back to PAFFENDORF. The Regiment marched back to PAFFENDORF area and were billetted as follows :- "A" Sqdn. WIDDENDORF. "B" Sqdn. GLESCH. "C" Sqdn. THORR and GROUVEN. Headquarters. PAFFENDORF.	
	31st.			

C Callaghan
CAPTAIN & ADJT.
THE ROYAL DRAGOONS.

DUPLICATE.

Army Form C. 2118.

Instructions regarding War Diaries and Intelligence Summaries are contained in F. S. Regs., Part II. and the Staff Manual respectively. Title pages will be prepared in manuscript.

WAR DIARY
or
INTELLIGENCE-SUMMARY.
(Erase heading not required.)

M 54 Covers

Place	Date	Hour	Summary of Events and Information	Remarks and references to Appendices
PAFFENDORF.	March.1919.		NOTES. ***** The weather throughout the month was bad being particularly cold the last fortnight. The situation as regards men and horses was very serious as we are now about 1 man to 9 horses. APPENDIX I. " " NIL. APPENDIX II. " " NIL. APPENDIX III. 36 other ranks re-posted from Royal Scots Greys.19/3/19. 30 " " " " " 2nd.Dragoon Guards 26/3/19 C.Callahan Capt. & Adjt. The Royal Dragoons.	

www.ingramcontent.com/pod-product-compliance
Lightning Source LLC
Chambersburg PA
CBHW080922230426

43668CB00014B/2175